# Teacher Education across
# Minority-Serving Institutions

# Teacher Education across Minority-Serving Institutions

## Programs, Policies, and Social Justice

EDITED BY

EMERY PETCHAUER

LYNNETTE MAWHINNEY

RUTGERS UNIVERSITY PRESS

NEW BRUNSWICK, CAMDEN, AND NEWARK, NEW JERSEY, AND LONDON

LIBRARY OF CONGRESS CATALOGING-IN-PUBLICATION DATA

Names: Petchauer, Emery, editor. | Mawhinney, Lynnette, 1979– editor.
Title: Teacher education across minority-serving institutions : programs, policies, and
  social justice / edited by Emery Petchauer and Lynnette Mawhinney.
Description: New Brunswick, New Jersey : Rutgers University Press, [2017] | Includes
  bibliographical references and index.
Identifiers: LCCN 2016025794| ISBN 9780813588667 (hardcover : alk. paper) |
  ISBN 9780813588650 (pbk. : alk. paper) | ISBN 9780813588674 (e-book (epub)) |
  ISBN 9780813588681 (e-book (web pdf))
Subjects: LCSH: Minority teachers—Training of—United States.
Classification: LCC LB1715 .T399 2017 | DDC 370.71/1—dc23
LC record available at https://lccn.loc.gov/2016025794

A British Cataloging-in-Publication record for this book is available from the British
Library.

This publication was supported in part by
the Eleanor J. and Jason F. Dreibelbis Fund.

∞ The paper used in this publication meets the requirements of the American
National Standard for Information Sciences—Permanence of Paper for Printed Library
Materials, ANSI Z39.48-1992.

www.rutgersuniversitypress.org

Manufactured in the United States of America

# CONTENTS

# ACKNOWLEDGMENTS

Many people helped us, both directly and indirectly, to assemble this volume. We are grateful to Marybeth Gasman, Andrés Samayoa, Alice Ginsberg, and the Center for Minority Serving Institution at the University of Pennsylvania for brainstorming with us in Philadelphia during the early stages of this project and for supporting us throughout its entirety. Funds from the Research Support Committee in the School of Education and Human Services at Oakland University allowed us time together to conceptualize this project. We appreciate Cheryl Crazy Bull and Tarajean Yazzie-Mintz at the American Indian College Fund, who were instrumental in helping us secure chapters on teacher education at Tribal Colleges and Universities. Along similar lines, Lisa Azure, Constance Frankenbery, Cindy O'Dell, Regina Sievert, Cheryl Medaris, Chris Fried, Cyndi Pyatskowit, Teresa Delorme, Geraldine Garrity, and JT Shining Oneside all provided vital information about the future of teacher education in Indian Country. Carl Walton, our former colleague at Lincoln University in Pennsylvania, directed us to the important work happening at Savannah State University, and through him we received helpful direction from Marshalita Sims Peterson and Elazer Barnette. Andrew Arroyo, Kira Baker-Doyle, Cathy DeCoursey, Bettina Love, Rich Milner, and Decoteau Irby all sent good vibes our way. Lauren Carley, Katie Brandt, and Anthony Conte diligently completed some technical work behind the scenes for us. I (Emery) started my academic career at an HBCU because of Louis Gallien, my mentor and a former Spelman College professor. I remain grateful to him for this and much, much more. And I (Lynnette) am grateful to both my graduate school mentor, James Earl Davis, for pushing me to apply to teach at an HBCU—a decision for which I am forever grateful—and Emery for deciding to hire me at Lincoln.

Completing this volume prompted us to remember and retell many joys from working with our former students at Lincoln University, the *first* HBCU. From the Urban Ed Ridas to intense Praxis exam study sessions, this project reminded us of how much richer we are professionally and personally from having had each of you as students. We miss you all.

# Teacher Education across
# Minority-Serving Institutions

# Introduction

## Teacher Education across Minority-Serving Institutions

EMERY PETCHAUER
LYNNETTE MAWHINNEY

Teacher education programs are as diverse as the students who attend them. Many programs are nested within large, flagship state institutions with long histories of educating teachers. For some institutions, even smaller ones, this history began as normal schools responsible for training teachers. In these programs, teacher candidates move through advisors, field instructors, adjunct instructors, full-time professors, cooperating teachers in the field, and other supports during their professional matriculation. The most effective of these programs exhibits certain qualities: they maintain a cohesive vision of good teaching, have well-defined standards of performance, carefully align field experiences with other parts of the program, and lead students to confront their preexisting beliefs and assumptions about students (Darling-Hammond 2006). Most often, education students at these institutions are white women who come from middle-class backgrounds (NCEI 2011). Many preservice teachers in these programs had positive experiences in schools, saw themselves becoming teachers since they were young, and enter the profession in schools similar to the ones they attended (Su 1997). Much of what we know about teacher education in the United States comes from institutions like these.

Other teacher education programs are nested in institutions that sit closer to the periphery of higher education. Thriving more on committed faculty members than state funding, these programs build up instead of weed out; more important, they take a holistic approach to preparing teachers and build supports around their students' needs. Sometimes these needs concern passing a licensure exam. Other times they are financial or personal due to situations back home that are outside students' control. In most cases, these programs educate a more racially and socioeconomically diverse population of teachers— a demographic that more closely matches US classrooms today. These institutions receive students perhaps not admitted into more elite institutions and not always afforded the best opportunities and resources in their K–12 school-ing experiences. Yet such programs view these potential teachers as possessing a set of assets precisely because of the challenges they have overcome. They view these assets as necessary for the deep, messy battle of teaching for justice in today's shifting school landscape. Many of these programs are housed at Minority-Serving Institutions (MSIs).

MSIs, a family of higher education institutions, serve significant per-centages of low-income and underrepresented students of color (Gasman and Conrad 2013). Four types of institutions, as defined by the federal govern-ment, constitute MSIs: Historically Black Colleges and Universities (HBCUs), Tribal Colleges and Universities (TCUs), Hispanic-Serving Institutions (HSIs), and Asian American and Native American Pacific Islander–Serving Institutions (AANAPISIs). MSIs comprise a diverse group of institutions—both public and private offering two-year and four-year programs.

In the case of HBCUs, many were founded more than one hundred years ago and were initiated through federal legislation during Reconstruction for the specific purpose of educating and training African Americans recently eman-cipated from slavery (Anderson 1988). One of the earliest of these institutions is Lincoln University in Chester County, Pennsylvania, founded in 1854, where both of us began our careers as professors in teacher education. Federal legisla-tion also helped initiate the conditions for TCUs. With power granted through the Indian Civil Rights Act of 1968, many tribal communities created their own colleges in the spirit of self-determination, and subsequent acts offering finan-cial assistance helped stabilize and expand these institutions (Gasman, Nguyen, and Conrad 2014).

Unlike HBCUs and TCUs, many HSIs and AANAPISIs were not founded for the education of a specific group of people. Rather, these institutions have grown to enroll high percentages of students from ethnic minority groups owing to, among other factors, demographic changes in the United States and civil rights victories that expanded access to higher education for young adults of color (Gasman, Nguyen, and Conrad 2014). Mirroring the larger demographic shifts in our country, some predominantly and historically white institutions have become HSIs or AANAPISIs. A few institutions as well, though not founded as such historically, have become Predominantly Black Institutions (PBIs) through significant changes in student enrollment. Collectively, more than five hundred MSIs enroll approximately 25 percent of all undergraduate students in the United States (Gasman and Conrad 2013).

The uniqueness of MSIs expands beyond the racial demographics of their students. As many researchers have noted, their contributions to higher education derive from their approach to organizing the development, educa-tion, and care of students (Conrad and Gasman 2015; Fries-Britt and Turner 2002; Gasman, Baez, and Turner 2008; Gasman and Conrad 2013; Hale 2006;

Hirt et al. 2006; Outcalt and Skewes-Cox 2002; Palmer and Gasman 2008; Palmer, Maramba, and Gasman 2013; Teranishi 2011). Clifton Conrad and Marybeth Gasman (2015) make many aspects of this approach evident in their rich case study of twelve MSIs by focusing on mission, environment, programs, and practices. MSIs build their missions and educational approach around the social and economic barriers that low-income students and students of color often experience. Access to higher education and a meaningful experience that builds upon culture and heritage is at the center of these missions. These institutions also take a holistic approach to student support and development by not only paying as much attention to what happens outside class as to what happens inside class but also sharing the obligation for student success among all campus personnel through a "lift as we climb" ethos.

MSIs also create comprehensive and nurturing environments that advocate for academic development connected to racial self-development. Their programs often center on what is needed for students who have had inadequate preparation for college to compete across the higher education and employment landscapes. Integral components of this include effective remediation programs, meaningful community-centered research projects, and accessible faculty members committed to teaching. At their most successful, MSIs have done much of the heavy lifting that majority, predominantly white institutions either cannot or will not perform.

MSIs have been seen as separate institutional types with unique histories tied to racial and ethnic groups, justice movements, or federal legislation and classifications. At this particular moment, however, MSIs are becoming more visible as a collective unit to scholars and policymakers. On March 14, 2014, the Senate Committee on Health, Education, Labor, and Pensions held a hearing entitled "Strengthening Minority Serving Institutions: Best Practices and Innovations for Student Success," the first of its kind and a notable expansion beyond prior congressional hearings that focused primarily on HBCUs. Charitable and advocacy organizations such as the Southern Education Fund (2014) have similarly expanded their focus beyond HBCUs to include MSIs in their policy reports. Finally, major philanthropic organizations have made significant investments in MSI scholarship and capacity building. The Center for Minority-Serving Institutions at the University of Pennsylvania is a clear example. Established in 2013, the center has, within three years, received more than 8 million dollars from the Kresge Foundation, W. K. Kellogg Foundation, Andrew W. Mellon Foundation, and other charitable organizations. These funds have been used to establish capacity-building projects, faculty development opportunities, PhD pipelines for graduate students of color, and other projects to support MSIs and thrust them into national conversations about education. Once seen as separate silos, MSIs are becoming more visible when viewed as a diverse, rich, and collective unit with many lessons to teach higher education.

As MSIs have come into focus, little attention has been paid to their roles in preparing and educating our nation's teachers. Yet a look at the programs MSIs offer indicates they play a significant role in preparing students for a variety of roles in schools and educational settings. Of the 105 HBCUs in the United States, 76 offer an education degree program. Most of these programs are four-year, undergraduate degree certification programs in early childhood, elementary, and various secondary education subject areas. This concentration of traditional teacher training across HBCUs corresponds to many of their institutional beginnings as teacher training schools. Of the 34 accredited TCUs, 29 offer an education degree program. The majority of these programs are associate degrees in early childhood education or associate degrees that transfer to bachelor degree programs at nearby four-year institutions. This concentration of associate degrees corresponds to the status of most TCUs as two-year colleges, although ten institutions have bachelor degree programs leading to elementary or secondary certifications, and two offer master's degrees. Of the 136 AANAPISIs and 233 (of 264) HSIs, 128 have education degree programs. AANAPISIs and HSI are spread equally over two-year and four-year institutions, and the education programs across their curricula reflect this status as well. Most two-year institutions offer associate degrees in early childhood education or child development, and most four-year institutions offer bachelor's degrees and certifications in elementary education and a variety of secondary education subjects. These figures illustrate a broad range of education degrees, programs, and certifications across MSIs.[1]

Program offerings are one lens to understand the landscape of teacher education programs across MSIs. Another helpful perspective comes from looking at what these programs have produced. In the 2012–2013 academic year, MSIs produced 8.6 percent of all four-year degrees in education. Keeping with the MSI commitment to racial diversity, these programs were responsible for an impressive percentage of degrees awarded to students of color:

- 54.1 percent of Latino/a students who received undergraduate degrees in education;
- 32.8 percent of Black or African American students who received undergraduate degrees in education;
- 57.7 percent of Native Hawaiian and other Pacific Islander students who received undergraduate degrees in education;
- 17.4 percent of Asian American students who received undergraduate degrees in education; and
- 11.7 percent of American Indian and Alaskan Native students who received undergraduate degrees in education.[2]

Beyond these figures, scholars report that MSIs have awarded half of all education degrees and certifications earned by African Americans, Latino/as, and

American Indians; in addition, MSIs make an oversized contribution to high-need areas such as math and science education (Alliance for Equity in Higher Education 2000).

In our years at Lincoln University, we saw clear evidence of how the teacher education program produced a critical mass of Black teachers for the Philadelphia and tristate region. The most vivid reminder of this came during our first year participating in the Philadelphia Urban Seminar, a two-week summer immersion course that brought five hundred preservice teachers from sixteen institutions across the state to serve in Philadelphia public schools. For preservice teachers who were thinking about becoming urban teachers, this was an opportunity for a meaningful field experience internship in an urban school, something unavailable in rural and suburban parts of the state. Among the five hundred potential urban teachers, sixteen were African American. All but one came from Lincoln University. Like the larger figures on MSI teacher education programs and teacher diversity, our small HBCU of fewer than two thousand students supplied an oversized proportion of African American teachers in the region.

The contributions that MSIs have made to the racial diversity of the teaching profession are important, yet discussions on this topic, both scholarly and popular, often end with simple statistics. Missing are the enormous contributions to teacher education from MSIs that extend well beyond racial demographics. Principles of freedom, justice, and service are woven into the mission of many MSIs, and many of these principles are woven into their teacher education programs. HBCUs have a distinct legacy of situating teacher education within the lineage of service, freedom, and cultural transmission of Black communities (Dilworth 2012). This legacy has played out in many Black teachers' educational philosophies and pedagogies that focus on the nexus of education and academic, political, social, and economic advancement (e.g., Foster 1993; Irvine and Fenwick 2011; Ladson-Billings 2005; Mawhinney 2014).

Programmatically, HSIs have partnered with American Indian nations to prepare either culturally sustaining Indigenous teachers (e.g., Becket 1988; White et al. 2007) or culturally responsive educators to teach immigrant children in high-need schools along the US-México border (e.g., Zapata 1988). Education programs at many TCUs infuse Native languages, cultures, and epistemologies into the education of their teachers (e.g., Lamb 2014). Thus, MSIs have done much more than help increase racial diversity in the teachers' lounge; instead, they have pushed and advanced teacher education in ways not always evident in studies of teacher education program design and effectiveness. Although vital to the field, much existing knowledge about teacher education is derived from white teachers within the predominantly white programs that educate them.

Moreover, our own years as teacher educators at an MSI attest to the available, but untapped knowledge. While at Lincoln University, a collective "lift as we climb" ethos was part of the program's culture, as is the case at many HBCUs. Students often saw their individual success as aspiring teachers bound to the collective success of their classmates and their future students. Given the obstacles many of them had overcome as low-income students, first-generation students, and/or students of color, many resisted the push to use higher education as a way to escape their communities; instead, they felt called to return, serve, and grow more roses in concrete (Duncan-Andrade 2009). Others understood the impact they could make as teachers of color in a majority white or suburban school and felt called accordingly. They understood that who they *were* as teachers would be as important as what they *did* as teachers.

Instead of an abstract sense of "wanting to give back" or (much worse) a sense of guilt, a deep commitment to justice motivated many preservice teachers. This commitment often grew from coming to understand the systemic reasons behind their substandard schooling experiences: for example, why had their schools often employed inexperienced teachers and outdated technology? We saw their commitment to justice manifest when our students tackled their academic deficiencies head-on, demonstrated an unusual level of commitment to their fieldwork and students, and challenged one another to grow. Like many MSI faculty members, the hours we dedicated to our students outside the classroom far exceeded our job descriptions.

Teacher education has a great deal to learn about developing, educating, and supporting teachers from the legacy of MSIs. Now is the appropriate time to learn from this legacy. Over the next decades, teacher education in the United States must respond to many pressing issues: an emerging majority student population of color, more multilingual students, a widening socioeconomic gap between wealthy and poor, the erosion of the middle class, a higher concentration of students with exceptionalities in classrooms, shrinking public education funding, and new education legislation and standards, among others. We must prepare teachers for *this* world. While some may see this forecast as ominous, we see possibility and an opportune time to learn from MSIs and their teacher education programs. Institutional mission, US-México border proximity, immigration patterns, local rootedness, and other variables have put many MSIs ahead of the curve in responding to the complicated teacher education mission. Many teacher education programs at MSIs have arguably been confronting and responding to these demands—doing more with less—well before they became unavoidable to the entire field and country. Teacher education programs writ large have been criticized as disconnected from practice, ineffective at preparing teachers for "real" work, and slow to adopt new and innovative models (Darling-Hammond 2006). MSIs form a largely untapped resource for teacher education innovation and promise.

Policy demands facing teacher education at this contemporary moment also make this the right time to see MSIs as a collective unit in teacher education. These demands originate from policies that pressure schools, among other things, to equate program quality with graduates' professional performance (most often their students' standardized test scores), to adopt new professional standards, to seek (re)accreditation by changing professional bodies, and to respond to controversial metrics of teacher quality. Challenges such as these provoke education scholars and practitioners to frequently describe their profession as "under attack." Although all teacher education programs must respond to these demands, they have an acute impact on smaller teacher education programs, many of which operate at MSIs. The continued success of many MSI teacher education programs entails responding to these demands in proactive ways.

This volume on teacher education across MSIs sits against this backdrop of possibility and challenge. Our collection of chapters speaks to the range of teacher education work happening at MSIs. In part I, Community Connections and Justice-Oriented Teacher Education, the authors address the ways that MSIs orient their teacher education programs to the needs and assets of surrounding community in meaningful ways. A commitment to justice and equity with regard to race, ethnicity, culture, language, and other dimensions is integral to this orientation. This volume opens with "The Promise of Equity: Preparing Future Teachers to Be Socially Just Educators," where Mae S. Chaplin and Annette M. Daoud look across two institutions in the California State University system—one designated an HSI and the other an AANAPISI—to unpack how these programs use social justice, equity and action planning, and critical pedagogy to prepare teachers to work with linguistically and ethnically diverse student populations. Chaplin and Daoud's recommendations for other education programs are practical, grounded in data from preservice teachers, and housed within a model that encompasses multiple stages of teacher professional growth. In chapter 2, "Learning from the Community: Innovative Partnerships That Inform Tribal College Teacher Education Programming," Danielle Lansing draws from the Wakanyeja "Sacred Little Ones" early childhood initiative to illustrate how Southwestern Indian Polytechnic Institute has built an education program based upon needs identified by the local Native community. Lansing offers a rare picture of the powerful work underway at Tribal College education programs that is instructive for all institution types looking to build programs around the needs of their local communities in authentic ways. In chapter 3, "Teacher Preparation for Our Communities: Building Co-teaching Collaborative Schools from the Ground Up," Cheryl A. Franklin Torrez, Jonathan Brinkerhoff, and Irene Welch move far beyond the traditional, ineffective model of fieldwork and student teaching to offer a fresh approach to clinical preparation and collaboration among university, schools, and community in New Mexico. The authors draw from data and reflection from five cohorts of teachers in their Co-teaching Collaborative School model to offer practical directions for other programs seeking to develop organic partnership for clinical preparation. In chapter 4, "From Our Own Gardens: Growing Our Own Bilingual Teachers in the Southwest," Sandra Browning brings insight from higher education scholarship to bear on teacher education by applying nine design principles for Hispanic student success. Browning illustrates how these principles guide a collaborative partnership between the University of Houston–Clear Lake, four community colleges, and four local school districts to create opportunities for Hispanic students to become teachers.

In part 2, Program Responses to Contemporary Demands, authors confront the tough challenges facing teacher education programs. Instructive for a variety of institution types, authors outline practical methods to address these challenges. In chapter 5, "Lifting Gates and Building Skills: Preparing Diverse Candidates to Pass New Certification Exams," Joni S. Kolman, Laura M. Gellert, and Denise L. McLurkin effectively address an aspect of data-driven accountability with the most direct impact on preservice teachers: the changing battery licensure exams they must pass. The authors chronicle the rapid and profound changes to these exams in New York and unpack the specific steps they took to support their preservice teachers to pass these exams. In chapter 6, "Special Education Teacher Preparation Reform in Context: Lessons from a Decade of Program Support," Mary Bay, Norma Lopez-Reyna, and Rosanne Ward draw from their work supporting special education program development at the Monarch Center at University of Illinois, Chicago (an AANAPISI). By outlining the steps that faculty teams across sixteen MSIs took to improve their special education teacher education programs, the authors provide an excellent opportunity for others in higher education to learn from the program improvement work done by special education faculty members at MSIs. In chapter 7, "Becoming a Black Institution: Challenges and Changes for Teacher Education Programs at Emerging Minority-Serving Institutions," Byung-In Seo, DeWitt Scott, and Emery Petchauer identify some challenges to and related solutions for institutions that are becoming MSIs by serving a more racially, linguistically, and socio-economically diverse student body. Using the history and growth of Chicago State University—a historically white institution that has become predominantly Black—the authors provide important guide points so that institutions traveling a similar path today will provide their preservice teachers the support they deserve. In chapter 8, "The Future of Teacher Preparation at Tribal Colleges and Universities: A Talking Circle of Education Warriors," Carmelita Lamb introduces readers to the landscape of teacher education across TCUs. From her own experience working in Indian Country and through interviews with department chairs (i.e. Education Warriors) at nine TCUs, Lamb paints a picture of the harsh challenges stacking up against TCU teacher education programs and the self-determination of faculty members who have carried them thus far. In chapter 9, "Teacher Preparation at Historically Black Colleges and

Universities: Remaining Relevant in a Climate of Accountability," Brian Harper and Lynnette Mawhinney identify some ways that contemporary policy and accreditation pressures have made it increasingly difficult for HBCU teacher education programs to honor their mission of service, activism, and justice. Ever hopeful, the authors highlight some ways that current HBCU teacher education programs are still fulfilling this mission despite current challenges. We conclude this volume with a call for thinking differently about the education work at MSIs so that innovations in research and practice can spread a wider presence across this family of institutions.

The contributors to this volume come from a range of institutions. Many hold faculty positions in education departments at MSIs. Insights from these scholars, particularly ones at smaller institutions with hefty teaching loads, have been missing from our knowledge base. A few contributors are housed at predominantly white institutions but conduct work relevant to MSIs. These connections across institution types are important to start thinking about teacher education at MSIs in new ways. Some chapters in this volume derive from the work happening at specific institutions, but other chapters derive insights from the work happening across a specific institution type, like HBCUs. Furthermore, some chapters look among MSIs as a whole to draw insights about general teacher education. Consequently, the contents of this volume operate at three different scales: *at, among,* and *across* MSIs. We believe thinking about MSI teacher education work according to these three scales is a useful framework to forge a meaningful path of research and practice, and this becomes the essence of our conclusion to the volume. As a whole, we present this volume as a resource to spark growth and improvement within teacher education programs at all types of institutions and to initiate a long line of work connected to teacher education across MSIs.

We offer a final word on language and terminology: We have an aversion for the word "minority" because its contextuality masks the larger systems that *minoritize* a person or group. We typically use the term "of color" in the place of "minority." We also see shortcomings and problems with the term "Hispanic" and some other terms used in this volume. As the title and introduction of this volume indicates, we and the contributors use "minority" and other limited terms throughout the text in order to align with federal classification. We hope readers are mindful of the limitations of such terms and think through their implications with regard to institutional descriptions as they read the volume.

NOTES

1 We used the 2015 report from the Penn Center for Minority-Serving Institutions for our total numbers of institutions in each MSI category, which includes an institution on the brink of becoming an AANAPISI in the classification. Additionally, we excluded MSIs in US territories such as Guam and Puerto Rico. It should be noted that

the total number of institutions in each category varies from year to year due to enrollment trends and other variables. Additionally, fifty-four institutions hold the designation of both AANAPSIS and HSI.

2  We are grateful to the Penn Center for Minority-Serving Institutions for providing us with this IPEDS data.

## REFERENCES

Alliance for Equity in Higher Education. 2000. "Educating the Emerging Majority: The Role of Minority-Serving Colleges and Universities in Confronting America's Teacher Crisis." http://www.ihep.org/sites/default/files/uploads/docs/pubs/educatingemerging majority.pdf.

Anderson, James D. 1988. *The Education of Blacks in the South, 1865–1930*. Chapel Hill: University of North Carolina Press.

Becket, Diane R. 1998. "Increasing the Number of Latino and Navajo Teachers in Hard-to-Staff Schools." *Journal of Teacher Education* 49: 196–205.

Conrad, Clifton, and Marybeth Gasman. 2015. *Educating a Diverse Nation: Lessons from Minority-Serving Institutions.* Cambridge, MA: Harvard University Press.

Darling-Hammond, Linda. 2006. *Powerful Teacher Education: Lessons from Exemplary Programs.* San Francisco: Jossey-Bass.

Dilworth, Mary E. 2012. "Historically Black Colleges and Universities in Teacher Education Reform." *Journal Negro Education* 81: 121–135.

Duncan-Andrade, Jeff. 2009. "Note to Educators: Hope Required When Growing Roses in Concrete." *Harvard Educational Review* 79(2): 181–194.

Foster, Michelle. 1993. "Educating for Competence in Community and Culture: Exploring the Views of Exemplary African American Teachers." *Urban Education* 27(4): 370–394.

Fries-Britt, Sharon, and Bridget Turner. 2002. "Uneven Stories: Successful Black Collegians at a Black and White Campus." *Review of Higher Education* 25(3): 315–330.

Gasman, Marybeth, Benjamin Baez, and Caroline Sotello Viernes Turner, eds. 2008. *Understanding Minority-Serving Institutions.* Albany: State University of New York Press.

Gasman, Marybeth, and Clifton Conrad. 2013. "Minority-Serving Institutions: Educating All Students." Report from the Center of Minority Serving Institutions. http://www.gse. upenn.edu/pdf/cmsi/msis_educating_all_students.pdf.

Gasman, Marybeth, Thai-Huy Nguyen, and Clifton Conrad. 2014. "Lives Intertwined: A Primer on the History and Emergence of Minority Serving Institutions." *Journal of Diversity in Higher Education* 8(2): 120–138.

Hale, Frank W., ed. 2006. *How Black Colleges Empower Black Students: Lessons for Higher Education.* Sterling, SC: Stylus.

Hirt, Joan B., Terrell L. Strayhorn, Catherine T. Amelink, and Belinda R. Bennett. 2006. "The Nature of Student Affairs Work at Historically Black Colleges and Universities." *Journal of College Student Development* 47(6): 661–676.

Irvine, Jacqueline Jordan, and Leslie T. Fenwick. 2011. "Teachers and Teaching for the New Millennium: The Role of HBCUs." *Journal of Negro Education* 80(3): 197–208.

Ladson-Billings, Gloria. 2005. *Beyond the Big House: African American Educators on Teacher Education.* New York: Teachers College Press.

Lamb, Carmelita. 2014. "Growing Our Own: A Sustainable Approach to Teacher Education at Turtle Mountain Community College." *Tribal College Journal* 26(2): 30–31. http:// www.tribalcollegejournal.org/archives/28935.

Mawhinney, Lynnette. 2014. *We Got Next: Urban Education and the Next Generation of Black Teachers.* New York: Peter Lang.

National Center for Education Information. 2011. *Profile of Teachers in the U.S. 2011.* Washington, DC: National Center for Education Information.

Outcalt, Charles L., and Thomas E. Skewes-Cox. 2002. "Involvement, Interaction, and Satisfaction: The Human Environment at HBCUs." *Review of Higher Education* 25(3): 331–347.

Palmer, Robert T., and Marybeth Gasman. 2008. "'It Takes a Village to Raise a Child': The Role of Social Capital in Promoting Academic Success for African American Men at a Black College." *Journal of College Student Development* 49(1): 52–70.

Palmer, Robert T., Dina C. Maramba, and Marybeth Gasman, eds. 2013. *Fostering Success of Ethnic and Racial Minorities in STEM: The Role of Minority-Serving Institutions.* New York: Routledge.

Southern Education Foundation. 2014. "Performance Funding at MSIs: Consideration and Possible Measures for Public Minority Serving Institutions." http://www. luminafoundation.org/files/resources/performance-funding-at-msis.pdf.

Su, Zhixin. 1997. "Teaching as a Profession and as a Career: Minority Candidates' Perspectives." *Teaching and Teacher Education* 13(3): 325–304.

Teranishi, Robert T. 2011. "Asian American and Native American Pacific Islander–Serving Institutions: Areas of Growth, Innovation, and Collaboration." *AAPI Nexus: Asian Americans & Pacific Islanders Policy, Practice, and Community* 9: 16–22.

White, Carolyne J., Clara Bedonie, Jennie de Groat, Louise Lockard, and Samantha Honani. 2007. "A Bridge for Our Children: Tribal/University Partnerships to Prepare Indigenous Teachers." *Teacher Education Quarterly* 34(4): 71–86.

Zapata, Jesse T. 1988. "Early Identification and Recruitment of Hispanic Teacher Candidates." *Journal of Teacher Education* 39: 19–23.

# PART ONE

# Community Connections and Justice-Oriented Teacher Education

# 1

## The Promise of Equity

### Preparing Future Teachers to Be
### Socially Just Educators

MAE S. CHAPLIN

ANNETTE M. DAOUD

Minority-Serving Institutions (MSIs) play an integral role in recruiting and preparing students from traditionally underserved populations for careers that require postbaccalaureate education. For K–12 teacher education programs at MSIs, justice-oriented pedagogies are essential components in developing and retaining transformative educators from various backgrounds (Gasman and Conrad 2013). Educators who enter the field of public education must not only prepare to work with students from varied backgrounds but also possess the capacity to navigate a system that often dehumanizes its students and teachers through high-stakes standardized measures of "proficiency" and other such deficit-based practices (Valdés 2001; Valencia 1997). Given these contexts, faculty members who work with preservice teachers at MSIs have unique opportunities to prepare future teachers for the systemic realities they will face in the field and to develop the advocacy skills necessary to promote systemic transformation.

### Background: Two Different MSIs

The two MSIs detailed in chapter 1 are part of the California State University (CSU) system. The CSU system contains twenty-three campuses serving both urban and rural areas. As of 2014, fifteen of these universities, designated Hispanic-Serving Institutions (HSIs), are primarily located in the southern portion of the state. There are additional noteworthy facts from 2014 enrollment figures for the CSU system:

- Of the students, 54 percent are Latino/a, Asian American/Pacific Islander, African American, or Native American.
- More than one-third of the systems' graduates are first-generation college graduates.

- Of CSU's students, 76 percent receive financial aid (California State University Enrollment Data 2015).

Educators and policy makers interested in diversifying California's overwhelmingly white, female, and middle-class teaching force should pay close attention to such numbers and enrollment trends, especially because they indicate a clear source for teacher recruitment. The need to recruit, prepare, and retain teachers from diverse backgrounds is a pressing issue that MSIs are poised to address.

### Sacramento State University

The first MSI we discuss is located near the center of Sacramento, California. Sacramento State University has become an increasingly diverse campus during the past decade. For example, according to the Sacramento State University 2014 assessment survey, enrollment demographics from fall 2013 paint a diverse picture : White (37%), Asian/Pacific (21%), Latino/a (22%), Other (11%), African American (6%), Foreign (2%), and Native American (1%). These numbers indicate a shift from the 2003 fall enrollment demographics, most noticeably in the increase of Latino students from 13 percent of the student body in 2003 to 22 percent in 2013, as well as the growth in population of Asian/Pacific students from 17 percent in 2003 to 21 percent in 2013 (Sacramento State University 2014). By the spring of 2016, Sacramento State University was already recognized as an Asian American and Native American Pacific Islander–Serving Institution (AANAPISI) and had recently been granted status as an HSI.

The College of Education at Sacramento State University offers programs and certificates, including six minors in education and child development fields as well as several options for postbaccalaureate students seeking to earn a teaching credential. Each of these programs evidences an emphasis on social justice and equity. Specifically, the programs and their associated courses offered by Sacramento State's College of Education align with their TEACHing for Change Framework: T = Transformative Teaching, Learning, and Leadership Roles; E = Equity and Social Justice; A = Active Civic Engagement; C = Collaboration and Communication; and H = Human Capital and Diversity (California State University, College of Education, 2015). According to the TEACHing for Change framework, the College of Education "prepares educators, counselors, administrators and other school personnel to become active change agents—candidates that recognize, understand and create responsive programs and activities to transform and reform curriculum and programs within our P/K–12 schools, communities and other agencies" (California State University, College of Education, 2015). The focus on producing educators, administrators, and counselors who will serve as "change agents" helps to create a foundation for the curriculum and teaching methods across programs within the College of Education at Sacramento State. Together, these intentions guide efforts to recruit and prepare diverse educators dedicated to serving marginalized students.

### California State University, San Marcos

The second MSI, California State University, San Marcos, is located in north San Diego County and was established in 1989. Its current growth, reflecting its primary draw of student population from regional school districts, attests to the university's recognition as both an AANAPISI and a HSI. Approximately 12,000 students were enrolled during the fall 2014 semester: Latino/a (39%), White (33%), Asian/Pacific Islander (10%), Other (9%), Multiple Ethnicities (5%), African American (3%), and Native American (<1%). Of the 2014 graduation class, approximately 52 percent represented the first in their family to earn a bachelor's degree (California State University, San Marcos, Office of Communications, 2015).

The School of Education at California State University, San Marcos, offers programs and credentials primarily for postbaccalaureate students pursuing teaching credentials and/or a master's degree in education. The mission statement of the School of Education is to collaboratively transform education, and programs in the School of Education align with both the mission and conceptual framework: engaging diverse communities through leading and learning for social justice (California State University, San Marcos, School of Education, 2015). Through the years, the School of Education faculty members have worked collaboratively to develop programs and design curricula that explicitly address issues of diversity, social justice, and educational equity. Additionally, the School of Education has established policies ensuring preservice teachers enrolled in all their programs are placed in school sites with diverse K–12 student populations.

## Conceptual Frameworks

To prepare teachers who will become transformative change agents, these teacher education programs use pedagogies rooted in the theoretical foundations of multicultural education, critical pedagogy, and tenets of social justice and equity (Banks 1993). Improving educational experiences through understanding and respecting all students anchors the theories and practices of multicultural education (Sleeter 2005). Students learn when the curriculum is meaningful, comprehensible, and relevant to students' lives, and achievement improves when instructional practices address students' cultures, experiences, and learning styles (Gay 2010). Culturally relevant pedagogy, based on academic achievement, cultural competence, and sociopolitical consciousness, clearly enhances academic and social performance of all students (Ladson-Billings 2001). Moreover, culturally responsive (relevant) pedagogy is validating, affirming, comprehensive, multidimensional, empowering, and transformative (Gay 2010). Curricula should exceed simple snapshots of diversity in certain lessons or units to focus on culturally relevant big ideas that still address standards (Sleeter 2005). Teacher education programs should be rooted in these multicultural education principles by offering a relevant and meaningful curriculum to serve as a model for preservice teachers while they learn how to become transformative educators.

Teacher education programs that are explicitly rooted in tenets of social justice and equity see teaching as the act of enhancing students' learning and expanding their opportunities both in and beyond school (Cochran-Smith et al. 2009). Social justice teacher education programs highlight inequities that exist in schools and guide preservice teachers in understanding theories and practices that will help them provide equitable educational opportunities for all their future students (Darling-Hammond, French, and Garcia-Lopez 2002). These teacher education programs approach social justice through a framework similar to one described by Sharon Chubbuck on conceptualizing and implementing socially just teaching (Chubbuck 2010). By using both individual and structural orientations, preservice teachers reflect upon and design their individual socially just and equitable pedagogy to address student learning difficulties (Chubbuck 2010).

In studying teacher education programs with an explicit focus on teaching for social justice, Marilyn Cochran-Smith and her colleagues (2009) classify preservice teachers' definitions of social justice and equity into four categories: pupil learning, relationships and respect, teacher as activist, and recognizing inequities. Across the categories, preservice teachers define and enact social justice through their own individual actions rather than through policy change or political actions. In her study of two teacher education programs in California, Morva McDonald (2005) examined how each program implements social justice and equity across their programs and found that translating these definitions into actions could be challenging for preservice teachers.

Although implementing a teacher education program focused on social justice and equity offers challenges, both ensuring that preservice teachers have experiences in school sites with diverse student populations and providing a supportive environment in their multicultural education courses in which to discuss those experiences, can begin to address these challenges (Hill 2012). In her study of fifty-two undergraduate elementary teacher candidates, Nayda Capella-Santana (2003) found that internships in culturally and ethnically diverse urban public elementary schools contributed to candidates' positive multicultural attitudes and knowledge. Also contributing to positive multicultural attitudes and increased knowledge were forums in multicultural education courses where preservice teachers could openly discuss issues and share concerns they had with their peers.

Analyzing the experiences of two teacher candidates in a program centered on social justice and equity, K. Dara Hill (2012) found similar results. The program placed candidates in urban schools with diverse populations where they participated in one-on-one tutoring with students in the classes they were teaching. Additionally, caring, cooperating teachers supervised the candidates who engaged in class discussions and course activities that provided an appropriate support system to reaffirm their desire to teach for social justice (Hill 2012).

Drawing from these studies, teacher education programs should take the following steps: (1) present social justice in ways that allow candidates to understand how they can become change agents; (2) teach candidates to define social justice in terms of the realities faced by their students; and (3) help candidates use their expanding definition of social justice to challenge inequities and promote systemic change. Teacher educators who teach multicultural education courses may face instructional, institutional, and sociopolitical challenges, such as dealing with preservice teachers' privileged identities or the influences of conservative ideologies on teacher education (Gorski 2012). These challenges, however, only underscore the importance of ensuring future generations of teachers who are empowered to address these issues and, in turn, empower their future students.

## Justice, Equity, and Empowerment

As indicated by our review of literature, justice-oriented pedagogies provide faculty, working with preservice teachers, the foundation to transform their individual methods courses and thus influence the larger field of public education (Cochran-Smith et al. 2009). The concepts that emerged from both the literature and the missions of these two California teacher preparation programs lead to the development of the Justice, Equity, and Empowerment framework (see figure 1.1).

The three circles represented in figure 1.1 illustrate the spiraled process of the Justice, Equity, and Empowerment framework, particularly as each relates to preparing socially just educators. Each stage of this process is designed to build on the learning and experiences fostered in the previous stages, regardless of where students and educators are in terms of their own social justice identities. For example, during their credential coursework, which starts after they have obtained their bachelor's degree, preservice teachers take methods courses that apply the foundations developed in their undergraduate education courses. In California, they typically complete such coursework during a one-year postbaccalaureate credential program. Later, this foundation expands as these preservice teachers graduate their credential programs, begin their careers as educators, and return to the university to seek higher degrees.

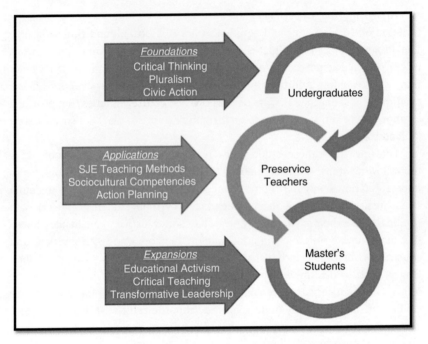

FIGURE 1.1 Justice, Equity, and Empowerment Framework

The final circle representing the master's candidates indicates the self-sustaining nature of this process; that is, the process does not end but continues to spiral as teachers working in the field reach more students and broader communities.

Despite the fact that the two teacher preparation programs we feature are in different parts of the state, each is grounded in similar missions of social justice and equity with preservice teachers who, in their respective programs, follow similar social justice and empowerment pathways. As illustrated in figure 1.1, such a pathway could include:

1. Foundations: Preservice teachers at this level are beginning to develop their overall awareness of social inequities and diversity. Undergraduates fulfill prerequisite requirements for teacher credentialing programs by taking courses designed to develop their ability to think critically about societal issues, particularly those connected to educational access and equity. Such courses also push the preservice teachers to consider the varying stages of multiculturalism and pluralism as well as what they can do to become more civically aware and active in their own communities.

2. Applications: The initial awareness developed during the foundations stage continues after preservice teachers have graduated with their bachelor's degrees and started the fifth year of methods coursework necessary to

earn a teaching credential in California. Preservice teachers learn how to apply their knowledge of the sociocultural factors and their students' backgrounds to their lesson design and implementation. Teacher candidates in this stage of their development as social justice educators build on their sociocultural competencies through researching the backgrounds of their students and forming action plans to provide their students with equitable access to educational opportunities.

3. Expansions: The final stage presented in figure 1.1 builds on the previous two stages for the express purpose of making justice-oriented pedagogies and self-sustaining curriculum. As graduates of the credential programs serve in their various school communities, they do so through community activism and by implementing social justice pedagogies and curriculum. The use of such pedagogies in their practice further allows educators at this stage of social justice development to become critical educators who not only serve their communities but also strive for systemic transformation. Additionally, these educators represent various levels of transformative leadership, whether they become administrators or teacher leaders at their school sites. Such practices allow the elements of justice-oriented pedagogies to become self-sustaining while these teacher leaders continue to work with students and colleagues in the field.

The teacher education programs at Sacramento State and California State University, San Marcos, have implemented ideas from the Justice, Equity, and Empowerment framework. We share narratives from these programs to illustrate how both undergraduate and postbaccalaureate levels of instruction for preservice teachers can apply elements from the Justice, Equity, and Empowerment framework.

## Applications of the Justice, Equity, and Empowerment Framework

As previously noted, teacher preparation programs at MSIs play an important role in the recruitment and preparation of socially just educators. Specifically, using justice-oriented pedagogies throughout the course sequence for preservice educators can help to develop the dispositions they require to meet the needs of their diverse students and become civically engaged with their school communities. The following sections detail how such a process might look with both undergraduate students and preservice teachers.

Thirty-four undergraduates who completed a writing-intensive course dedicated to children's and adolescent multicultural literature at Sacramento State University during the 2015 spring semester produced the work we feature. This course meets both the writing intensive and multicultural requirements necessary to graduate from Sacramento State University. Undergraduates earning a minor in education must also complete this course, and it tends to attract undergraduates from a wide variety of majors and backgrounds, including those on the "preservice teacher" pathway. For this reason, this course is often viewed as a method of recruiting a more diverse population of K–12 educators. For undergraduates minoring in education, this course begins the process of breaking down any personal assumptions or biases they may have, particularly as these assumptions relate to disenfranchised groups. Of the undergraduates enrolled in this particular section of the children's and adolescent multicultural literature course, twenty-five (74%) were seniors, and nine (26%) were juniors; moreover, twelve (35%) self-identified as either earning their minor in education or developing an interest in becoming teachers.

### Foundations: Critical Thinking

As indicated by the Justice, Equity, and Empowerment framework, undergraduates are at the initial stages of developing their social justice awareness and capacity for civic action. Programs used three specific course objectives to formalize this development:

1. Examine a range of high-quality multicultural children's and adolescent literature that reflects the underrepresented groups of the United States. Students will study the many genres of children's and adolescent literature from diverse cultural and pluralistic perspectives.
2. Identify bias-free, age-appropriate, relevant, and multicultural literature and employ it as a means of motivating children and adolescents to engage in meaningful literacy activities and develop a love of reading.
3. Explain how an exposure to multicultural children's and young adult books can foster an understanding and appreciation of the cultural values, identity, and heritage of diverse populations.

These particular objectives indicate that educators designed this course to promote ideas of pluralism while developing student capacity to think critically about multicultural children's and adolescent literature. For the future preservice teachers in this course, such objectives are essential in building foundations for future growth and applications of the social justice work they will continue in their methods course.

Given the writing-intensive requirement for this course, undergraduates who enroll in EDUC 121 must complete at least five thousand words of formal writing assignments throughout the semester. They mainly accomplished this through a series of literary analysis pieces specifically designed by the instructor to push the future preservice teachers to think beyond summarizing literature and instead to write essays that critically examined the issues. For this purpose, instructors asked the undergraduates to evaluate books using three main lenses: (1) quality as children's/adolescent literature; (2) quality as a multicultural selection; and (3) level of multicultural education represented by the book. For many of these future preservice teachers, these instructions—that is, being asked to move beyond providing a synopsis of a given piece of literature and using multiple lenses for evaluation—presented them with a new way of thinking about children's and adolescent literature. Because the instructor strategically designed class activities and lectures to support this process, preservice teachers were able to meaningfully apply their understanding and reflection on the content through a series of analytical essays and a final research project.

The course instructor specifically created an assignment that demonstrated the future preservice teachers' ability to think critically about the material: literature circles. Instead of completing the traditional literature circle roles during their discussions, the class rotated through a series of four roles: (1) critical questioner, (2) social justice and equity analyst, (3) big-picture detector, and (4) reviewer. The course instructor modified these roles for the express purpose of helping the future preservice teachers in the course develop their overall social justice awareness. With the exception of the critical questioner, these roles called for the future preservice teachers to analyze how the events in their group's chosen young adult novel connected to social justice and equity issues and areas of otherness. For example, one future preservice teacher who read the novel *Never Fall Down* (McCormik 2012) pointed out how the main character's struggle to pronounce the "th" sound when he was learning English connected to her own experience learning English when she entered an American high school after emigrating from Ukraine. She commented on her ability to "connect to Arn [the main character] on a personal level" and on his sense of "frustration and aloneness," something that she personally had experienced. Her ability to share her experience with her American-born monolingual classmates caused them to think differently about the topic of immigration and adapting to life in a completely new environment. One such classmate reflected this shift in thinking in her reflective essay on *Never Fall Down*; she wrote that she was "able to understand the process that people may go through in times of sheer desperation" and that she could understand the protagonist's sense of alienation in an American high school due to the fact that his peers were "completely unaware" of the "tragedies" that caused him to move to the United States. The fact that this particular undergraduate self-identified as a "future teacher" gives additional importance to her thoughts. Furthermore, she promised to try to both remember that students' experiences could "influence" them before they enter her future classroom and be "respectful" of what students might have undergone before immigrating to the United States. Such reflections are necessary for preservice teachers to be able to identify how the larger sociopolitical context can influence their work with students, especially those from immigrant populations. These thoughts indicate that this future preservice teacher was starting to think more critically about the larger context of human migration as a result of reading and discussing *Never Fall Down* with her classmates.

Besides thinking critically about literature, the instructor designed the curriculum and assignments to push the future preservice teachers in the course to consider how the master narrative, written by dominant societal groups, influences society's understanding, or often misunderstanding, of various areas of otherness. As they analyzed literature related to diverse populations, the future preservice teachers considered how literature and popular media either portray or omit certain groups. Because a majority of the future preservice teachers enrolled in this course had identified gender roles and sexism as something that they were interested in researching at the start of the semester, the course instructor decided to begin the discussion of mainstream media portrayals of subordinate groups by focusing on issues related to gender.

The course instructor then expanded on this discussion topic with an activity designed to challenge the future preservice teachers to expand their thinking regarding traditional gender roles. This activity called for the class to categorize certain adjectives as either "masculine" or "feminine." After viewing a series of images depicting popular cartoon characters and individually writing adjectives for each character, the instructor asked them to compare their lists with a classmate. With this same classmate, the student then had to decide which of the chosen adjectives were more "masculine" and which were more "feminine" in nature. Given the fact that the course instructor wanted the future preservice teachers to see how labels and rigid categories often repress a more accurate discourse of a given topic, each word had to be put into one specific category. During this activity the class came up with several lists:

- Masculine—strong, brave, troublemaker, hero, angry, lazy, courageous, protector, athletic, tough, confident, fearless, powerful
- Feminine—sweet, nice, teacher's pet, pretty, kind, sexy, shy, smart, innocent, polite, selfless, intelligent, fragile, creative, romantic, beautiful

During the following class discussion, several future preservice teachers were quick to point out that both lists contained stereotypes, especially the use of terms such as troublemaker, lazy, and angry as masculine terms and shy, sexy, and innocent as feminine terms. Furthermore, many future preservice teachers then commented that they disliked being forced to categorize the terms as belonging to a single gender. This led to a wider conversation about society's tendency to place labels into well-defined categories and how this process did not, as a whole, accurately reflect the many nuances of one's gender and individual identity. In their reflective journals, the future preservice teachers commented that such categories were "limiting" because they did not account for "differences." In particular, one student compared the class discussion to being "forced" to choose one category for his race/ethnicity on demographic forms and that he constantly "struggled" with making a choice. Another future preservice teacher wondered how being "told to use set categories" could influence one's ability to present a "true picture of sexual orientation and gender" to others.

Such connections indicate how the instructor was able to encourage the future preservice teachers to see beyond the separate groups of otherness and consider the different ways such areas shared interlocking themes of societal silencing. The ability of the future preservice teachers in the course to recognize how the process of labeling words as either "masculine" or "feminine" was limiting and thereby not reflecting the many different nuances a single term can include was extremely valuable. The focus on cultural pluralism, as guided by the instructor, further enhanced the process of moving beyond stereotypes and narrow-minded labeling.

### Foundations: Pluralism

The ability to think in terms of cultural pluralism was another focus that the instructor intentionally added to the course. The class discussions, activities, and assignments to expand their thinking about diversity challenged future preservice teachers in this class. The questionnaires at the start of the semester asked the undergraduates in this section of EDUC 121 (N=34) to quantify whether they had a "good understanding" of multiculturalism. Their responses indicated that four (12%) felt they had "no understanding," twenty (58%) had "some understanding," and ten (33%) had a "good understanding." Despite the fact that not all undergraduates in this course had identified themselves as being on the credential pathway, the instructor selected certain course readings for the express purposes of expanding the future preservice teachers' knowledge of multicultural education, particularity as it pertained to children's and adolescent literature. For example, the class was asked to read a series of articles related to the stages of multicultural education (Banks 1993; Gorski 2012). In a corresponding journal entry, one future preservice teacher commented that it was important to expose children to a variety of perspectives in literature because "the dominant group might come up with something they take for granted" when reading from a different point of view. Another future preservice teacher remarked that the awareness of others could foster "interest and respect for the differences and can give everyone more strength in fighting for social justice against racism, sexism, heterosexism, etc." These reflections indicate a willingness on the part of these future preservice teachers to use literature to expose children to multiple viewpoints and use those viewpoints as methods for promoting social justice and transformation. Yet another future preservice teacher summed up her ideas about using multicultural materials to teach for social justice: "I don't want them [students] scared of other cultures because of what mainstream media teaches them."

To help future preservice teachers, as well as the additional undergraduates in the course, conceptualize how others could view their individual identities, the class participated in an activity where they decorated individual paper dolls with images and words representing how they saw their own identities. During this activity, the class had to walk around and view others' work while trying to figure out whom they thought created each paper doll. This viewing led to an instructor-facilitated discussion of assumptions and stereotypes and how these views can harm students. Furthermore, several future preservice teachers commented that they did not realize how much one's native language related to identity formation, given the many paper dolls that contained words in Spanish, Vietnamese, Tagalog, and Russian. Reflecting on this activity, one future preservice teacher wrote that she did not realize how many languages her classmates represented and that she "assumed" that most of the class spoke English as a first language. Another future preservice teacher indicated that he was "surprised" by his assumptions concerning which classmate created which doll; he realized how quickly he "judged" others based on his own arbitrary set of beliefs about identity.

The previous examples show that the future preservice teachers, already on the teaching credential pathway, were starting the process of thinking about the multiple realities and experiences their future students will bring to the classroom. The sooner preservice teachers, in either their prerequisite or methods courses, can begin the process of rethinking concepts of both multiculturalism and identity, then the better able they will be to work in marginalized communities and challenge the status quo when they become practicing teachers.

### Foundations: Civic Action

The final component of the "Foundations" section of the Justice, Equity, and Empowerment framework is civic action. Given that the future preservice teachers whose voices are included in this narrative represent various levels of societal awareness, it was important for the course instructor to differentiate how they applied their learnings from the course through individualized research projects. For this purpose, the course instructor designed a multistep culminating project for the class to complete. This project required a series of activities: (1) name a social issue of personal importance; (2) discuss why that issue should be included in children's/adolescent literature; (3) read and analyze children's/adolescent books related to that issue; and (4) make recommendations for authors, teachers, parents, and others on how to present the issue to children and young adults. By guiding the future preservice teachers through the process of naming a personal issue of importance, they began to develop skills related to critical pedagogy and action research through a personally meaningful assignment. Furthermore, learning how to use action research and critical pedagogy also allowed the future preservice teachers to start developing the skills necessary to become responsive educators in the future.

Overall, the final projects from this course represented a wide range of topics: immigration, gender roles, family structure, war and conflict, racial stereotyping, and mental and physical abilities. In particular, the future preservice teachers' writing indicated their own varied stages of developing social justice awareness. Specifically, many future preservice teachers who wrote about gender roles realized that the literature they found did not "accurately" portray a variety of roles for girls and boys and that "traditional" gender roles were still being promoted by the dominant narrative regarding gender, but they did not make the additional realization that many of the books they analyzed were written from a mainly white, middle-class perspective. Moreover, they did not explicitly state that the dominant discourse surrounding race and language works in a similar manner to oppress other marginalized groups. Such connections are necessary for preservice teachers to make in order to understand how their students' lives may have been shaped by such societal factors. As these future preservice teachers progress through their methods courses, their initial awareness of societal oppression must, therefore, be expanded through course readings and assignments to include discussions of both other disenfranchised groups and the power of hegemony.

Despite the fact that some future preservice teachers did not explicitly connect the children's and adolescent literature they reviewed and its implications for their future careers as educators, other future preservice teachers used their own backgrounds to help them select their research topic. For example, a student who described herself a "Latina with strong ties to both Mexico and the United States" decided to explore the presentation of immigration through children's literature. This student was particularity curious about the role that children's literature could play in not only helping immigrant children navigate their new environment but also breaking down current myths regarding immigration. After reviewing several children's books including *From North to South/ Del Norte al Sur* by René Laínez and *My Name Is María Isabel* by Alma Flor Ada, this future preservice teacher reflected that, "literature is a very strong instrument for communication and for learning." Furthermore, she commented that her selection of topics was important to her own identity and that the books she read helped her begin form her "identity as a future teacher." By reading about the experiences of the immigrant youth portrayed in the books and connecting them to her own experience as an immigrant, this future preservice teacher was able to find "hope" from the literature. Given that the literature she reviewed "touched her on a personal level," she saw how it might also do the same for her future students. Such a discovery led her to realize that there was "hope" for her to present her future students with "realistic" literature relevant to their own lives and experiences.

*Applications: Social Justice and Equity Teaching Methods*

The course content and corresponding student work that exemplifies the application phase of the framework is from a secondary multilingual education course taught at California State University, San Marcos. This is a required course for all preservice teachers in the secondary (single subject) credential program where they learn how to equitably teach English learners content and English-language development in their content area classrooms. As with other methods courses, students take this course at the postbaccalaureate level. Preservice teachers learn about schooling experiences of secondary English learners both in and out of the classroom and how their pedagogy and actions can address inequities English learners encounter in school. Enrolled in two sections of the course during the 2014 fall semester were fifty-two candidates pursing single subject credentials in the following areas: English language arts (N=6), foreign languages—Spanish (N=2), mathematics (N=17), physical education (N=1), science (N=13), and social studies (N=13).

The instructor intentionally selected course readings and activities and designed assignments to guide preservice teachers through the application stage of the framework with the goal of taking action for social justice. To begin this process of taking action, candidates engage in a series of activities and assignments that help them start understanding their students as English learners. During an in-class assignment, preservice teachers work in small groups to develop questionnaires they will administer to their class; through these questionnaires the teachers will learn about their students' academic needs, cultural backgrounds (including languages they are proficient in), social, personal, and emotional considerations, and individual interests. Combined with data collected at their school sites (i.e., standardized test scores, information from their cumulative files), the preservice teachers create a learning profile for each student in their classes. They use this information throughout the semester to design lesson plans that meet the identified needs and address the interests of their students. This assignment helps the preservice teachers move beyond a deficit-based model of defining their English learners in terms of standardized language and content proficiency to understanding how to build upon the unique assets of each student when designing lesson plans.

Social justice and equity teaching methods also focus on culturally responsive teaching. The course instructor has selected course readings that highlight the need for culturally responsive pedagogy, defined as using the knowledge, prior experiences, and learning styles of diverse students to make learning more relevant and effective for them (Gay 2010). These course readings provide a base of knowledge for preservice teachers to then engage in class activities that guide them in understanding the importance of making their curriculum relevant to students, particularly their English learners. In content area groups, preservice teachers research what resources they can include in their lesson plans to match the interests and backgrounds of their students; these lesson plans offer preservice teachers guides not only for teaching their class, but also for submitting an assignment toward the end of the semester. For example, a science teacher incorporated an article, "Women Who Discovered Elements," into a lesson on the periodic table to make the content relevant to the girls in her class who had indicated their interest in careers in the science fields on their questionnaires.

Finally, throughout all courses in the program, preservice teachers learn how to design differentiated lesson plans that address the learning profiles of all students in their class. In the multilingual course, the instructor introduced differentiated lesson planning as a pedagogical approach that addressed inequities in the education of secondary English learners. The instructor designed a series of activities and assignments that ensure that preservice teachers understand the specific focus of lesson planning in this course: differentiation based on their English learners' proficiency levels, specific academic content area needs, and interests. Preservice teachers learn how to implement strategies and design student activities that allow their English learner students both access to the core curriculum and progress in their English-language proficiency. For many preservice teachers, this is a challenging task because they are specialists in their content area, such as math or science, not in teaching English-language development. To compensate, preservice teachers are given ample class time to work with their peers to reflect upon decisions they make during each phase of their lesson planning to ensure they are meeting the needs of their English learners. In an analysis of the final lesson plan submitted at the end of the semester, fifty out of fifty-two (96%) preservice teachers included language objectives aligned to their English learners' proficiency levels. Forty-five out of fifty-two (87%) included differentiated strategies, and thirty-five out of fifty-two (67%) included differentiated assessment plans specifically designed on their English learner students' learning profiles.

### Applications: Sociocultural Competencies

In concert with learning equitable and socially just teaching methods, instructors also ask the preservice teachers to continually reflect upon their own sociocultural competencies throughout the course. Acknowledging the challenge of addressing language development needs within content area classes, the instructor ensures that course readings and class discussions center on sociopolitical aspects of English learner students' schooling experiences such as parental involvement with, societal attitudes toward, and/or misconceptions about bilingual education. The instructor presents the societal and political context of an English learner's schooling experience to guide preservice teachers in discussions about their role as change agents, specifically how they can become advocates for their English learner students. During these class discussions, instructors encourage preservice teachers to identify and reflect upon any biases they have and understand the importance of not acting upon such biases as a teacher. Moving beyond addressing biases, preservice teachers discuss actions they can take to either counter some societal attitudes or proactively address shortcomings they see in their English learners' educational experiences. For example, after reading about Latino/a parent involvement, preservice teachers work in small groups to discuss strategies their cooperating teachers use to communicate with caregivers, particularly those who may not speak English. They then decide which of these strategies matches their teaching styles and communication abilities and design their own caregiver-teacher communication plan. Plans designed by the preservice teachers include securing translators at their school sites for phone calls and parent-teacher conferences and creating newsletters in the languages spoken by the caregivers of the English learner students in the class.

In addition to course readings, activities, and assignments, during the fall semester, instructors assess preservice teachers on several professional dispositions, including one on social justice and equity: "Candidates appreciate the languages, communities, and experiences learners bring to the classroom. Candidates advocate for and support marginalized communities and individuals." At the semester midpoint, they assess themselves on a three-point rubric (unacceptable, approaching, meets) on each disposition. Course instructors and university supervisors then provide their collective assessment of each disposition, followed by preservice teachers comparing the collective assessment to their self-assessments. Because it is the first semester of their program, the vast majority of preservice teachers score themselves as "approaching" on the social justice and equity disposition because they cannot cite sufficient evidence to indicate they are "doing" each aspect of the disposition. Their self-assessments are accurate as indicated by the collective scores given by course instructors and university supervisors. During the fall semester, all fifty-two preservice teachers scored themselves as "approaching" on their self-assessments and received the same score on the collective assessment from instructors and supervisors. The preservice teachers repeat the process during the second semester with the expectation that they will grow as educators and "meet" all dispositions by the end of the program.

### Applications: Action Planning

As a culminating activity of the course, the instructor guides the preservice teachers to reflect upon the course information focused on the inequities in the schooling experiences of secondary English learners. Using the information about their English learner students, as well as through their experiences at their school sites, preservice teachers develop social justice and equity action plans addressing an inequity they have identified. Based on Joan Wink's book

*Critical Pedagogy: Notes from the Real World*, preservice teachers use a framework of "To Name, To Reflect Critically, and To Act" that is used as the foundation for the final social justice and equity action plans (Wink 2010). Their action plans consist of three sections corresponding to Wink's framework: identifying the problem to be addressed, reflecting critically on the problem through research and critical examination of practices, and producing the action plan itself. Throughout the course, preservice teachers meet in small groups to discuss and analyze their action plans, receive feedback from their group members, and revise their plans accordingly. Their final action plans form the culmination of this reflective peer review process.

Based on the reflective process described above, the instructor specifically guides preservice teachers through an individual analysis of how they define socially just and equitable actions to address identified inequities. Through this process, the instructor helps preservice teachers focus on socially just and equitable actions they are willing to take. Acknowledging their own competencies, the instructor then encourages preservice teachers to create a "doable" action plan, based on how they individually apply their definition of social justice and equity. Through this process of identifying a doable action plan, the instructor connects preservice teachers with other preservice teachers at their school sites who many want to work collaboratively on similar ideas to address complex issues; the instructor separates these ideas into doable plans for each of them. For example, one school site team addressed the issue of college and career readiness for the school's English learner population. Each preservice teacher designed a workshop for English learner students focused on the following aspects of the issue: filling out a college application, creating a budget for college, preparing for the SAT/ACT, and understanding community college pathways to a four-year university.

Working individually or collaboratively, the intent of the assignment is for preservice teachers to design an action plan that reflects their commitment to the identified issue. During the Reflect Critically stage, preservice teachers investigate their identified problem and how it is being addressed (if at all) at their school sites. Throughout the semester, preservice teachers use this information to refine their plans so they become doable within their school site systems. In small groups, they continually talk through their ideas and efforts with their peers and refine the specific steps they need to take in order to implement their plans.

During the fall 2014 semester, the social justice and equity action plans designed by the fifty-two preservice teachers can be grouped into four categories: (1) academic support (67.3%), (2) building community (15.4%), (3) support for families (9.6%), and (4) other efforts (7.7%). In the academic support category, the action plans were categorized further into four subcategories; (a) tutoring (n = 8 or 15.4%), (b) college preparation (n = 15 or 28.8%),

(c) standardized test (state language assessment) support (n = 8 or 15.4%), and (d) career readiness (n = 4 or 7.7%). In the academic support category, preservice teachers designed workshops on STEM careers, lunchtime tutoring sessions focused on Common Core math literacy, and information sessions/workshops on test taking strategies. Action plans that focused on building community (n = 8 or 15.4%) included a wide range of efforts, such as creating a weekly multicultural book club, facilitating bilingual conversations between English learners and students in advanced Spanish classes, and establishing a "family" support system for super seniors. Action plans in the support for families category (n = 5 or 9.6%) included workshops to help parents understand student placements (in Spanish) and a computer lab to help parents gain skills. Finally, the other efforts category (n = 4 or 7.7%) contained plans centered on providing information to parents and teachers on students in foster care and establishing an annual book drive to supplement bilingual resources in school libraries. The plans preservice teachers designed are representative of their ability to apply the knowledge learned about social justice and equity issues into concrete actions each of them were willing to take to address these issues.

## Conclusion and Recommendations

Teacher credential programs at MSIs play an important role in the recruitment, preparation, and retention of educators who understand how the larger sociocultural and sociopolitical realities influence students and learning. Furthermore, programs that place a strong focus on justice-oriented pedagogies throughout the various academic levels of their programs prepare their graduates to become effective teachers. Such programs also help preservice teachers to develop educational activists able to navigate the educational system while seeking ways to name and abolish existing inequities in the larger field of education. Making such justice-oriented practices self-sustaining is a challenge that social justice educators must address to counter the current deficit-based discourse being perpetuated by the so-called accountability movement and related federal policies.

We make five recommendations for building on the work we presented in this chapter and creating a self-sustaining movement of socially just and aware educators:

1. Clearly define the articulation of social justice and equity themes among coursework and fieldwork at the various academic levels.
2. Explicitly state the expected social justice and equity outcomes within course syllabi and assignments.
3. Sequence coursework to build on students' existing social justice and equity awareness and challenge them to expand and act upon such understandings.

4. Foster a connection (e.g., create activist networks) between the university and communities through teacher activists.
5. Define various pathways for transformational leadership at both teacher and administrator levels.

Given the spiraled nature of the process outlined in this chapter, these recommendations serve as interconnected methods for building and expanding capacities for applying social justice methods in actual teaching practices and policies. For example, at the foundations level, undergraduates need a thoughtful progression of assignments and fieldwork to help them think critically about their future roles as change agents. At the applications level, this requires coordination among course instructors, university supervisors, and cooperating teachers so that preservice teachers are getting a consistent social justice and equity message and applying it accordingly. At the expansions level, master's students must continually reflect upon their pedagogy and learn how to apply such reflection in research and community activism.

As educators and future educators move through the process of naming and acting on the inequities they encounter in the field, they must have the resources and networks to form communities of socially just educators. Such communities will provide the space for the critical dialogue, action planning, and reflection necessary to continue striving for social transformation. These recommendations represent the initial stages of what could become a larger movement to create classrooms and school communities that truly serve students and families. By putting such practices into action, the promise of equity may become reality.

### REFERENCES

Banks, James. 1993. "Approaches to Multicultural Curriculum Reform." In *Multicultural Education: Issues and Perspectives*, edited by James Banks and Cherry Banks. Boston: Allyn & Bacon.

California State University. 2015. "Enrollment Data." http://www.calstate.edu/externalrelations.

California State University, College of Education. 2015. "TEACHing for Change Framework." http://www.csus.edu/coe/index.html.

California State University, San Marcos, Office of Communications. 2015. "2015 Cougar Stats: Facts and Figures." http://news.csusm.edu/fast-facts.

California State University, San Marcos, School of Education. 2015. "Mission and Vision Statements." http://www.csusm.edu/education/index.html.

Capella-Santana, Nayda. 2003. "Voices of Teacher Candidates: Positive Changes in Multicultural Attitudes and Knowledge." *Journal of Educational Research* 96: 182–190.

Chubbuck, Sharon. 2010. "Individual and Structural Orientations in Socially Just Teaching: Conceptualization, Implementation, and Collaborative Effort." *Journal of Teacher Education* 61: 197–210.

Cochran-Smith, Marilyn, Karen Shakman, Cindy Jong, Diana Terrell, Joan Barnatt, and Patrick McQuillan. 2009. "Good and Just Teaching: The Case for Social Justice in Teacher Education." *American Journal of Education* 115: 347–377.

Darling-Hammond, Linda, Jennifer French, and Silvia Paloma Garcia-Lopez. 2002. *Learning to Teach for Social Justice*. New York: Teachers College Press.

Gasman, Marybeth, and Clifton Conrad. 2013. *Minority-Serving Institutions: Educating All Students*. Philadelphia: Center for Minority-Serving Institutions.

Gay, Geneva. 2010. *Culturally Responsive Teaching: Theory, Research, and Practice*. New York: Teachers College Press.

Gorski, Paul. 2012. "Stages of Multicultural Curriculum Transformation." http://edchange .org.

———. 2012. "Instructional, Institutional, and Sociopolitical Challenges of Teaching Multicultural Teacher Education Courses." *Teacher Educator* 47: 216–235.

Hill, K. Dara. 2012. "We're Actually Comfortable with Diversity: Affirming Teacher Candidates for Culturally Relevant Reading Pedagogy in Urban Practicum." *Action in Teacher Education* 34: 420–432.

Ladson-Billings, Gloria. 2001. *Crossing Over to Canaan: The Journey of New Teachers in Diverse Classrooms*. San Francisco: Jossey-Bass.

McCormik, Patricia. 2012. *Never Fall Down*. New York: HarperCollins.

McDonald, Morva. 2005. "The Integration of Social Justice in Teacher Education: Dimensions of Prospective Teachers' Opportunities to Learn." *Journal of Teacher Education* 56: 418–435.

Sacramento State University. 2014. "Student Demographics." http://www.csus.edu/oir/ Assessment/Nonacademic%20Program%20Assessment/Survey%20Instruments.html.

Sleeter, Christine. 2005. *Un-standardizing Curriculum: Multicultural Teaching in the Standards-Based Classroom*. New York: Teachers College Press.

Valdés, Guadalupe. 2001. *Learning and Not Learning English: Latino Students in American Schools*. New York: Teachers College Press.

Valencia, Richard. 1997. *The Evolution of Deficit Thinking: Educational Thought and Practice*. London: Routledge-Falmer.

Wink, Joan. 2010. *Critical Pedagogy: Notes from the Real World*. Boston: Pearson.

# 2

# Learning from the Community

## Innovative Partnerships That Inform
## Tribal College Teacher Education Programming

DANIELLE LANSING

After three weeks without a meeting, the families barreled into the preschool conference room full of updates and stories to tell. They started with making their way around the room greeting one another with hugs and smiles. We had a lot to catch up on! Several of the children had moved on to kindergarten. They each took time to hug their preschool teachers who also participated in the meeting. They missed them and their former classmates as well. It took us at least twenty minutes to settle into the room and begin our business at hand. We couldn't help but reflect on what had transpired over our three years together. An important commitment we had made to each other to carefully collaborate to make our preschool program more responsive to our community and to make our voices heard. We planned unique learning experiences that incorporated local culture, planted our community garden, and developed special community events and projects. All of which reflected the tribal communities we each represented. As a result, our children had moved on to kindergarten as confident individuals grounded in a strong Native identity. It was then that we realized that our relationships would always be the strong foundation for their futures. As a community we had built strong connections and systems that have changed the way we support our children. Our community would continue to flourish as new families joined our efforts. It is then that I realized the impact our tribal college has had on the greater community. I began to realize how our partnerships benefited countless tribal community members including my own. I further appreciated the unique context of our tribal college and my special role as a tribal college faculty member. I couldn't help but think about my own teacher training. I could only remember the typical mainstream developmental theories I had read about in textbooks. Only now did I understand that the skills I needed had been realized through years of trial and error as I tried my best to meet the expectations of the tribal communities I had worked within. If only I had been given the chance to learn this much earlier. I can't help but think how much more I could have accomplished as an educator. (Lansing, observational note, September 10, 2015)

Tribal Colleges and Universities (TCU) play a fundamental role in developing future educational leaders for tribal nations across the United States. Teacher education programs at TCUs continue to be integral in developing Native teachers for early childhood centers and K–12 schools that serve tribal nations. These TCU teacher education programs are unique because the collaborative partnerships maintained within their local communities deeply inform the education programs. Notions of service and reciprocal capacity build the relationships between TCUs and their respective tribal nations. To exemplify how TCUs engage in culturally based and responsive teacher education programming, this chapter describes how the Southwestern Indian Polytechnic Institute (SIPI), funded by an American Indian College Fund's *Wakanyeja* "Sacred Little Ones" early childhood initiative grant, partnered with the local Native community to build culturally based curriculum within their early learning center and within the SIPI early childhood teacher education program. This chapter explains the threefold process: (1) I illustrate how the SIPI team utilized the photovoice methodology to systematically document their process in strengthening early childhood education with the local community; (2) I describe the impact on Native preservice teachers as they participate in the community of practice resulting from SIPI's unique partnerships; and (3) I discuss the lessons learned from engaging the local community. Chapter 2 concludes with recommendations for reenvisioning Native teacher educational programming from within TCUs to meet the distinct needs of tribal communities and nations.

## Tribal Colleges and Universities

TCUs were founded under the notion that they would directly meet the needs of tribal communities by providing access to higher education. For the most part, they are located within tribal communities, on tribal lands, or within close proximity. In 1968, the Navajo Nation founded the Navajo Community College. Now renamed Diné College, Navajo Community College opened its doors as the first tribally controlled community college located on an Indian reservation (Pavel et al. 1998). Several other tribal communities followed suit and opened the doors of their own community colleges between 1969 and the 1990s.

The number of TCUs has steadily increased to thirty-seven institutions (thirty-four of which are fully accredited postsecondary institutions) that serve more than nineteen thousand students in a range of tribal communities across the United States (American Indian Higher Education Consortium [AIHEC] 2012). Common principles are apparent in their mission statements, which often include providing higher education and technical training for tribal members, preserving tribal language and culture, and allocating resources for tribal economic development and self-determination (Pavel et al. 1998).

In additional, TCUs have been recognized as distinct institutions that directly support Native nation-building within tribal communities through unique programs that honor Indigenous knowledge systems (Stull et al. 2015). These institutions directly provide not only higher education programs but also opportunities for community engagement. This extends the benefits of TCUs to the greater community because they provide needed resources while contributing to community change and revitalization. Robust engagement with local communities provides avenues for students to take part in social change within their communities (Crazy Bull 2015).

## Southwestern Indian Polytechnic Institute

Southwestern Indian Polytechnic Institute was established as a direct response to the request of the All Indian Pueblo Council together with the Navajo, Jicarilla Apache, Mescalero Apache, and Southern Ute Nations as well as other southwestern tribes who hoped for the establishment of an institution of higher learning to serve local Native American communities. Their vision was realized in the fall of 1971 (Southwestern Indian Polytechnic Institute 2014). The institution began as an individualized training institute but developed into a community college in 1993. Accredited by the Higher Learning Commission, SIPI now offers advanced technical education as well as university transfer degree programs. As one of two federally funded Bureau of Indian Education postsecondary institutions, SIPI serves American Indian and Alaskan Native (AIAN) students from not only New Mexico and Arizona tribal communities but also many tribes from states across the United States. The unique location within the metropolitan city of Albuquerque, New Mexico, is convenient for students from local New Mexico tribes who often commute daily. Residential students represent local tribal communities as well as various tribes from across the country. As a result, SIPI has a 100 percent AIAN student body. At times the student population can represent more than one hundred different tribes, which makes SIPI a truly intertribal community. Like other TCUs, SIPI often serves as a hub of activity and resources for the local Native American community of Albuquerque. Community workshops, cultural and informative events, powwows, and community runs are examples of events that SIPI often hosts for students, surrounding tribal communities, and greater Albuquerque.

In 2003, the Higher Learning Commission granted SIPI approval to provide an associate of arts degree in early childhood education in response to the needs of local tribal communities whose Head Start programs were working toward compliance with Head Start mandates (Southwestern Indian Polytechnic Institute 2011). Head Start mandates included requirements to elevate teacher quality through credentialing and higher education; for example, the mandates required Head Start teachers to obtain associate degrees in early childhood education. Beginning in 2000, SIPI began offering a three-course series leading to the National Association for the Education of Young Children's Child Development associate credential. Owing to the success of this pilot, SIPI then evolved to become the early childhood education associate of arts degree program (Martin et al. 2003). As a result, SIPI became a valuable resource to tribal communities who struggled to meet these mandates. The institution then began offering its courses via distance learning through videoconferencing. Through local agreements, SIPI has worked with tribal communities to train Head Start teachers from numerous tribal communities in New Mexico.

Southwestern Indian Polytechnic Institute ensures a quality educational experience for early childhood education students through a curriculum that includes practicum experiences. In 2010, SIPI opened an early childhood learning center on campus to serve as a laboratory school for early childhood education students. The center also provides a much-needed resource for SIPI students who are also parents. The Youth Development Incorporated, contracted to operate the center as an Early Head Start and Head Start program, offers income eligible families full-day services for infants, toddlers, and preschoolers (Southwestern Indian Polytechnic Institute 2011). Early childhood education students at SIPI complete two practicum experiences at the center, including sixty hours in infants and toddler classrooms and sixty hours with preschool children. The center primarily serves SIPI students, but it also serves the greater Albuquerque community.

## Community-Based Partnerships within Higher Education

There is a paucity of academic literature regarding teacher education and community-based partnerships specific to TCUs, which have, however, been continually recognized as pivotal in developing community capacity through their certificate and degree programming. Since their inception, TCUs have also been instrumental in developing teachers: twenty-nine TCUs offer early childhood and elementary education degree programs; of these, twenty-one house early childhood learning centers that meet the needs of the community and often serve as lab schools for students (AIHEC 2012). These teacher education programs are essential for the development of early childhood centers, Early Head Start, Head Start, and K–12 education in many rural reservation communities. In fact, for many communities, TCUs not only present the sole access point for training the next cadre of Native teachers but also meet the training needs of paraprofessionals and community members who lack access to postsecondary education. For this reason, many tribal communities have chosen to partner with TCUs to prepare early childhood personnel (Jacobs et al. 2001).

Although very little has been written regarding community partnerships and TCUs, we can learn a great deal from higher education and

community-based partnerships. Mainstream institutions have developed partnerships with tribal communities and documented their efforts. The Navajo
and Hopi nations have successfully partnered with Northern Arizona University
to increase the number of culturally responsive Indigenous teachers (White
et al. 2007). Many of these partnerships mostly include non-Native graduate
students or university faculty as partners. For example, the University of Idaho
partnered with Coeur d'Alene reservation communities to build local capacity
to solve problems associated with poverty. Experiential learning motivated and
improved learning outcomes among non-Native graduate students involved in
the partnership, but problems remain with regard to community leadership
and faculty and staff effectively engaging with tribes (Salant and Laumatia 2011).

For many TCUs, their missions specifically address commitments to partner with local communities. In turn, as TCUs value these connections, they
become the ideal setting for partnerships with tribal communities. TCU faculty
members offer a greater understanding of tribal communities, given their
experience in collaborating with Native communities, and position them for
possible partnerships. Moreover, a greater propensity for the sustainability of
community partnerships emerges because TCU students often return to tribal
communities for employment.

Through the support of the American Indian College Fund, TCUs were
supported in opportunities to develop unique early childhood partnerships
with tribal communities (Yazzie-Mintz 2012, 2014a, 2014b, 2014c). Early childhood programs in four TCUs have engaged local early childhood centers and
schools through the Wakanyeja "Sacred Little Ones" early childhood initiative
(Crazybull 2015; Yazzie-Mintz and Lansing 2014). Throughout this initiative, four
TCUs—including Iḷisaġvik College, College of Menominee Nation, Northwest
Indian College, and SIPI—have engaged their partners to develop culturally
infused curriculum, learning materials, language immersion programs, and
teacher training and education (Wakanyeja—ECE Initiative; Yazzie-Mintz 2015).
These partnerships have positively impacted the quality of teacher education at
each site, which has systematically documented their practices and built their
capacity to engage in meaningful research to strengthen their early childhood
programs (Yazzie-Mintz et al. 2014; Yazzie-Mintz and Lansing 2015).

## Innovative Community Partnerships at SIPI

American Indian and Alaskan Native families have hardly received meaningful
opportunities to participate in the educational lives of their children. In the past,
Native American parents, often seen as obstacles to assimilating their youth into
mainstream society (Lomawaima and McCarty 2006), experienced educational
programs that intentionally excluded parental input and participation. For
generations, educators continued to withhold the educational matters of their

children from Native parents; for example, many parents sent their children to school without knowing anything about their children's curriculum. As a result, educational systems in many tribal communities have reflected not the local values or cultures of the communities they serve; instead, they simply replicate mainstream curriculum and programs. Simultaneously, AIAN communities continue to grapple with complex problems that impact the well-being and perpetuation of Native language and culture within their communities. To develop tribal citizens who are able to contribute to the livelihood of their communities, it is imperative that educators engage Native communities in determining the priorities of educational programs that serve their children, a goal that requires defining the unique contexts of tribal communities. To define community culture, educators must consult parents and community as partners (Yazzie-Mintz 2014).

In 2011, SIPI was one of four TCUs awarded a grant under the College Fund's Wakanyeja "Sacred Little Ones"—Tribal College Readiness and Success by Third Grade Initiative (W. K. Kellogg Foundation Grant, P3015070). As part of the Wakanyeja ECE Initiative, SIPI's early childhood education associate degree program began laying the foundation for integrating Native language and culture into early childhood curriculum within both its partner early learning center and its teacher education programming. In doing so, SIPI has made a concerted effort to collaborate with families to define the local community culture along with the needs of community members in hopes of building culturally responsive programs.

## Overview of the Photovoice Project

As SIPI began to consider the development of culturally based early childhood education programs, it determined that a period of self-study was necessary. Faculty at SIPI, who also direct the initiative, were convinced that understanding the community culture was foundational for developing programming that was responsive to the community. The ultimate goal of the self-study was to garner a deeper understanding of SIPI's community in order to better determine the educational needs of the Native children and families they serve. A community-based inquiry moved AIAN parents to act as agents of change with regard to their child's education, and through this evolutionary process, SIPI documented practices that would inform and further develop SIPI's early childhood teacher education program.

After the College Fund selected and provided initial photovoice training in Year I of the initiative, SIPI chose to fully employ the photovoice methodology to engage the local community in a community-based qualitative inquiry. Based upon its use in a local tribal community, SIPI's team deemed photovoice an appropriate methodology (Romero-Little 2010). SIPI faculty, teachers, and parents developed as a team through intensive training.

Participatory qualitative inquiries promote collaboration as a means to solve community problems. Participatory action research allows professionals and nonprofessionals to become coresearchers in order to evoke community change (Patton 2002). Photovoice, a form of participatory needs assessment, allows individuals to act as researchers and recorders of the strengths and concerns within their own communities (Wang and Burris 1997). Through the photovoice methodology, participants receive cameras to photographically document their answers to research questions, which become the basis for the narratives of reflecting upon community needs and strengths. Group reflection then promotes dialogue through large and small group discussions that inspire community change (Wang and Burris 1997). Thus, the process provides a vehicle for community aspirations to reach policy makers. Originally developed for community health issues, photovoice has been utilized in a variety of contexts. It is partly based upon critical educational theories so it is especially suitable for educational settings (Whitfield and Meyer 2005), and educators have used it in a variety of contexts, including AIAN communities (Markus 2012; Romero-Little 2010). Photovoice is an especially suitable methodology for SIPI's context; for example, culturally responsive early childhood programs based upon Native American community values at the Pueblo of Jemez, a community served by SIPI's programs, developed through using photovoice (Romero-Little 2010).

SIPI recruited parents from its early childhood learning center to voice their interests, desires, and concerns with regard to the education of their children. Parents answered the research question: What knowledge is needed to become a healthy Native American?

Researchers crafted the question to encourage parents to reflect upon whole child development with the recognition that their tribal affiliation and knowledge was an important aspect of development. Educators provided digital cameras to parents and allowed time to develop photo collections that answered the research question. Since January 2013, a core group of ten parents have become engaged in SIPI's photovoice project. Parents have attended up to two meetings per month. Over the course of two years, parents developed photo collections depicting their expectations and desires regarding their child's education. Throughout this time, parents participated in group analysis sessions, where they reflected on the community's hopes and dreams, while mobilizing to develop community-based learning opportunities for their children.

## Selected Photovoice Findings

Several key themes have emerged from the parent photovoice data. A consistent theme with parents is the notion that AIAN children should know more about their tribal heritage, including an understanding of their connection to their ancestral homelands. For many parents in the SIPI community, strong connections to their tribal communities remain intact. Although they may have relocated for educational or economic reasons, they value the knowledge and understanding of their connections to the land of their people. Stan, a father in the program, shared a photo of his tribal community and the traditional dwellings of his people. He reflected on both the importance for his young son to understand their connection to the land and the kinship connections that are inherent in tribal communities: "I wanted to share this photo because it shows [Sonny] how beautiful one of the places he comes from is and how important it is to remember where he comes from as a young Indigenous man. We felt that it was also a good reminder of why we need to continue to help one another because in one way or another we are all related."

Parent data also illustrate the loss of culture that many Native communities recognize and that many parents realize—a realization that provides a powerful shared history among all Native families. Parents have expressed the strong desire to maintain their identities through exposure to their tribal culture, especially because many have relocated from their tribal communities. Stella shared an image of a tribal gathering in her community that reminded her of the need to reinforce the development of her child's identity as a Native person. Stella stated: "Our tribe is losing their identity slowly, and they are trying their best to keep this ceremony intact without drastic changes. There is always a way to evolve a traditional belief, and I believe that children need to be taught at a young age about who they are and where they come from."

Parents have also expressed the value of Native American teachings and knowledge, including storytelling, songs, dances, art, and understanding of meanings behind Native regalia. Throughout the ongoing dialogue, parents shared aspects of their tribal backgrounds and recognized that they represent an intertribal community—a real asset of the group. Many parents expressed their belief that knowledge and exposure to various tribal teachings are important aspects of learning for the children. Cecilia shared a photo of a recent tribal dance event held on campus and described it as a valuable experience to learn different tribal traditions. Cecilia reflected: "Introducing different cultures and traditions into children's lives can provide an understanding of one another. Understanding each other's beliefs and customs may bring harmonious peace among people."

Throughout this process, parents have come to understand their collective realities and have developed a narrative based upon their values, strengths, and hopes for the future. Families have become engaged in the inquiry process and systematically shared their photos with each other. They participate in an ongoing reflection process that honors each of their voices. Through this inquiry, the perspectives of Native parents became the central voice in shaping aspects of the early childhood learning center's curriculum. Deep reflection and dialogue have motivated parents and teachers to develop curriculum and learning opportunities for SIPI's youngest learners. After decades of Native parents' exclusion from the educational lives of their children, parents at SIPI are developing strength-based narratives that articulate their hopes and dreams for their children. Educators hear these parent voices and directly shape the educational experiences of their children. As a result of the partnership, an ongoing dialogue discusses how to develop early learning experiences that are relevant to meet the needs of child, family, and community. SIPI's early learning center brought together parents, teachers, and SIPI faculty to develop a curriculum framework based upon parental input that has produced three culturally based curriculum units developed for the early learning center as well as numerous collaborative projects across the campus community.

## Photovoice Inquiry Impact on Early Childhood Education Program

The photovoice project at SIPI has developed a true community of practice that has evolved to include TCU faculty, preschool teachers, TCU preservice teachers, and parents. These reciprocal relationships provide opportunities for preservice teachers to experience the implementation of a locally developed curriculum. In addition, this initiative improves SIPI's early childhood education program because preservice teachers benefit firsthand from the community-based programming, wherein the infusion of Native language and culture is visible. These experiences consequently provide a robust educational program that includes fully developed practicum experiences, strong connections with preschool teachers, practical examples of the infusion of Native culture into curriculum, and opportunities to volunteer and facilitate community events. Selected reflections from a focus group, including SIPI preservice teachers, evidence the program's success.

After preservice teachers were able to see the practical application of SIPI's own community-based curriculum, they set a higher standard for themselves as they witnessed the integration of Native language and culture into early childhood curriculum. Native American teachers hoped to achieve and uphold a higher standard founded upon inclusion of Native language and culture. Leila spoke to this effort:

> I would describe my experience at SIPI's early childhood program as an eye-opening experience. The standards are set much higher for teachers entering the early childhood field, especially for Native American teachers, because language and cultural preservation is very important for our future generations. I was able to get hands-on experience at SIPI's early

childhood center, and how the center integrates Native American culture. I gained a lot of knowledge and had amazing support from my teachers and my fellow co-students. It was a great experience.

For many preservice teachers, new co-curricular opportunities enhanced their training and supported their development of academic and nonacademic skills for the better. Students who volunteered for the initiative often took on leadership positions that enabled them to direct projects, including direct work with the local community, and therefore gain skills associated with those experiences. Annabelle described her experiences:

> Sacred Little Ones has improved my experience at SIPI by first opening up volunteer opportunities for me and all the other students here at the SIPI community. I remember being approached by my advisor and the teacher saying, "Volunteer, volunteer for these opportunities." But I wasn't really eager to volunteer until I found out more about the Sacred Little Ones project and their purpose. Then I started to volunteer more, and then I started getting involved more, and then this involvement turned to an internship and just really collaborating with everyone here, but with that—within the SIPI community, the early childhood program at the Head Start center, working with the families and children—it just really expanded my skills and I really gained a lot. My communication skills have, I would say, improved a whole lot. My presentation skills have tremendously gotten better because I used to be afraid and . . . now like I feel more confident speaking to a class—or a group of students, speaking to a group of people or just presenting anywhere now. I just feel more confident and more proud of myself.

For many SIPI students, opportunities to become involved in community events including cultural projects resulted in an increased sense of pride. As they became advocates for integrating Native language and culture, students often took pride in their AIAN heritage and their personal offerings to the children. Students then felt motivated to engage other students on campus and became instrumental in developing partnerships with various student groups. Annabelle praised the initiative that provided them an opportunity to work toward the common goal of providing community-based cultural learning experiences for young children:

> I just feel more proud of myself as a Native American student, and it just really taught me to collaborate with others as well and to reach out to others within the SIPI community or within the local communities, such as we've been collaborating with the SIPI clubs, such as the Apache Club, the Intertribal Dorm Council, Early Childhood students, Phi Theta Kappa,

and Head Start families and the children . . . making those connections and those relationships with them and just building the relationships with everybody because that's really important now as a teacher because you want to work with everybody. Because the more people that you work with I'm learning you create this unique, awesome team that can really impact the community, and could really make a difference together. Because it's not a one person thing, it's a community thing, just like the saying always goes, "it takes a community to raise a child." And I'm finding out more and more that this is very true, and as a teacher I need to learn all these things. Because if I really want to be a great teacher, um, I need to gain the skills right now to really implement them later down the road.

Students also realized that engaging the local community in developing culturally relevant learning is part of becoming a responsive Native teacher, which became part of their career aspirations. Many students expressed the intention of working with tribal communities in the future to develop culturally responsive curriculum within educational settings.

For those who possessed either special talents or cultural knowledge to share, SIPI's initiative provided opportunities for them to share their knowledge within various projects. These preservice teachers gained valuable experiences in the practical application of cultural knowledge within early childhood class-rooms. These meaningful experiences have helped students to develop and integrate Native knowledge into learning experiences. John, a recent graduate, discussed his involvement with SIPI's initiative:

I also was involved with the gardening. I had some students or the Head Start students come out, and I taught them how to take care of their garden. I taught them how to hoe the weeds around the chili that they planted, the corn they planted, the melons, how to . . . cut down the corn—so actually the main stalk will grow taller and produce more corn . . . put up the chili mounds so the chili doesn't fall down once the chili is produced. So we had a good time out there. We had children get in there and actually do the work themselves too. And the other thing that I helped out with was with the Native American 5K. I was able to collaborate with the students' families and, you know was able to give them a little bit of information on how to stretch and how to be there for their kids as far as whatever activities that they want to be in, you know, just be there to support them as a father. So, you know, I gave words of wisdom in that way.

As students participated in cultural projects, they saw the value of the relationships that developed between the early learning center and the greater community. June, a student who participated in the community garden project, discussed the benefits of participating in a healthy collaboration with families.

> One of the experiences that I enjoyed too was my first one, which was during the summer of 2014, which was a planting event. During this time I saw how the preschool staff and families work together. I saw them build healthy relationships. I also like how this event implemented culture by teaching children the morals of planting. Sacred Little Ones has involved early childhood students to experience collaborating with families and to practice working as a team.

By becoming immersed in SIPI's collaborative community partnerships, SIPI's early childhood education students have gained valuable lessons and skills that they can take to their communities. As SIPI students participate in a community of practice, they build their capacity to engage families and community members to develop responsive educational programs. Through photovoice and other collaborative projects with the community, SIPI has developed reciprocal systems that benefit all stakeholders. As illustrated in figure 2.1, SIPI has leveraged its community partnerships to build systems that support the documentation and development of best practices that directly inform its ECE programming.

Students learned valuable lessons from engaging the local community in a collective inquiry process. Moreover, SIPI's early childhood education program has benefitted from its partnership with its early learning center in countless ways. It is imperative to document and integrate these lessons into future praxis. The institution has developed place-based practices, grounded in a unique local community and founded in responsive educational practices

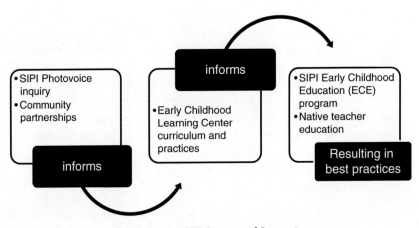

FIGURE 2.1 SIPI Systems of Support

for the children and families it serves. We learned valuable lessons from SIPI's community partnerships:

- The institution has developed systems for engaging Native families in processes to develop culture-based Native early childhood curriculum. These systems include taking time to develop processes for listening to community voices. These partnerships demonstrate the impact of privileging the knowledge of the families and community served by the program and develop a strong sense of trust and commitment among all involved stakeholders.

- The early childhood education program at SIPI documented the value of real-world experiences. Meaningful engagement with children and families has positively impacted TCU student learning as they experience firsthand knowledge regarding best practices for engaging Native communities. Students, learning to become teachers, are able to directly connect early childhood theory to real world examples, which results in increased understanding and achievement.

- As preservice teachers participate in SIPI's early childhood education initiative to develop culturally relevant early childhood education, they begin to imagine the possibilities for change within their own communities. Preservice teachers have witnessed culturally based curriculum developed directly from community voices and collective photovoice inquiries to work toward developing educational programs that honor AIAN community values.

## Conclusions and Recommendations

The early childhood education program at SIPI has developed an authentic partnership that engages the local community in a collective effort to develop culturally responsive curriculum for Native children, wherein both partners benefit in a reciprocal relationship. This has occurred in part due to the longstanding commitment SIPI has to its community. Tribal Colleges and Universities are ideal institutions for community-based partnerships, given their unique missions and commitments to tribal communities. These partnerships provide unique opportunities for TCU students to build the capacity to make change within their own communities.

Meaningful community-based partnerships take time and careful consideration of community needs and input. Tribal Colleges and Universities can capitalize on their existing community relationships to develop research-based best practices. Documenting lessons learned from these partnerships is essential for developing a research community and discourse within TCUs, and faculty members need opportunities to engage in meaningful relationships with community partners. For teacher education programs at TCUs, the potential is great. Meaningful partnerships with local community schools and early childhood centers can undoubtedly result in innovative practices that can inform Indian education.

Teacher education programs at TCUs have a responsibility to push beyond current mainstream educational theories to create place-based and relevant learning opportunities for preservice teachers so they may reach their full potential as leaders for their respective tribal nations. Tribal institutions are the ideal training ground for tribal early learning centers and K–12 schools. Steeped in nation-building principles, TCUs have the potential to develop teacher education programs that provide opportunities to reimagine educational systems serving Native families and children. In these innovative learning communities, AIAN preservice teachers can develop place-based education innovations with the potential to lead the reenvisioning of educational systems that capitalize on the strengths of Native nations.

## ACKNOWLEDGMENTS

This research was supported by the "Wakanyeja 'Sacred Little Ones'–Tribal College Readiness and Success by Third Grade Initiative," W. K. Kellogg Foundation (Grant # P3015070).

## NOTE

I use pseudonyms for all parent and student names.

## REFERENCES

American Indian College Fund. 2011. "Wakanyeja 'Sacred Little Ones' Early Childhood Education Initiative." http://www.collegefund.org/content/wakanyeja.

American Indian Higher Education Consortium. 2012. "2009–2010 AIHEC AIMS Fact Book: Tribal Colleges and Universities Report." http://www.aihec.org/our_stories/docs/reports/AIHEC_AIMSreport_May2012.pdf.

Crazy Bull, Cheryl. 2015. "Engaging Life: TCUs and Their Role Building Community." *Journal of American Indian Higher Education* 27: 20–24.

Jacobs, Geralyn M., Joanne Wounded Head, Sue Forest, Judy Struck, Keenan Pituch, and Gerard A. Jacobs. 2001. "Forming Partnerships with Tribal Colleges to Meet Early Childhood Personnel Preparation Needs." *Journal of Early Intervention* 24: 298–305.

Lomawaima, Tsianina K., and Teresa L. McCarty. 2006. *"To Remain an Indian": Lessons in Democracy from a Century of Native American Education.* New York: Teachers College Press.

Markus, Susan F. 2012. "Photovoice for Healthy Relationships: Community-Based Participatory HIV Prevention in a Rural American Indian Community." *American Indian and Alaskan Native Mental Health Research Journal* 19: 102–123.

Martin, Joe, James Lujan, Valerie Montoya, Gail Goldstein, and Kathy Abeita. 2003. "Request for Approval: Institutional Change in Educational Offerings." Unpublished report, Southwestern Indian Polytechnic Institute.

Patton, Michael Q. 2002. *Qualitative Research and Evaluation Methods*. Thousand Oaks, CA: Sage Publications.

Pavel, D. Michael, Rebecca R. Skinner, Margaret Cahalan, John Tippeconnic, and Wayne Stein. *American Indians and Alaska Natives in Postsecondary Education*. Washington DC: US Department of Education, National Center for Education Statistics, 1998. http://nces.ed.gov/pubs98/98291.pdf.

Romero-Little, Mary E. 2010. "How Should Young Indigenous Children Be Prepared for Learning? A Vision of Early Childhood Education for Indigenous Children." *Journal of American Indian Education* 49: 1–16.

Salant, Priscilla, and Laura Laumatia. 2011. "Better Together: Coeur d'Alene Reservation Communities and the University of Idaho." *Journal of Higher Education Outreach and Engagement* 15: 101–112.

Southwestern Indian Polytechnic Institute. 2011. "Southwestern Indian Polytechnic Institute Early Childhood Education Program 2000–2010 Self Study Report." www.scribd.com/document/50982434/Sipi-2011-Self-Study-Report-with-links./

———. 2014. "2014–2016 Catalog." http://www.sipi.edu/ acadprog/catalog/SIPI%202014–2016%20Catalog.pdf.

Stull, Ginger, Demetrios Spyridakis, Marybeth Gasman, Andrés Castro Samayoa, and Yvette Booker. 2015. "Redefining Success: How Tribal Colleges and Universities Build Nations, Strengthen Sovereignty, and Persevere Through Challenges." https://www2.gse.upenn.edu/cmsi/sites/gse.upenn.edu.cmsi/files/MSI_TBLCLLGreport_Final.pdf.

Wang, Caroline, and Mary A. Burris. 1997. "Photovoice: Concept, Methodology, and Use for Participatory Needs Assessment." *Health Education and Behavior* 24: 369–387.

White, Carolyn J., Clara Bedonie, Jennie de Groat, Louise Lockard, and Samantha Honani. 2007. "A Bridge for Our Children: Tribal/University Partnerships to Prepare Indigenous Teachers." *Teacher Education Quarterly* 34: 71–86.

Whitfield, Dean, and Helen Meyer. 2005. "Learning from Our Students: Photovoice and Classroom Action Research." *Science Education Review* 4: 97–103.

Yazzie-Mintz, Tarajean. 2012. "Wakanyeja 'Sacred Little Ones' Early Childhood Education Initiative: Highlights from Four Tribal College Funded Projects." Presentation at Native Children's Research Exchange, Denver, Colorado, October 3–5.

———. 2014a. "Engaging Community-Based Partnerships to Strengthen Early Childhood Educational Opportunities." Presentation at Native American Conference on Special Education, Albuquerque, New Mexico, March 26–28.

———. 2014b. "To Become a Teacher of the Next Generation: Counting Coup with Education in Honor of Our Youngest Tribal Members." Presentation at American Indian Higher Education Consortium—Student Conference, Billings, Montana, March 16–18.

———. 2014c. "Wakanyeja 'Sacred Little Ones' ECE Initiative: Creating Systems of Care and Learning for Native Children." Presentation at National Indian Education Association Expert-Driven Presidential Session: Building Strong Foundations for Early Learning, Anchorage, Alaska, October 17.

———. 2015. "Drawing upon Places of Strength and Knowing: Wakanyeja Communities of Inquiry Strengthen Early Childhood Learning Opportunities with Native Children and Families." Presentation at Inequality, Poverty, and Education: An Ethnography Invitation, Communities of Inquiry Symposium, Philadelphia, Pennsylvania, February 27–28.

Yazzie-Mintz, Tarajean, and Danielle Lansing. 2014. "Re-envisioning Early Childhood Education from Tribal Colleges and Universities." Presentation at National Indian Education Association 2014 Research Forum, Anchorage, Alaska, October 16.

———. 2015. "Theory and Institutional Practices: Policy Implications and Transformation of Early Childhood Education from TCUs to the World." Presentation at Native Early Childhood Education Symposium, Albuquerque, New Mexico, June 1–2.

Yazzie-Mintz, Tarajean, Cyndi Pyatskowit, Danielle Lansing, Devin Bates, Shelley Macy, and Ashia Smock. 2014. "Imagining Our Indigenous Knowledge within Reach of Our Children: Lessons from the Wakanyeja 'Sacred Little Ones' ECE Initiative." Presentation at 2014 World Indigenous Peoples Conference on Education (WiPC:E), Honolulu, Hawaii, May 19–24.

# 3

# Teacher Preparation for Our Communities

## Building Co-teaching Collaborative Schools from the Ground Up

CHERYL A. FRANKLIN TORREZ

JONATHAN BRINKERHOFF

IRENE WELCH

In this chapter we describe an innovative model of clinical preparation for teacher candidates. Our collaborative model, co-teaching collaborative schools (CTCS), has been successful for all participants. This equitable and organic university-school partnership model of clinical preparation may inform other teacher preparation programs as we all endeavor to better prepare future teachers and positively impact current and future elementary classrooms. We describe this innovative model by providing a background and framework for the CTCS, a description of what the schools look like in practice, the impact of CTCS, and the lessons we learned.

## Background

The University of New Mexico (UNM) is one of four universities in the United States that holds both the designation of Hispanic-Serving Institutions (HSI) and the Carnegie classification of Research University–Very High Research Activity. As a Minority-Serving Institution (MSI) in a state of two million residents, more than half our students self-identify as Hispanic and/or Native American, and 36 percent of our undergraduates self-identify as white (University of New Mexico 2015). This breakdown is representative of the state as a whole. In addition to elementary teacher preparation on the main campus, we have field centers located in several rural communities across the state. In a typical academic year, more than 275 elementary teacher candidates enroll in our undergraduate teacher preparation programs, and our teacher candidates reflect the composition of New Mexico. For example, at one branch campus,

80 percent of the undergraduates identify as Native American (University of New Mexico 2015). Many of our teacher candidates have a strong sense of community, heritage, and cultural affinity. Victoria Derr (2002) noted that when people experience nature, culture, and family as interwoven entities, their connections and attachments are strong and meaningful. These types of attachments and experiences are inherent in many of our teacher candidates. Community and cultural heritage are fundamentally parts of self and represent strengths for many of our teacher candidates. We consistently see dispositions of caring and understanding among them as well as a willingness to engage with families and communities during their clinical preparation.

Without a doubt, New Mexico is a diverse state and unique in the southwest with twenty-two tribal nations (New Mexico Indian Affairs Department 2015), including nineteen Pueblos. More than 20 percent of the state's population lives below the federal poverty level (U.S. Census Bureau 2015). According to a recent *Kids Count* report, 35 percent of the children in the state live in poverty, which makes New Mexico among the lowest in the nation for child well-being (Annie E. Casey Foundation 2015; New Mexico Kids Count 2015). Albuquerque, the state's largest metropolitan area, is home to nearly half of the state's population as well as the University of New Mexico's main campus.

Many of these factors not only contribute to the richness and uniqueness of New Mexico but also, at times, present challenges. For example, many bilingual teacher candidates do not earn bilingual teaching endorsements, owing to a number of factors, including the lack of educational funding to attend the university for an additional year. The state of New Mexico also offers a Native American Language and Culture certificate with each tribal nation "determining an acceptable standard of competence and language proficiency to teach the language and culture" (New Mexico Administrative Code, title 6, sec 6.63.14.8).

Often, and erroneously, New Mexico is clumped together with other states in the Southwest such as Arizona or Texas. The common discourse among New Mexicans is that New Mexico—historically, culturally, and currently—is unique among all other southwestern states. Native New Mexicans bristle when the state is likened to neighboring southwestern states, emblematic of the subtle and gross distinctions that are not always visible to non–New Mexicans; in fact, the differences between the numerous tribal nations are often not evident to nontribal members. In our CTCS, we strive to enhance the teacher candidates' dispositions of caring and sense of heritage and consciously avoid overgeneralizing and stereotypes as the teacher candidates develop culturally sustaining pedagogies (McCarty and Lee 2014).

Twenty years ago our award-winning teacher preparation program served as a model for clinical preparation at MSIs and HSIs. Over time, budget cuts, political influences, and changes in leadership resulted in threadbare clinical preparation. The faculty recognized our program was no longer meeting the needs of students, their future students, or the state as effectively as possible, a recognition that prompted change in the spring of 2010.

In response to a query from a local elementary school, we initiated a partnership to develop an innovative model of clinical preparation to better meet the needs of our students and the needs of elementary students across our majority-minority state. University-based teacher educators and elementary classroom educators, instructional councils, and community members co-implemented and co-evaluated the co-developed CTCS model. Hence, the CTCS model, organic in nature, developed from the ground up rather than being imposed from the top down.

Fundamental to the CTCS teacher preparation model is co-teaching (Bacharach, Washut Heck, and Dahlberg 2010). The CTCS student teaching experience differs substantially from most teacher preparation programs. Both the Council for the Accreditation of Educator Preparation (CAEP) and the state of New Mexico require student teaching, the most widely accepted part of teacher preparation programs (Zeichner 2002), for licensure. Traditional models of student teaching have not changed significantly in the last sixty years (Guyton and McIntyre 1990). This practice of learning to teach in isolation may not provide the teacher candidate with an authentic experience; after all, a practicing educator must often learn to collaborate with other classroom teachers, paraprofessionals, parent volunteers, community experts, and special educators to meet the academic needs of their students (Brownell and Walther-Thomas 2002; Darling-Hammond 2000). An alternative approach to student teaching is a co-teaching model, which allows both the cooperating teacher and teacher candidate to work collaboratively throughout the student teaching experience.

In a co-teaching model, cooperating teachers mentor teacher candidates by sharing the planning, organization, delivery, and assessment of instruction within the classroom. When meeting regularly with teacher candidates to plan instruction, the instructors spend at least two hours in co-planning sessions each week. During the co-planning sessions, cooperating teachers and teacher candidates select from a range of co-teaching strategies that align with lesson goals and objectives to promote maximum student engagement and effective teaching. In addition to co-planning and co-teaching, teacher candidates also participate in professional learning communities, state-mandated assessments and testing of students, and community initiatives as well as all meetings and professional development in which cooperating teachers participate. Taken together, the components of the CTCS model—collaboration, co-planning, and co-teaching—represent an innovative model of teacher preparation.

One goal of the CTCS is to prevent praxis shock, or the feeling of being underprepared, reported by many first-year teachers. Geert Kelchtermans and Katrijn Ballet (2002) used the term *praxis shock* to describe the feelings faced by many teachers during their induction years: "Praxis shock refers to the teachers' confrontation with the realities and responsibilities of being a classroom teacher that puts their beliefs and ideas about teaching to the test, challenges some of them, and confirms others" (Kelchtermans and Ballet 2002, 105).

Praxis shock is a common result of traditional models of student teaching that focus on the teacher candidate, often an isolated student teacher at an elementary school, spending numerous hours as an observer/helper, gradually assuming the role of teaching, and eventually leading to a short full assumption. Such models are typically ineffective (Cochran-Smith 1991). In contrast, through the CTCS model, a cohort of ten to fifteen teacher candidates completes three semesters of student teaching totaling 900 hours of clinical preparation in collaboration with their cooperating teachers. The extended hours support teacher candidates in better meeting the needs of the elementary students, school site, district, and university, while being part of a cohort also allows teacher candidates to actively support one another. The cohort of teacher candidates becomes a visible, active, and pivotal component of the school community. The teacher candidates often volunteer to coordinate afterschool programs, to work alongside community members in school gardens, and to assist with school fundraisers. Additional support for teacher candidates comes from an embedded university faculty member who is on site at the school with the teacher candidates at least one full day each week. Along with support for teacher candidates, the embedded faculty serves as a liaison between the school site and the university and conducts professional development for the cooperating teachers. The embedded faculty also works with the school site instructional coach to implement the various components of the CTCS.

The CTCS model, including the embedded university faculty member, addresses the focus some researchers have placed on partnerships between universities and K–12 schools (Darling-Hammond 1994, 2006; Sirotnik and Goodlad 1988; Teitel 2003). These researchers believe that closer connections between university teacher education programs and K–12 schools can improve the quality of teaching and influence student achievement. We believe the purposeful, supportive community that forms within CTCS better prepares teacher candidates, especially when compared to the traditional, often isolating, models of student teaching. Our students, for whom the sense of community is profound, confirm the impact of this model.

The numerous components of the CTCS were thoughtfully and purposefully developed. An initial inquiry from an elementary school in spring 2010 led to a series of development and planning meetings that continued through the following fall semester. These meetings led to the inaugural cohort that began in spring 2011. Although the elementary school faculty and instructional council were eager to implement sooner, it was vital to spend the extra time to ensure that we met all participants' needs and that we arranged all administrative and organizational pieces. Too often, we find ourselves flying the plane while still building it; we did not want this to be the case while we developed this new model of clinical preparation.

During the initial planning, the members of the collaborative team jointly decided to use a co-teaching model, along with more clinical preparation time. The cooperating teachers and members of the instructional council simply did not believe our traditional student teaching model was providing enough meaningful clinical preparation time for teacher candidates. Additional planning outcomes focused on including an embedded faculty member, conducting the student teaching seminar at the elementary school site, and supporting the concept (from all participating classroom teachers) that their school should be a CTCS. In fact, the school site coined the term *co-teaching collaborative school*. As a result of this comprehensive planning, the College of Education and the public school district produced a well-developed memorandum of mutual understanding.

## Our Timeline

In spring 2016, we were working with our fifth teacher candidate cohort at the original site and have expanded the CTCS model to two additional elementary schools that are currently engaged with their second cohorts. While students are inducted into the university's elementary teacher preparation program in both fall and spring semesters, candidates are able to begin student teaching at a CTCS site only in the spring semester with admission to the CTCS cohort occurring in late fall. Initially, we attempted to admit a new cohort each semester, but this proved overwhelming for the school site. As a result, each spring semester a CTCS will have ten to fifteen third-semester teacher candidates and ten to fifteen first-semester teacher candidates. School-site capacity determines the size of each cohort.

### Admission

Each fall semester, after the elementary teacher preparation program admits its students, we hold an orientation meeting during which teacher candidates learn about the CTCS option and its potential benefits through a presentation by the embedded faculty and current teacher candidates. Students indicate their interest in student teaching at a CTCS site; within a few weeks, they participate in site-based interviews in groups of three or four conducted by a panel of cooperating teachers, the instructional coach, the embedded university faculty, and current teacher candidates. During our early development of the CTCS, two veteran cooperating teachers suggested the idea of an interview process; they had previously experienced not knowing or lacking input into the selection of their student teachers in our traditional model of student teaching.

Following the interviews, the committee agrees on the candidates to be invited to form the new cohort. All interviewees are sent an e-mail congratulating them on their acceptance or thanking them for their interest. The e-mail to new candidates includes an invitation to a formal half-day CTCS workshop for incoming teacher candidates and cooperating teachers. The workshops are co-designed and co-facilitated by the school instructional coach and the embedded faculty member. The content of these workshops varies from site to site; however, several components are essential: an introduction to co-teaching, icebreaker and get-to-know-each-other activities, administrative paperwork, establishment of expectations by the school principal, instructional coach, and embedded faculty, and a tour of the school. We adopted many of these activities from a co-teaching handbook developed at St. Cloud University (Teacher Quality Enhancement Center 2010).

### Program Induction

During the first semester in our program, the new teacher candidate cohort attends methods classes at the university Monday through Wednesday, and they spend Thursday and Friday at the CTCS. Teacher candidates arrive and depart from the CTCS according to the school district schedule. For the first three weeks, we divide teacher candidates into groups of two or three for visits to classrooms hosting a teacher candidate that semester. They spend mornings in one classroom and afternoons in another. The embedded faculty member provides teacher candidates with a classroom observations form, including questions to focus their observations. Teacher candidates complete the form as they observe each classroom. To support their ability to recognize the implementation of various classroom management strategies they might observe, we also provide teacher candidates with a handout describing a variety of strategies and techniques.

After the teacher candidate groups observe all the hosting classrooms, they attend the first session of the required student teaching seminar. The embedded university faculty member conducts all seminar meetings on-site throughout the program. At the initial seminar meeting, we discuss responses to the classroom observations form before we ask students which grade level they are most interested in teaching. Following the seminar, the embedded faculty member meets with the school's instructional coach to jointly decide on classroom placements.

For the three semesters of clinical preparation, we place teacher candidates in one classroom for spring semester (semester one) and in a different classroom for the remaining two semesters the following full academic year (semesters two and three). We make an effort to place teacher candidates in their preferred grade level for the second and third semesters. To provide experience at both upper and lower grade levels, we make first semester placements in opposition to teacher candidates' preferred grade level. The embedded faculty member and instructional coach also consider teacher candidates' grade level preferences as well as the personalities of both teacher candidate and cooperating teacher.

### Supporting Cooperating Teachers

During the weeks when teacher candidates are visiting classrooms, the embedded university faculty member meets with cooperating teachers who have agreed to host a teacher candidate. The agenda includes a discussion of strategies for making teacher candidates feel welcome and integrating them into classroom procedures and routines while establishing teacher candidates as teachers rather than students. Critical to this process is referring to the preservice teachers as teacher candidates and not student teachers (Teacher Quality Enhancement Center 2010). Strategies include placing teacher candidates' names alongside the teachers' names outside classroom doors, providing a desk or other place for teacher candidates to work, and having teacher candidates take responsibility for routine procedures such as attendance, lunch count, and leading lines. Cooperating teachers are encouraged to engage teacher candidates immediately by teaching with the co-teaching strategies. Most often, one teach/one observe or one teach/one assist are used first, although there is no hierarchy within the seven co-teaching strategies. In the cooperating teacher meetings, the embedded faculty member addresses all seven co-teaching strategies and encourages use of the co-teaching strategies in each lesson each day.

An additional critical topic in these meetings focuses on the differences between more typical student teaching models and co-teaching. It is not uncommon to find many cooperating teachers who have hosted student teachers in the past or vividly remember their own student teaching experiences. Naturally, these individuals envision co-teaching as essentially equivalent to their prior experiences. Accordingly, we use these meetings to remind cooperating teachers of the far closer relationship represented by co-teaching in both planning and instruction. In terms of planning, we also remind cooperating teachers that the verbalization of their thought process during the first semester significantly benefits teacher candidates. In terms of instruction, the embedded faculty and cooperating teachers review the various co-teaching strategies and discuss what examples of each might look like in their classrooms to support cooperating teachers in faithfully and effectively implementing the co-teaching strategies.

At the beginning of the first semester, one of the most frequently used strategies is one teach/one observe. It is critical that cooperating teachers understand this represents an active strategy where the teacher candidate takes notes focused on a previously agreed-upon topic, such as classroom management or effective teaching techniques. Following the lesson, the teacher candidate and cooperating teacher should meet to discuss the observations with the intent of expanding the teacher candidate's awareness and understanding of the lesson.

### Becoming Part of the School Community

Starting in the spring semester and continuing through the entire clinical experience, teacher candidates actively participate in all teacher in-service trainings, professional learning communities, individualized education plan meetings, and other meetings attended by their cooperating teacher. In addition, both teacher candidates and cooperating teachers actively participate in school fund-raising activities. They also frequently create or support afterschool clubs. In these ways, teacher candidates are purposefully integrated into all aspects of the school community.

An understanding of the schools' surrounding neighborhood community can also help teacher candidates to recognize and manage diverse cultural classroom environments and student needs. Accordingly, when they first arrive at their assigned schools, we ask teacher candidates to explore both the school and the neighborhood communities. In one aspect of exploring the school community, the teacher candidates work alongside/shadow for two or three days a nonclassroom-teacher school employee—an instructional assistant, custodian, administrative assistant, or cafeteria personnel. When exploring the neighborhood community we ask teacher candidates to identify a neighborhood gathering or support locations such as grocery stores, libraries, health and counseling centers, community centers, and so forth. After identifying these locations, the teacher candidates, while spending several afternoons observing in these locations and talking with volunteers and employees, seek to better understand the neighborhood's services and needs.

Throughout the remainder of the spring semester, the embedded faculty member spends one full day on-site conducting informal visits to teacher candidates in their classrooms. These visits and the informal feedback they allow, coupled with interactions during lunch, support the development of deeper relationships with teacher candidates than is allowed by typical student teaching models. Additionally, the embedded faculty member meets once or twice more with cooperating teachers and weekly at the student teaching seminar with teacher candidates. Seminars universally include teacher candidates sharing ideas or concerns, discussing readings, and exploring various topics such as classroom management techniques, constructivist learning theory and its implementation through Socratic dialogue, and other effective teaching strategies and techniques.

A focus on the basics of designing and implementing effective instruction helps meet the needs of diverse students. The CTCS serves a variety of student populations with different needs, yet the foundation for successfully meeting diverse student needs is a solid understanding of research-based, effective teaching strategies (Bransford, Brown, and Cocking 2000). These foundational instructional design skills include, but are not limited to, using student-centered, constructivist instructional strategies that focus on building understanding. In addition, we cover specific skills and concepts: creating well-written instructional objectives; differentiating instruction and language support for English learners; breaking instruction into logically sequenced and manageable steps; checking for understanding during instruction, including assessments aligned with both the objectives and the instruction; and distributing practice of lesson content over time. With the widespread availability of interactive white boards at our CTCS, whenever possible, we encourage teacher candidates to include images and other interactive features in instruction to make it more concrete, visual, and culturally relevant.

Teacher candidates develop an understanding of these foundational skills and learn how their successful implementation can meet the needs of a diverse student body in the first semester seminars. We reinforce these understandings throughout seminars in the remaining two semesters and both formal and informal teaching observations. At each CTCS, the pool of experts, including the cooperating teachers who are chosen for their record of instructional success as well as the embedded faculty and instructional coach, support development of skills in implementing instructional designs.

### Moving into Semester 2 and 3: The Final Placement

At the end of the spring semester, the embedded faculty member and instructional coach meet to assign teacher candidates to their placement for the following year. This assignment takes place in the spring because we expect teacher candidates to be in contact with their second/third semester cooperating teacher during the summer so they can participate in opening the classroom and preparing for the new school year. The teacher candidates begin work at the CTCS two or three weeks prior to the university's official fall semester start date. Thus, we intend to provide teacher candidates with a hands-on understanding of the planning and procedures required to set up a classroom in preparation for a new school year.

During the fall semester, teacher candidates attend methods classes at the university on Mondays and Tuesdays while reporting to the school site for the remainder of the week. As before, teacher candidates are on site for the same hours as their cooperating teachers and attend all teacher trainings and meetings. They continue attending weekly student teaching seminars where the embedded faculty member addresses concerns and issues, discusses weekly readings, and covers topics related to effective instruction. During the semester, informal visits to classrooms by the embedded faculty member continue; however, during the semester, the embedded faculty member conducts two formal teaching observations, and the cooperating teacher conducts an additional two observations. Formal teaching observations consist of a preconference where teacher candidates share their detailed lesson plan, observation of the lesson implementation, and a postconference where they discuss instructional successes and possibilities for improvement. During this semester, teacher candidates continue participating in fund-raising activities (as do the other faculty members at the school) and often volunteer to run clubs after school.

The final student teaching semester begins in the spring. During the university's winter break, teacher candidates must follow the school district's calendar, which means they return to their student teaching placement immediately after the start of the new year, despite the fact that this is several weeks before the second semester of university classes officially begin. Within the final semester, both the embedded faculty member and cooperating teacher conduct three formal teaching observations each.

## Benefits of CTCS

The CTCS model offers a multitude of benefits for teacher candidates, cooperating teachers, embedded faculty, the school and the university, and the elementary school students. While the model is not free of challenges, it holds great promise for providing our diverse population of teacher candidates with clinical experiences needed to succeed as teachers of diverse students. Particular to this model, teacher candidates receive support and interaction provided by both the embedded university faculty member and their cooperating teachers. The strong presence of an embedded university faculty member helps teacher candidates negotiate their university coursework and clinical experiences to build their teaching repertoires. The CTCS model provides high expectations and a network of support for the teacher candidates to assure their effectiveness as future teachers.

### Elementary Students

The CTCS prepares our teacher candidates for teaching in diverse settings in ways that significantly benefit elementary students. Consistent implementation of the co-teaching strategies and lessons derived from extensive co-planning with their cooperating teachers results in an enhanced learning environment. The New Mexico Legislative Finance Committee (2012) reported that the fifth-grade test scores in co-teaching classrooms at the initial CTCS were better than those of classrooms without co-teachers and far exceeded achievement scores of fifth-grade classrooms across the state. Ongoing program evaluations indicate that student achievement in co-teaching classrooms is enhanced by the CTCS model (Center for Education Research Policy 2014).

These findings are consistent with those of other researchers. In an interview Nancy Bacharach, a teacher education professor at St. Cloud University, stated (von Zastro 2009), "Four years of research show that students in co-taught classrooms outperform students in classrooms using other models of student teaching. They even outperform students taught by a single experienced teacher." The CTCS model creates a collaborative synergy between the cooperating teacher and teacher candidate that promotes K–12 students' engagement.

### Teacher Candidates

Within the CTCS model, the teacher candidates are actively engaged from the first day of their clinical experience. In traditional teacher preparation programs, student teachers often sit in the back of classrooms observing, tutor individual students, or complete small tasks such as making copies, getting supplies, and so forth. In contrast, the CTCS model views the teaching dyad as a team in the classroom. The introductory workshop places a strong emphasis on co-planning of lessons, and the pairs learn to integrate co-teaching strategies when presenting lessons.

In addition to their productive teaching roles in the classroom, the cohort of teacher candidates becomes part of the school culture, which further supports their evolving identities as teachers. They participate in parent-teacher conferences and attend IEP and student assistance team meetings. They also become involved in schoolwide events such as math night, design and run afterschool clubs, serve as science fair judges, and participate in fundraisers and celebrations, all of which encompass the role of a classroom teacher. As a result, the teacher candidates feel a sense of belonging at the school and thrive on the challenges and demands of their role.

The strong connection to school and community continues to evolve throughout the three semesters at the same CTCS site. The embedded faculty member supports the teacher candidates by building community through the weekly seminar and addressing themes and issues particular to the school and community context. We consistently revisit and explore more deeply the co-planning and the use of co-teaching strategies. These fundamental aspects of the CTCS model, continuously developed during the 900 hours for each teacher candidate at the school site, afford teacher candidates a strong sense of community. The embedded faculty members get to know the teacher candidates well and work with each individually and the cohort collectively to further their development and evolving sense of identity as culturally responsive teachers learning culturally sustaining/revitalizing pedagogies (Ladson-Billings 1995; McCarty and Lee 2014). In turn, the teacher candidates get to know the elementary students well and become adept at differentiating instruction to incorporate students' diverse funds of knowledge into their learning opportunities. For example, at one CTCS site, several bilingual teacher candidates contributed ideas for supporting recent immigrant students using the co-teaching strategies of supplemental teaching and differentiated teaching to work with students in their home language. They developed small group literacy and math lessons using the co-teaching strategy station teaching that incorporated students' home languages. At another CTCS site, a first grade co-teaching dyad implemented one teach/one assist using English and Spanish to initiate a lesson.

When asked to name the benefit derived from participating in our CTCS model, one graduate, who is currently a classroom teacher, responded, "The largest impact working as a co-Teaching candidate has had on my professional career is the ability to work effectively with my peers. The co-Teaching program prepared me for the challenges faced when working with a group of professionals and illustrated to me the importance of collaboration. It also prepared me for the idea of being observed and held accountable for my classroom" (Center for Education Research Policy 2015, 58). The long-lasting benefits of participating in a CTCS as a teacher candidate are profound. A recent study found 80 percent of the teacher candidates from CTCS remain employed as teachers in 2016; one teacher candidate wrote: "I felt much more prepared walking into my first year" (Center for Education Research Policy 2015). This rate of persistence in the field is higher than that found by the Alliance for Excellent Education, which reported that 50 percent of teachers leave within the first five years (Hayes 2014).

### Cooperating Teachers

Cooperating teachers experience a renewed energy and excitement for teaching, which can often be isolating work. Serving as a cooperating teacher within the CTCS model allows the co-teaching dyad to develop a strong professional relationship that often becomes a camaraderie that benefits both dyad members with mutual rewards. One cooperating teacher described her experience: "I love seeing teaching through another set of eyes. I learn a lot from just her throwing out her thoughts and then us morphing them into either one thought or working two different strategies to the same end. Getting more ideas, and the more current. They're at the cutting edge of the new research and learning theories. It's nice to be able to tap into that" (Center for Education Policy Report 2014, 17). Their co-planning sessions provide a context to explain curriculum decisions, goals, and objectives as well as an opportunity to collaborate on which co-teaching strategies to implement for the lessons. This process "thrives on collaborative practice between the cooperating teacher and teacher candidate whereby the experience of the cooperating teacher and the new perspectives brought in by the teacher candidate 'cross-pollinate' each other" (Center for Education Policy Report 2014, 3).

Unlike traditional student teaching, the cooperating teacher is not required to leave the classroom for weeks at a time to allow the student teacher to teach alone. Instead, the cooperating teacher stays in the classroom as a co-teacher; therefore, the elementary students continue receiving the benefits of an instructional team. We know individual teaching time is important for teacher candidates, and these times are negotiated by the co-teaching dyad.

The embedded faculty member adds another layer of support for the cooperating teacher through their regular communication and meetings, which provide the cooperating teachers with opportunities to learn about and reinforce content presented within the student teaching seminars and to address questions and concerns with the university faculty member. In addition, the embedded faculty member reviews the co-teaching strategies and issues related to co-planning and co-teaching. Cooperating teachers value the benefit of having scheduled time to communicate with one another and the embedded faculty.

Overall, serving as a cooperating teacher can be invigorating. According to Janine Darragh and colleagues (2011), "Co-teachers participate in simultaneous renewal because the collaborative nature of co-teaching encourages a mutual exchange of knowledge and skill among partners" (89). In one instance, at one of our CTCS, a cooperating teacher was considering leaving teaching altogether until she experienced the benefits of participating in the program. During a panel presentation at a national conference, she shared that her relationship with the embedded faculty and her role as a cooperating teacher resulted in renewed excitement about teaching and mentoring a teacher candidate.

### Of and for Embedded Faculty

The embedded faculty member teaches the teacher candidates' seminar course on site and visits classrooms to perform both informal and formal teaching observations while supervising the teacher candidates. As a result, the faculty member becomes well acquainted with the teacher candidates and their classrooms and, accordingly, is better able to design relevant and meaningful seminar content. The teacher candidates appreciate the embedded faculty member and the consistent support and communication they receive. The students have a key person to go to for any issue that arises, and they recognize this distinction from the traditional student teaching model or solo practice at a school. Course evaluations for the on-site seminar reveal overwhelming gratitude for the embedded faculty member, with comments such as, "I wouldn't have made it through this semester without [embedded faculty]." In a recent survey, one graduate of the CTCS program responded enthusiastically to a question about the benefit of the embedded faculty: "What benefit did the faculty member *not* [emphasis added] add to my overall experience?" (Center for Education Research Policy 2015, 59).

The embedded faculty role is rewarding on both personal and professional levels. Being actively engaged at the school, meeting with teachers and administrators, being there for students, and forming relationships greatly benefit the university faculty member. The close relationship the embedded faculty member develops with the teacher candidates creates opportunities for meaningful professional growth. For example, at one CTCS site, the embedded faculty worked closely with two bilingual teacher candidates, both native Spanish speakers, and encouraged them to apply for student internships at a national bilingual conference. They were accepted, and their attendance at the conference affirmed their goals of becoming bilingual teachers, which are in high demand, in New Mexico.

Notably, the positive relationships between the embedded faculty member and the teacher candidates are often long-lasting. Graduates of the CTCS have participated in conference sessions to describe their experiences as teacher candidates. One graduate, now in her third year of teaching, invites current teacher candidates and the embedded faculty member to her middle school each year to allow the teacher candidates a middle-grade-level experience in a different school setting.

## Conclusion

The CTCS model represents a promising, innovative teacher preparation program that answers the call for meaningful, highly effective clinical preparation experiences. The CTCS reduces the praxis shock described by Geert Kelchtermans and Katrijn Ballet (2002) that teacher candidates often experience during their first years in the classroom. Through collaboration, co-teaching, and co-planning, teacher candidates are supported and challenged as they prepare to meet the needs of diverse students and communities. As a result, they are more likely to engage in a long-term, successful teaching career.

Within our MSI and within the communities we serve, the CTCS has moved us beyond traditional models of teacher preparation into a model that effectively prepares teachers to teach with persistence in the profession. The CTCS model also positively impacts all participants and continues to be seen as an important partnership between the university and local school districts. As we continue to expand the CTCS model, we trust that other institutions may find components within the model that may benefit their teacher preparation programs and communities.

REFERENCES

Annie E. Casey Foundation. "Kids Count Data Book." http://www.aecf.org/resources/the-2015-kids-count-data-book.

Bacharach, Nancy, Teresa Washut Heck, and Kathryn Dahlberg. 2010. "Changing the Face of Student Teaching through Coteaching." *Action in Teacher Education* 32: 3–14.

Bransford, John D., Ann L. Brown, and Rodney R. Cocking. 2000. *How People Learn: Brain, Mind, Experience, and School.* Washington, DC: National Academy.

Brownell, Mary T., and Chris Walther-Thomas. 2002. "An Interview with Dr. Marilyn Friend." *Intervention in School and Clinic* 37: 223–228.

Center for Education Policy Research. 2014. *University of New Mexico Co-teaching Collaborative School Initiative 2014 Report.* Albuquerque: Center for Education Policy Research at the University of New Mexico.

———. 2015. *Co-teaching Collaborative Schools Initiative: Fall 2014 Follow-up Survey.* Albuquerque: Center for Education Policy Research at the University of New Mexico.

Cochran-Smith, Marilyn. 1991. "Reinventing Student Teaching." *Journal of Teacher Education* 42: 104–118.

Darling-Hammond, Linda, ed. 1994. *Professional Development Schools: Schools for Developing a Profession.* New York: Teachers College Press.

———. 2000. "Teacher Quality and Student Achievement." *Education Policy Analysis Archives* 8: 1–44. http://dx.doi.org/10.14507/epaa.v8n1.2000.

———. 2006. "Assessing Teacher Education: The Usefulness of Multiple Measures for Assessing Program Outcomes." *Journal of Teacher Education* 57: 120–138.

Darragh, Janine J., Kathryn E. Picanco, Debbie Tully, and Suzie A. Henning. 2011. "When Teachers Collaborate, Good Things Happen: Teacher Candidate Perspectives of the Co-teach Model for the Student Teaching Internship." *Association for Independent Liberal Arts Colleges of Teacher Education Journal* 8: 83–104.

Derr, Victoria. 2002. "Children's Sense of Place in Northern New Mexico." *Journal of Environmental Psychology* 22: 125–137.

Guyton, Edith, and John D. McIntyre. 1990. "Student Teaching and School Experiences." In *Handbook of Research on Teacher Education,* edited by W. Robert Houston, 514–534. New York: Macmillan.

Hayes, Mariana. 2014. "On the Path to Equity: Improving the Effectiveness of Beginning Teachers." Alliance for Excellent Education. http://all4ed.org/reports-factsheets/path-to-equity/.

Kelchtermans, Geert, and Katrijn Ballet. 2002. "The Micropolitics of Teacher Induction: A Narrative-Biographical Study on Teacher Socialization." *Teaching and Teacher Education* 18: 105–120.

Ladson-Billings, Gloria. 1995. "But That's Just Good Teaching: The Case for Culturally Relevant Pedagogy." *Theory into Practice* 34: 159–165.

McCarty, Teresa L., and Tiffany S. Lee. 2014. "Critical Culturally Sustaining/Revitalizing Pedagogy and Indigenous Education Sovereignty." *Harvard Educational Review* 84: 101–124, 135–136.

New Mexico Indian Affairs Department. 2015. "New Mexico's 22 Tribes and the Indian Affairs Department." http://www.iad.state.nm.us/history.html.

New Mexico Kids Count. 2015. "2015 Kids Count in New Mexico." http://www.nmvoices.org/archives/5491.

New Mexico Public Education Department. 2015. *New Mexico Administrative Code.* Title 6. Primary and Secondary Education.

Sirotnik, Kenneth A., and John I. Goodlad, eds. 1988. *School-University Partnerships in Action: Concepts, Cases.* New York: Teachers College Press.

State of New Mexico Legislative Finance Committee. 2012. *Report #12–13. Public Education Department. Teacher and Administrator Preparation in New Mexico,* December 5.

http://www.nmlegis.gov/lcs/lfc/lfcdocs/perfaudit/Public Education Department—
Teacher and Administrator Preparation New Mexico.pdf.

Teacher Quality Enhancement Center. 2010. *Mentoring Teacher Candidates through Co-teaching: Collaboration that Makes a Difference.* St. Cloud: St. Cloud State University College of Education.

Teitel, Lee. 2003. *The Professional Development Schools Handbook.* Thousand Oaks, CA: Sage Publications.

United States Census Bureau. 2015. "New Mexico Quick Facts." http://quickfacts.census.gov/qfd/states/35000.html.

University of New Mexico. 2015. "Office of Institutional Analytics Enrollment Report." http://oia.unm.edu/documents/enrollment-reports/spr-15-oer.pdf.

Von Zastro, Claus. 2009. "Breaking New Ground in Teacher Education: A Conversation with Teacher Educator Nancy Bacharach." Learning First Alliance. http://www.learningfirst.org/visionaries/NancyBacharach.

Zeichner, Ken. 2002. "Beyond Traditional Structures of Student Teaching." *Teacher Education Quarterly* 29: 59–64.

# 4

## From Our Own Gardens

### Growing Our Own Bilingual Teachers in the Southwest

SANDRA BROWNING

In the Southwest of the United States, the growth of the Hispanic population has established the need for universities and colleges to seek ways to best serve this population (Benítez 1998; Santiago 2006; De Los Santos and De Los Santos 2003). According to University of Houston's Hobby Center for Public Policy (2012) and the United States Census Bureau (2014), the Hispanic population in Texas has grown 38.4 percent and will continue to grow at a faster rate than other ethnic groups. Many Hispanic immigrants coming to Texas have settled in major urban areas in search of jobs (Laden 2001). With the booming Houston economy, the Hispanic population in Houston has increased at an even greater rate than the rate in Texas as a whole (United States Census Bureau 2014). To address this population growth, institutions of higher education with a minimum 25 percent Hispanic enrollment have been designated as Hispanic-Serving Institutions (HSIs) (Hispanic Association of Colleges and Universities 2014).

The percentage of the Hispanic population earning bachelor's degrees, however, remains significantly less than the percentage of white and Asian Americans (Brown, Santiago, and Lopez 2003; Miller and García 2004; De Los Santos and De Los Santos 2003). According to studies spanning several decades, several factors may influence the low attainment rate among Hispanic students in higher education: many are first-generation students, come from low-income families, attend school part-time due to work and family responsibilities, enroll in community colleges prior to transferring to a four-year university, and are more likely to eventually drop out of school prior to obtaining a degree (Dayton et al. 2004; Merisotis and McCarthy 2005; Nora et al. 1996).

For higher education institutions, these trends present not only many challenges but also great opportunities. The challenges include meeting the various needs of these students within the constructs of the university setting. And the many opportunities include the prospect of meeting the ever-growing need for bilingual teachers to serve students in Texas for whom English is not their first language. The growth in the Hispanic population, in general, necessitates an increase in Hispanic teachers to be role models for the schoolchildren. Having a diverse teaching staff benefits all students. All students, but especially Hispanic students, should see Hispanic teachers as positive role models who are successful in their chosen profession.

English as second language students and English-language learner students require teachers who are certified to adequately serve them in their native language as well as to assist them in transitioning to English. Language is an important component of one's self-identity; therefore, English as second language and English-language learner students need teachers who are proficient in Spanish. Teachers' ability to communicate with their students through native language provides a shared experience between the teacher and students. This shared language can establish a link between school and family, which is important because family is highly valued in most Hispanic cultures.

Programs that include cultural awareness and address the learning orientations of Hispanic students have the capability to motivate Hispanic students to reach their full potential. Bilingual teachers can enhance students' self-esteem, reinforce students' academic strengths, and perhaps motivate students to enter a career in education, thereby continuing the cycle of support and encouragement for future teachers.

L. Scott Miller and Eugene E. García (2004) suggest nine design principles to enhance the success of Hispanic students in HSIs: (1) institutional leadership, (2) targeted recruitment, (3) engaged faculty, (4) personal attention, (5) peer support, (6) comprehensive financial assistance, (7) enriched research opportunities, (8) accessible bridges to the next level, and (9) continuous evaluation. Implementing these nine design principles will allow universities to "enhance the academic success of racially diverse students [with] a purposeful and integrated approach" (Benítez and DeAro 2004). Keeping these nine design principles in mind, the University of Houston–Clear Lake (UHCL) is perfectly situated in an urban area of the Southwest to support the local school districts in their quest for qualified bilingual teachers.

## University of Houston–Clear Lake

The University of Houston–Clear Lake, is located in the southwest region of the Gulf Coast and is a relatively small institution with fewer than ten thousand students. In 2011, UHCL was designated an HSI by the Hispanic Association of Colleges and Universities (UHCL 2014c) with a student body that includes 26.4 percent Hispanic students in the university as a whole (UHCL 2014a). Even prior to this official designation, the School of Education at UHCL recognized the opportunity to address the unique needs and requirements of histori-cally underrepresented groups of students. The number of Hispanic students enrolled in the School of Education is larger than the number of Hispanic stu-dents in the entire university and has increased each year since 2010; in 2016, the number of Hispanic students exceeded 44 percent of the total university enrollment.

The institution realized the need to address the growing Hispanic popula-tion in the School of Education, while providing much-needed bilingual teach-ers for public schools through a grow-our-own-teacher education program. The community and local families have the potential to produce students who could fill the need for Hispanic role models and teachers. Therefore, UHCL created an environment where diversity is valued by instituting a program designed to attract students of color.

The mission of UHCL is to serve as a student-centered, community-minded, partnership-oriented university to enhance the educational, economic, and cul-tural environment of the region with a commitment to community engagement through partnerships with educational institutions, businesses, government agencies, and nonprofit organizations (UHCL 2010b). The School of Education is committed to implementing the UHCL mission to the fullest and considers the mission of creating a student-centered environment a necessity for the success of all students. This commitment to the students is well demonstrated through many avenues of support similar to those at other universities, such as provid-ing a student success center, tutoring, and financial aid programs. UHCL has, however, implemented two unique and integral programs: the Success Through Education Program (STEP) and the Center for the Professional Development of Teachers (CPDT). STEP is a collaborative entity whose partners work together to identify first-generation, diverse, economically disadvantaged students who have the potential to become highly qualified teachers in Texas. The CPDT, which facilitates the university's teacher preparation program, is structured to provide extensive school-based experiences for prospective educators by coor-dinating field experiences and providing a wide array of professional develop-ment opportunities with technological support for its students.

Each avenue of support employed by the School of Education includes and implements many of the nine design principles to enhance the success of Hispanic students enrolled in HSIs (see Miller and García [2004]). These nine design principles fall nicely into four major categories outlined by the School of Education to address the needs of Hispanic students: (1) recruitment, (2) retention with support, (3) graduation and employment, and (4) the circle of success (see figure 4.1). In each major category of the School of Education program, the nine design principles contribute to the success of the students and their goal of graduating as certified, highly qualified teachers with the promise of employment.

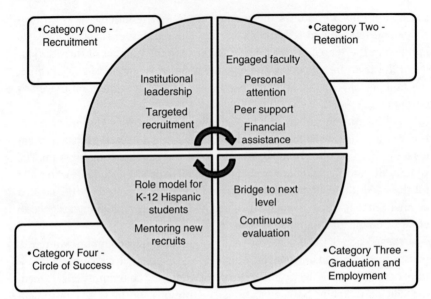

FIGURE 4.1 Categories and Design Principles to Enhance the Success of Hispanic Students

Incorporating the nine design principles into the four categories combines the theory often discussed in higher education with the practicality of teacher education. This unique intersection of research, theory, and practice benefits both the School of Education and the students graduating with teacher certification.

## Institutional Leadership and Targeted Recruitment

Education is one of the most exciting and rewarding careers, and the leadership of UHCL is dedicated to the declared vision of "learner-centered teaching and learning and equity and excellence for all learners" (UHCL 2010a, 3). As an institution dedicated to the community and the local environments, UHCL identifies diversity as a key value and is committed to equitable learning opportunities (UHCL 2014b). The School of Education has adopted a conceptual framework that places at the heart of all programs and policies learner-centered teaching and learning, the foundation of which is equity and excellence for all learners.

The School of Education strongly believes that success for all learners is the central and fundamental goal of education. For preservice teachers, success involves acquiring the necessary knowledge, skills, and dispositions to have a positive impact on their future students. Yet a fundamental question remains: how to provide an environment that will lead to the success of all students and, in particular, the growing Hispanic population attending the institution.

As noted by Sarita E. Brown, Deborah Santiago, and Estela Lopez (2003), Hispanic students do not fit the mold of a traditional college student. Many are older than traditional students, many have come from their home countries with limited formal literacy skills, and many have minimal formal education. Therefore, the leadership of the School of Education realized that "developing programs and practices that can promote minority student success requires a reconceptualization of the college experience from recruitment through graduation and beyond" (Benítez and DeAro 2004, 47).

The focus to provide a welcoming and supportive environment culminating in the success of all students led to the development and implementation of many programs. Perhaps the most unique is STEP, a partnership between the School of Education and four area public school districts involving six high schools, four local community colleges, and several businesses. Each partner school has significant percentages of economically disadvantaged students of color. STEP identifies and recruits students of color interested in becoming teachers. Through STEP, the recruitment of prospective students begins at the high school level. The School of Education provides academic advisors and faculty liaisons to collaborate with partner high schools and community colleges. These partners work together to identify first-generation, diverse, economically disadvantaged students who have the potential to become highly qualified teachers. Students' grade point averages, involvement and leadership roles in school organizations, and in many cases ability to manage school responsibilities while employed either part-time or full-time demonstrate this potential.

High school students interested in teaching are encouraged to enroll in Career and Technology Education (CTE). This one-semester course, taught by outstanding teachers in each public school district, introduces the students to the fundamentals of becoming an educator. Topics discussed in the course include the study/reading skills needed for college-level work, how to choose a career based on values and life goals, balancing school projects while working, the availability of scholarships, writing application essays, and what teaching looks like on a daily basis. The teachers also highlight these topics through workshops delivered on the UHCL campus by current STEP students and district college/career night events.

Various field trips to area community colleges as well as to UHCL include panel events and speakers providing information on several topics of interest for new students, including enrollment procedures. The panel events allow prospective students to interview current and former students, thereby providing prospective students a chance to hear directly from students with similar backgrounds who have made it to college and are succeeding. The students share their perceptions of the college experience including the challenges that they faced as well as the support they received to overcome their challenges and become confident in their ability to succeed. Through these tours, speakers, panel sessions, and interviews, prospective students gain a more detailed picture of the university experience. The visits to the university campus also provide information concerning financial assistance, a requirement of many Hispanic students (Benítez 1998; Benítez and DeAro 2004; Rodríguez et al. 2013). STEP students are eligible to apply for scholarships from their public school district, partner community colleges, and UHCL. These field trips motivate students to set their educational goals, identify values, and explore teaching as a career. Students add their names to a distribution list that allows them to receive e-mails and newsletters, and teachers invite the interested students to join the STEP Facebook page. The distribution list allows the STEP advisor and faculty liaison to provide resources and establish positive relationships with these students as they transition between schools.

Each semester, the high school students spend an entire day shadowing (observing) a teacher of their choice within their district. Students interested in teaching at the elementary level select the grade level they will observe, and students interested in teaching at the secondary level choose the subject area they will observe. Allowing students to focus on their preferred grade level or subject area makes this experience especially meaningful. After a day of shadowing, the students submit a written reflection on their observations of the day, and most state that the opportunity to shadow a teacher was an eye-opening experience concerning the many day-to-day responsibilities of teaching. The students often find that being in a classroom all day is exciting and inspirational. The CTE instructors then lead discussions and provide information concerning the degree plans available for students interested in pursuing a career in education.

Many students in the CTE classes also participate in work-study programs that involve tutoring K–12 students during the regular school day. Both the classroom teacher and the CTE teacher supervise the students while they are tutoring. Many school district partners continue this work-study program when the students transfer to community college and pay the students a small stipend for tutoring. Not only does this provide the students with a small income, but this also increases the students' personal interest in that school district. Because the tutoring sessions are during the regular school day, the CTE students are exposed to the routines and policies of public schools. These opportunities for experiential learning through tutoring while in high school or community college help to prepare students for student teaching at UHCL.

Recruitment efforts do not stop when students graduate high school. These efforts follow the targeted students to the area community college partnerships because many prospective students begin their college careers at community college due to financial concerns. As students transition to the community college, they receive information about the UHCL 2+2 plan through their STEP advisor. This plan ensures transfer courses from the community college (two years) will count toward their UHCL degree (+ two years). Advising students on these plans is a collaborative effort coordinated with community college advisors and faculty. Students are encouraged to participate in UHCL's Uni-link agreement, which allows them to utilize university services such as the library, career counseling, computer centers, community events, and membership in student organizations before they transfer.

Mentors, offering advice and support, talk regularly with potential students concerning their academic progress at the community college. Students attending area community colleges are also invited to the UHCL campus to participate in tours, panel discussions, and interviews. These visits, while similar to the visits for high school students, are conducted on days other than the high school student tours with greater emphasis on college acceptance, time management and study skills, interviewing, and résumé writing. To ensure a smooth transition, these sessions include more detailed information concerning financial opportunities, as well as the process involved in transferring to the university. Most students transfer a minimum of 54 hours that directly apply to a degree and teacher certification at UHCL.

While a key focus of STEP is to provide support and assistance to high school and community college students interested in teaching, paraprofessionals employed by the partner public schools are encouraged to attend the field trips, campus tours, and shadowing days. The School of Education participates in the state program that allows paraprofessionals to complete their student teaching in a nonstandard format because they are employed full-time and are therefore unable to complete their student teaching requirements during the regular school year. Once the paraprofessionals have completed their coursework toward a degree and teacher certification, they are eligible to complete their student teaching requirements during summer school sessions at area public schools. Paraprofessionals are able to use the classroom management skills they have developed while assisting in classrooms and further developing their skills in providing instruction. The summer school setting is an ideal situation in which to complete student teaching while fully employed in a school district. Many of these paraprofessionals are hired immediately upon graduation as teachers by the district in which they are currently paraprofessionals.

## Retention through Support

The largest and most intense category, Category Two, concerns the retention and support of the students. Without the support to retain the students that were recruited in Category One, the next two categories in the model—Category Three: Graduation/Employment and Category Four: The Circle of Success—would not be possible. Therefore, the major focus of student retention can be improved by aligning student support services with academic programs (Benítez and DeAro 2004; Flores et al. 2007; Hurtado and Ponjuan 2005).

Retention and support at the School of Education exist on many levels and involve numerous faculty and staff personnel. Continued encouragement is necessary as the students become acclimated to the teacher preparation program in the university setting. Therefore, this process involves the entire School of Education, which makes the students feel important and capable of succeeding; furthermore, from the students' first days on campus, faculty and staff encourage and assist the students to build personal relationships with them (Hoffman et al. 2002). At least thirty years of research indicate that building positive student-adult relationships is critical for the success of all students and especially Hispanic students (Pascarella et al. 1983; Pianta, Stuhlman, and Hamre 2002; Valenzuela 1999). Personalized academic advising, tutoring, and faculty mentoring create positive bonds between students and faculty/staff. Relationships with university adults can facilitate processes of perseverance and identity formation that are vital for historically marginalized youth, such as Hispanic students. University instructors must recognize, inspire, motivate, and support all students, especially Hispanic students, in and out of the classroom setting (Rodríguez 2012; Rodríguez and Oseguera 2015; Stanton-Salazar and Spina 2003). University professors involved in the bilingual teacher certification program provide the faculty with monthly professional development opportunities concerning topics such as understanding the cultural differences and language barriers of Hispanic students.

Thus, STEP is effective in recruiting prospective students from both the area high schools and community colleges through the partnership between the School of Education, area school districts, and area community colleges. The leadership of STEP, however, does not end with recruitment. Once the STEP partners identify area students as potential teachers, they collaborate as academic advisors, faculty, and administrators to retain, train, mentor, and support student development and success. The STEP partners provide a multitude of opportunities for students as they explore teaching as a profession. Throughout each semester that students are enrolled in UHCL, STEP continues to offer professional development sessions covering topics such as résumé building, time management, interactive strategies for the classroom, and implementing the English-language proficiency standards once employed in a school district. According to the Teaching English to Speakers of Other Languages International Organization (TESOL), the population of students coming from non-English-speaking backgrounds is the fastest growing section of school-aged children (TESOL 2006). Therefore, training STEP participants to fully and effectively implement the English-language proficiency standards into their classroom instruction will make STEP graduates more marketable when applying for teaching positions. Once hired, STEP graduates will then be able to bring public school students closer to the educational mainstream and improve their overall academic achievement.

The university offers many of the professional development sessions during the noon hour to allow all students the opportunity to attend, regardless of class schedules. The Lunch-n-Learn sessions focus on numerous practical topics: (1) setting goals for success, (2) getting to know each student, (3) managing time and tasks, (4) sharpening writing skills, (5) training for library searches, (6) improving résumé writing and mock interviews, (7) preparing for the Texas examinations of educator standards (required criterion-referenced examinations measuring knowledge of content and pedagogy), (8) connecting to campus resources and participating in resource fairs, (9) lesson planning for English-language learners, and (10) advising first-year teachers. Faculty mentoring and peer-to-peer meetings follow each professional development session to provide additional information and support, as well as to discuss any questions that students may have concerning the information provided in the sessions. Furthermore, many faculty members volunteer to provide training for job fairs, which includes demonstrating appropriate dress and conducting mock interviews with a panel of faculty to mimic an interview committee.

To graduate with certification and become a highly qualified teacher, students must demonstrate knowledge of subject matter and the competency needed for effective instruction. To demonstrate their knowledge and competency, students must pass state examinations pertaining to the subject matter that they will teach. Knowing that one must pass the examinations to become certified as a teacher is very stressful for students; therefore, tutoring sessions are available for the state examinations. Many faculty members and even adjunct instructors provide these tutoring sessions each week throughout the semester and on weekends. Instances of School of Education faculty dedication to student success are numerous. For example, faculty members provide three-hour workshops for the early childhood through grade 6 bilingual students on the Bilingual Target Language Proficiency Test, which is required for certification as a bilingual teacher. On their own time and without compensation, faculty review the components of the state examination with the students both in Spanish and English by sharing sample assessment activities and vocabulary terms that may be on the examination. Students find this workshop to be extremely beneficial in preparation for their state examination.

Another integral part of the plan to support students is the Center for the Professional Development of Teachers (CPDT), which is a state-approved provider of professional development for preservice teachers to support and improve teacher education. The primary purpose of the CPDT is to continually meet the changing needs of its public school partners along with the ever-changing role of the public school classroom teacher. Through the CPDT, the teacher preparation program offers extensive public school-based experiences for prospective educators as part of the certification program. The School of Education strongly believes that the more "real world" experience students gain during their training, the better prepared they will be as certified teachers. Each of the four core subject area methods courses (mathematics, science, English language arts, and social studies) involve field experiences in varying degrees dependent upon the content matter in the methods course. These field-based experiences culminate in the internship program at the School of Education; this last step prior to graduation is designed to provide students with hands-on experiences related to every aspect of the teaching profession by implementing a two-semester course consisting of Internship I and Internship II. Once a student is eligible for internship (student teaching), the School of Education places the students in the district where they attended high school and participated in the CTE course. This is part of the cycle of mentoring and giving back to the community.

Although the university provides many levels of student support, some students still struggle with internship, and thus an internship success committee evolved through the CPDT. This committee consists of the field supervisor, the CPDT director, the teacher education advisory chair, and additional faculty members, as needed. The committee meets with students who are facing challenges within the public school classroom, having difficulty understanding the responsibilities of teaching, or demonstrating inappropriate dispositions. When consulting with students concerning the causes of their difficulties, the committee provides the student with options and suggestions. The committee and the student then develop a plan of action for success, through which the student gains assistance in becoming proficient during Internship I and II. The rigorous requirements of the internship program enhance teacher quality through its successful partnerships with public schools as well as area businesses. Our partners share one common goal: student success. Many factors contribute to such success, including sustained renewal through student preparation, professional development, research, enhanced student learning, and technology integrated into the curriculum. The partners also share the common vision of preparing future teachers in learner-centered schools and intensively supervising and training the interns.

While STEP and the CPDT provide many supportive activities and sessions, students may still struggle with coursework. In addition to the aforementioned student success center, UHCL also offers supplemental instruction, which is a unique addition to tutoring and provides an intense level of academic support that, like tutoring, is based in skill development and guided practice. Supplemental instruction, however, is designed to deliver academic support to students in a specific course by embedding a supplemental instructor in the class. Faculty members, through close collaboration, choose supplemental instructors, who are required to attend the class for which they offer academic support. This allows the supplemental instructors to become familiar with not only the particular skills the faculty member is emphasizing but also how the professor uses the subject matter to engage and develop these skills. The supplemental instructor offers two to three sessions each week for students needing help in developing these skills. Through tutoring and supplemental instruction, the student success center regularly works together with faculty members to develop a network of student support aimed at addressing the changing needs of UHCL's diverse student body.

In addition to the support of faculty and staff, Hispanic students need and should have support from peers. More than a decade of student-centered, student-driven research has demonstrated that creating deliberate spaces for knowledge creation and critical school and community engagement are vital for engaging the nation's most marginalized students (Duncan-Andrade, Reyes, and Morrell 2008; Irizarry 2011). The institution has created a program called Strictly Speaking that matches a native English speaker with two to three non-native English speakers. We designed the informal program, largely staffed with students, to enhance the speaking skills of nonnative English speakers through conversation and immersion into the university culture. Tutors work one-on-one with a student or in a small group (generally no more than three students) once a week for approximately an hour. The structure is not rigid, which allows the tutor and student to shape their experience the way they feel most comfortable. Involvement in Strictly Speaking provides both student and tutor with an opportunity to build a sense of community through intercultural and interpersonal understanding. Permitting students to share their experiences and to participate in transforming their schooling experiences is critical in conveying a sense of self-efficacy concerning academic achievement (hooks 1994; Rodríguez 2014; Rodríguez and Brown 2009).

Of course, all of these support systems would be of little use if students could not attend UHCL due to financial issues. As with most universities, the UHCL financial aid office is open daily. The personnel in the financial office are willing and able to help students calculate the cost of attendance, complete forms for grants and scholarships, and locate possible employment opportunities. Many times, however, either this is not enough to cover the cost or students do not qualify for grants. Therefore, the School of Education, the school district partners, and business partners offer many scholarship opportunities for financial support. The partner school districts frequently provide students with opportunities for part-time employment and experiential learning while students are attending either UHCL or one of the partnering community colleges. Additionally, STEP has awarded well over $1.2 million in scholarships, with twenty-seven students receiving a total of $31,500 in scholarships in 2014 alone. The majority of these scholarship dollars are provided by financial supporters, including ExxonMobil, Fondren Foundation, Partnerships for Future

Teachers, Greater Texas Foundation, Kempner Fund, Meadows Foundation, and private donors; the participating school districts and UHCL also provide a percentage of these scholarship funds.

To measure the effectiveness of the numerous programs and processes implemented for student success, the School of Education monitors data regularly. Online surveys through Survey Monkey measure usefulness of opportunities provided, determine training needs as perceived by the students, and maintain current student information concerning course grades. The university's database program, known as ACCESS, contains demographics, retention, grade point averages, and graduation and certification rates for every student enrolled at the university. The university's writing and mathematics centers as well as the student success center also monitor and support student progress.

Each program works together to ensure that the students receive the support they need to continue on the path to graduation. This cooperation and collaboration is essential to support students' success as they progress through their degree plans toward graduating with teacher certification (Darling-Hammond et al. 2005).

## Graduation and Employment

Whether in high school, community college, or UHCL, students work together with faculty and advisors to design the best course of study for their particular choice of elementary or secondary teaching. Due to this support and the desire to give back to their community, many School of Education students graduate with certification in bilingual education or English as a second language. Because the largest limited-English-proficient population for area school districts is Spanish-speaking students, stipends are generally offered when bilingual teachers sign a letter of intent to hire. According to Lynne Diaz-Rico and Jerilynn Smith (1994), when the school district and the university share a common knowledge of practice and theory, the transition is easier for new teachers in terms of both classroom practice and confidence in their capability of performing their teaching responsibilities well. Therefore, providing training to STEP participants on implementing the English-language proficiency standards effectively makes STEP graduates more marketable to area school districts. This university is fortunate to have involved and caring bilingual faculty who currently work with two local districts and assist in developing their bilingual programs. In addition, the university teaches completely in Spanish three courses leading toward bilingual certification: an introductory course involves reading and writing skills with special emphasis on communication with the bilingual community; a second course investigates methods of teaching English to second-language learners in the bilingual classroom with emphasis on the relationship between native language and second language development; and a third course involves the study and design of the content area curriculum within a bilingual education program. Through these courses, along with other coursework, the School of Education prepares students to step into public school bilingual schools immediately upon graduation and meet the needs of the growing English-language learner populations.

With the support systems firmly in place, the School of Education has a high graduation rate at 74.9 percent (UHCL 2014d). While that is a very respectable rate, STEP students have a 93.6 percent graduation rate, which is higher than the graduation rate of the School of Education in general and the university at large. STEP students maintain a grade point average above 3.0 during their coursework taken at UHCL. Most STEP students transfer from local community colleges and enter UHCL with 45 to 60 semester hours. Once enrolled at UHCL, STEP students are able to complete the remaining hours of their degree plan in two to three years, which is an amazing accomplishment, considering that many are part-time students with work and family obligations. Hispanic youth enrolled at any HSI are usually first-generation college students and face cultural challenges such as lowered expectations from older generation Mexican Americans, a lack of motivation to pursue higher education, an expectation of Hispanic women to develop and care for home responsibilities, and the conflict between family and academia concerning the appearance of putting schooling above family (Dayton et al. 2004). The daily struggle of finding a balance between family and academia makes it difficult for students to develop the stability needed to progress educationally. Institutions can support Hispanic youth by providing many personal interactions with diverse faculty and staff communities. The faculty and staff can draw upon their personal experiences in establishing a commitment of support on behalf of the university while adding comfort, trust, and acceptance for the students (Dayton et al. 2004).

Upon graduation, many STEP students begin successful teaching careers and stay longer in teaching than the state average (National Commission on Teaching and America's Future 2007; UHCL 2014b). Many of these students return to teach in the elementary, middle, or high schools they attended as children. Through STEP, students have an increased likelihood of employment in their home district where they were recruited and through which they had mentors while at UHCL. The partner districts anticipate hiring the STEP students that they have mentored throughout high school, community college, and student teaching because these students have already demonstrated a vested interest in the district. These graduating students enter the teaching profession fully prepared to effectively serve contemporary students—largely a function of the elaborate support systems, the collaboration of the university leadership, the dedicated faculty and staff, the area partnerships developed by STEP and CPDT, and the rigorous internship program.

## Circle of Success

School of Education graduates, and particularly STEP graduates, travel full circle by giving back as they enter a highly rewarding career, become strong role models in the public schools, and mentor incoming STEP students who hope to become teachers. In addition, STEP students become leaders, positively impacting their communities by helping others realize that a college degree is possible and obtainable. Examples of the success of the program and the willingness of graduates to give back are numerous. Throughout the journey from high school through community college through UHCL, students are provided opportunities to make a difference in their community. Even the seemingly small activity of STEP students making and donating literacy book bags to high school and community college students who work and/or tutor in local schools helps to bridge the transition from just being a student to becoming a leader and one who serves the community. Beginning with tutoring students while still attending high school to becoming a role model for students when they have a classroom of their own, STEP students reinvest in their own neighborhoods. Due to the many volunteer hours STEP students and graduates willingly perform, the STEP program is consistently acknowledged on the president's Higher Education Community Service Honor Roll (Corporation for National and Community Service 2015).

The collaborative connections between public schools, community colleges, and UHCL create a shared vision of encouraging diverse and capable students to overcome challenges, graduate from high school, prepare to become highly effective teachers for area schools, and become role models for their communities. The institution, through STEP and the CPDT, provides a seamless transition from high school to becoming teachers in the neighborhoods from which the students come. When possible, students are tracked for six years after graduating from UHCL, and the data indicate that the support provided by the School of Education and its partners provides opportunities and rewards far beyond the initial goals of the program. A person who grew up in an economically challenged family or area and is a first-generation college student is an awe-inspiring role model to the young people in these communities. This person is a symbol of someone who worked hard and overcame daily challenges and obstacles to pursue the dream of becoming a teacher, thereby kindling the dream that others can do the same. These teachers have instant credibility and become difference-makers in the very communities in which they grew up.

Dozens of students who have gone through this program are now successful teachers, coaches, directors, and administrators and are giving back to the communities that believed in them. They are encouraging and leading future generations to get an education and to make a difference themselves someday. This program provides opportunities and points to a brighter tomorrow.

The excellent field experiences and support offered by the CPDT provides the students with opportunities to work with public school students and thereby develop the skills needed in the classroom, but the STEP program is the glue that holds all of these support systems together. STEP has proven to provide comprehensive support and advisement in a seamless transition from high school to community college to UHCL, which culminates in a college degree and teacher certification. Graduates are successful, and many are award-winning teachers in their school districts for their exemplary practices.

## Conclusion

Faculty members in the School of Education at UHCL are committed to the success of their students. Each faculty member plays a role in cultivating relationships with students and shares in the responsibility of assisting students in their quest to become educators. The personal attention combined with many support systems prepare our students to graduate while feeling competent and confident that they are highly qualified teachers and will succeed in their chosen career of educating the leaders of tomorrow. The School of Education is thus upholding the important mission of serving as a student-centered, community-minded, partnership-oriented university to enhance the educational, economic, and cultural environment of the region with a commitment to community engagement through partnerships with educational institutions, businesses, government agencies, and nonprofit organizations.

The combination of STEP and the CPDT provides a structure for sustained renewal, retention, and success for future generations, and the students who go through the program appreciate all the time and effort devoted to their success by the faculty, staff, and the university as a whole. The School of Education is, indeed, fortunate to have STEP and each component of the well-planned support system in place.

Through the many support systems implemented by the School of Education, Hispanic students are succeeding in their coursework, graduating with teacher certification, and obtaining employment. Data is continually analyzed to strengthen the program to better meet the needs of students. Demographics, first-generation status, retention rates, grade point averages, graduation and certification rates are assessed using ACCESS and databases. Data are monitored to ensure students receive support and resources to sustain success and attain their goals of becoming highly qualified, certified teachers. This study begins while the students are in high school and tracks their progress through the community college and UHCL. Surveys and other feedback from students, teachers, and administrators allow for continuous improvement at every level. For instance, as a result of feedback from high school partners, STEP reorganized

UHCL fieldtrips to focus on values exploration, goal-setting for college, applying for financial aid, and advisement. Another improvement initiative based on student surveys from the Lunch-n-Learn seminars led to increased individual advising sessions. The surveys provide advisors and faculty liaison the opportunity to address students' concerns and to provide needed resources either through follow-up phone calls or in person throughout the semester.

Costs associated with the program include travel to collaborative partnering schools, marketing the program, food for field trips and receptions, and incidental items (e.g. awards, books, and supplies). This is usually around $30 per student. Additional expenses include salaries for two university professionals, who commit 50 percent of their time supporting STEP, and a part-time administrative assistant. While financing the program is important, the key to the success of the program is a group of dedicated educators who spend time developing personally meaningful relationships with first-generation college students who often do not have access to the support system they need to be successful in college. Whereas money provides needed scholarships, resources, and support for the students, the most important thing is the personal contact that assures students that their success is important to all faculty members.

The benefits of the teacher education program are greater than we can measure. Graduates return to their home school districts to teach students who face the same challenges they once did. Moreover, the School of Education will continue to improve the program by developing new goals to improve the students' journey to becoming highly qualified teachers. Future plans include writing grants to increase scholarship funding, including Science, Technology, Engineering, and Mathematics (STEM) coursework where appropriate, and improving data collection strategies.

The path to the development of the grow-your-own teacher education program has taken many twists and turns. Faced with an alarming teacher shortage and lack of diversity in the workforce, the UHCL School of Education collaborated with one school district to address these mutual concerns. From the roots of this successful collaboration, partnerships expanded to several school districts. The community colleges were brought on board to meet the needs of minority students beginning their college careers. Then the university further developed the program goals of recruiting, training, and sustaining diverse, first-generation students to become highly qualified teachers and leaders in PK–12 classrooms. They have met these goals by providing scholarships, academic advising, professional training, mentoring, and field experiences. Now the first-generation, diverse, low-income students in STEP graduate classrooms have these wonderful and productive teachers as role models and living proof that earning a college degree is an attainable goal no matter the circumstances.

## REFERENCES

Benitez, Margarita. 1998. "Hispanic-Serving Institutions: Challenges and Opportunities." *New Directions for Higher Education* 102: 57–68.

Benitez, Margarita, and Jessie DeAro. 2004. "Realizing Student Success at Hispanic-Serving Institutions." *New Directions for Community Colleges* 127: 35–48.

Brown, Sarita E., Deborah Santiago, and Estela Lopez. 2003. "Latinos in Higher Education: Today and Tomorrow." *Change: The Magazine of Higher Learning* 35: 40–47.

Corporation for National and Community Service. 2015. "President's Higher Education Community Service Honor Roll." http://www.nationalservice.gov/special-initiatives/honor-roll.

Darling-Hammond, Linda, Karen Hammerness, Pamela Grossman, Frances Rust, and Lee Shulman. 2005. "The Design of Teacher Education Programs." *In Preparing Teachers for a Changing World: What Teachers Should Learn and Be Able to Do*, edited by Linda Darling-Hammond and John Bransford, 390–441. San Francisco: John Wiley & Sons.

Dayton, Boualoy, Nancy Gonzalez-Vasquez, Carla R. Martinez, and Caryn Plum. 2004. "Hispanic-Serving Institutions through the Eyes of Students and Administrators." *New Directions for Student Services* 105: 29–40.

De Los Santos, Alfredo G., and Gerardo E. De Los Santos. 2003. "Hispanic-Serving Institutions in the 21st Century: Overview, Challenges, and Opportunities." *Journal of Hispanic Higher Education* 2: 377–391.

Diaz-Rico, Lynne T., and Jerilynn Smith. 1994. "Recruiting and Retaining Bilingual Teachers: A Cooperative School Community-University Model." *Journal of Educational Issues of Language Minority Students* 14: 255–268.

Duncan-Andrade, Jeffrey, Michael Reyes, and Ernest Morrell. 2008. *The Art of Critical Pedagogy: Possibilities for Moving from Theory to Practice in Urban Schools*. New York: Peter Lang.

Flores, Belinda Bustos, Ellen Riojas Clark, Lorena Claeys, and Abelardo Villarreal. 2007. "Academy for Teacher Excellence: Recruiting, Preparing, and Retaining Latino Teachers through Learning Communities." *Teacher Education Quarterly* 34: 53–69.

Hispanic Association of Colleges and Universities. 2014. "Hispanic-Serving Institution Definitions." http://www.hacu.net/hacu/HSI_Definition.asp.

Hoffman, Marybeth, Jayne Richmond, Jennifer Morrow, and Kandice Salomone. 2002. "Investigating 'Sense of Belonging' in First-Year College Students." *Journal of College Student Retention: Research, Theory, and Practice* 4: 227–256.

hooks, bell. 1994. *Teaching to Transgress*. New York: Routledge.

Hurtado, Sylvia, and Luis Ponjuan. 2005. "Latino Educational Outcomes and the Campus Climate." *Journal of Hispanic Higher Education* 4: 235–251.

Irizarry, Jason. 2011. "Buscando la Libertad: Latino Youths in Search of Freedom in School." *Democracy and Education* 19: 1–10.

Laden, Berta Vigil. 2001. "Hispanic-Serving Institutions: Myths and Realities." *Peabody Journal of Education* 76: 73–92.

Merisotis, Jamie P., and Kirstin McCarthy. 2005. "Retention and Student Success at Minority-Serving Institutions." *New Directions for Institutional Research* 125: 45–58.

Miller, L. Scott, and Eugene E. García. 2004. "Better Informing Efforts to Increase Latino Student Success in Higher Education." *Education and Urban Society* 36: 189–204.

National Commission on Teaching and America's Future. 2007. "The High Cost of Teacher Turnover." http://www.nctaf.org/wp-content/uploads/2012/01/NCTAF-Cost-of-Teacher-Turnover-2007-policy-brief.pdf.

Nora, Amaury, Alberto Cabrera, Linda Serra Hagedorn, and Ernest Pascarella. 1996. "Differential Impacts of Academic and Social Experiences on College-Related

Behavioral Outcomes across Different Ethnic and Gender Groups at Four-Year Institutions." *Research in Higher Education* 37: 427–451.

Pascarella, Ernest T., Paul B. Duby, Patrick T. Terenzini, and Barbara K. Iverson. 1983. "Student-Faculty Relations and Freshman Year Intellectual and Personal Growth in a Nonresidential Setting." *Journal of College Student Personnel* 2: 395–402.

Pianta, Robert C., Megan W. Stuhlman, and Bridget K. Hamre. 2002. "How Schools Can Do Better: Fostering Stronger Connections between Teachers and Students." *New Directions for Youth Development* 93: 91–107.

Rodríguez, Louie F. 2012. "Everybody Grieves, but Still Nobody Sees: Toward a Praxis of Recognition for Latina/o Students in US Schools." *Teachers College Record* 114: 1–31.

———. 2014. *The Time Is Now: Understanding and Responding to the Black and Latina/o Dropout Crisis in the US*. New York: Peter Lang.

Rodríguez, Louie F., and Tara M. Brown. 2009. "Engaging Youth in Participatory Action Research for Education and Social Transformation." *New Directions for Youth Development* 123: 19–34.

Rodríguez, Louie F., Eduardo Mosqueda, Pedro E. Nava, and Gilberto Conchas. 2013. "Reflecting on the Institutional Processes for College Success: The Experiences of Four Chicanos in the Context of Inequality." *Latino Studies* 11: 411–427.

Rodríguez, Louie F., and Leticia Oseguera. 2015. "Our Deliberate Success Recognizing What Works for Latina/o Students across the Educational Pipeline." *Journal of Hispanic Higher Education* 14: 128–150.

Santiago, Deborah. 2006. "Inventing Hispanic-Serving Institutions (HSIs): The Basics." *Excelencia in Education*. http://files.eric.ed.gov/fulltext/ED506052.pdf.

Stanton-Salazar, Ricardo D., and Stephanie Urso Spina. 2003. "Informal Mentors and Role Models in the Lives of Urban Mexican-Origin Adolescents." *Anthropology and Education Quarterly* 34: 231–254.

TESOL (Teaching English to Speakers of Other Languages). 2006. "PreK–12 English Language Proficiency Standards." http://www.tesol.org/advance-the-field/standards/prek-12-english-language-proficiency-standards#sthash.QYrPBuWa.pdf.

United States Census Bureau. 2014. "QuickFacts, Texas." http://www.census.gov/quickfacts/table/PST045214/00.

University of Houston–Clear Lake (UHCL). 2010a. "Conceptual Framework." http://ncate.uhcl.edu/CF/ConceptualFramework.htm.

———. 2010b. "Mission Statement." http://prtl.uhcl.edu/portal/page/portal/PRE/UHCL_MISSION_STATEMENT.

———. 2014a. "Enrollment Management Trends: Fall Facts at a Glance." http://prtl.uhcl.edu/portal/page/portal/OIE/IR_PUBLICATIONS/FAST_FACT_SHEET/Fall%202014%20facts%20at%20a%20glance.pdf.

———. 2014b. "National Council for Accreditation of Teacher Education Board of Examiners Report [NCATE]." http://prtl.uhcl.edu/portal/page/portal/SOE/ntol/websites/NCATE/.

———. 2014c. "Office of Institutional Effectiveness." http://prtl.uhcl.edu/portal/page/portal/OIE/Content.

———. 2014d. "Student, Faculty, and Program Data." http://prtl.uhcl.edu/portal/page/portal/OIE/IR_PUBLICATIONS/ENROLLMENT_PROFILES.

University of Houston, Hobby Center for Public Policy. 2012. "Projections of the Population of Texas and Counties in Texas by Age, Sex, and Race/Ethnicity from 2010 to 2050." http://www.uh.edu/class/hcpp/_docs/research/population/2014%20PPRLE-SV2.pdf.

Valenzuela, Angela. 1999. *Subtractive Schooling: US Mexican Youth and the Politics of Caring*. Albany: State University of New York Press.

# PART TWO

# Program Responses to Contemporary Demands

# 5

# Lifting Gates and Building Skills

## Preparing Diverse Candidates to Pass New Certification Exams

JONI S. KOLMAN

LAURA M. GELLERT

DENISE L. MCLURKIN

Teacher effectiveness is a central concern of policy makers, educators, and the public at large. Within the national discourse on improving educational experiences for all children, debates endure on the appropriate gates for entry to the teaching profession and how to assess the readiness and fitness of teacher candidates (Cochran-Smith and Fries 2005; Goodwin and Oyler 2008; Zumwalt and Craig 2008). Often disputed is the value of teacher certification (certification exams in particular) in ensuring that quality teachers are in classrooms (Hess 2003; Wilson and Youngs 2005; Zumwalt and Craig 2008). Although some of these differences are rooted in ideology, the research also reveals mixed findings in terms of the benefit of teacher certification on student outcomes (Zumwalt and Craig 2008).

The adoption of occupational licensing regulations and accompanying exams began to increase at the beginning of the twentieth century as professional and technical occupations proliferated (Law and Kim 2005). For the teaching profession, however, standardized tests of basic skills were introduced in Pennsylvania as early as 1834 (Ravitch 2003), and their use for teacher licensing ebbed and flowed through the late twentieth century. By 1994, approximately 50 percent of public school districts required teachers to pass a test of basic skills, and almost 40 percent required teachers to pass tests of subject matter knowledge (Angus 2001). In 2016, almost all states require successful completion of exams to demonstrate subject matter competency and mastery of basic skills, although there is considerable variation in the content and number of certification exams by state.

Advocates for more rigorous teacher certification exams (e.g., Kate Walsh of National Council on Teacher Quality) argue that such exams are necessary to prevent weak individuals from entering classrooms—that the restricted entry effect is good and necessary. Few would argue about the imperative to have quality teachers in classrooms, but such arguments rest on the assumption that these tests are good measures of capacity to meet the needs of students and that they are indeed only restricting entry to those inappropriate for the profession.

The standardized tests offered, however, have been found to be poor measures of a candidate's ability to effectively teach all children (Darling-Hammond and Snyder 2000; Pecheone and Chung 2006) and of readiness (Mitchell et al. 2001; Wilson et al. 2007). Performance-based assessments (e.g., edTPA), introduced in part to be more predictive of these factors, are probably better indicators than the computer-based (or paper-and-pencil) tests that have dominated the certification testing landscape, yet little research has explicitly addressed such questions (Margolis and Doring 2013). Moreover, none of these tests explicitly measures what Mary E. Dilworth and Anthony L. Brown (2008) refer to as the other "value-added dimensions" (424) that teachers bring to classrooms. In particular, exams overlook two potential values: teacher candidates can often "offer their students broader and more complex interpretations of the education curriculum" (Dilworth 1990, xi), and they can support within schools the understandings of various students' cultural backgrounds.

The research also suggests that the cost of these exams is a barrier for many teacher candidates (Angrist and Guryan 2008; Berger and Toma 1994), which probably has a more profound effect on poor and working-class candidates' abilities to become certified and actually discourages many from entering the teacher pipeline (Angrist and Guryan 2008). Evidence also suggests that the exams may be racially biased (*Gulino v. New York State Education Department* [2006]); such bias restricts entry more profoundly for teacher candidates of color than for others (Angrist and Guryan 2008; Shapiro, Slutsky, and Watt 1989; Taylor 2015), and it therefore widens the demographic divide (Gay 2000). Indeed, studies have shown significantly lower passing rates on the Praxis exams for diverse teacher candidates than for their white counterparts (Gitomer 2007; Gitomer, Latham, and Ziomek 1999; Nettles et al. 2011). The research finds, for instance, that approximately 40 percent of African American Praxis I test takers passed the exam, as compared to 80 percent of white test takers (Nettles et al. 2011). This means that to become certified, African American teacher candidates would disproportionally bear the economic burdens of retakes despite an overall increase in the academic successes of all teacher candidates in the last decade (Gitomer 2007).

As teacher educators, we prepare those candidates who identify as racially/ ethnically, culturally, religiously, linguistically, and socioeconomically diverse and who often gain employment in low-resource, high-accountability public school environments, and thus we understand the importance of gatekeeping to the profession. The children in these underfunded schools often experience a cycle of inexperienced teachers (Ingersoll 2004) who are ill-prepared to meet students' needs (Darling-Hammond 2000). In chapter 5, we acknowledge the tension between certification exams, which we believe can be gatekeepers to capable, and often gifted, diverse teacher candidates from entering the profession, and the imperative to ensure that children in schools have well-prepared teachers who can meet their needs. These tensions parallel the mission of City College of New York (CCNY)—a Hispanic-Serving Institution (HSI) and an Asian American and Native American Pacific Islander Serving Institution (AANAPISI)—that focuses on both access and excellence. We illustrate our work around certification exams with a teacher candidate population that mirrors the diversity of New York City public schools by drawing on the voices of teacher educators and teacher candidates. In so doing, we aim to make visible the challenges that these certification exams present for these candidates and the ways in which the School of Education at CCNY has responded to them. Utilizing specific examples from our own teacher education program (which prepares teachers for grades 1 through 6), we present ways in which programs might conceptualize and engage in practices to ensure that capable teacher candidates are not being kept out of the teacher workforce.

## The Context of Teacher Certification Exams in New York State

New York State recently released a slew of new certification exams designed "to be more rigorous and raise the entry bar to the teaching profession" (D'Agati and Wagner 2015, 2); candidates are now required to pass four exams (three computer based and one performance based) as part of the requirements for licensure. While the state requires all of the exams for certifications, the teacher education programs determine when, during the course of the teacher education curriculum, candidates must pass these exams. Some of these exams, like the Academic Literacy Skills Test (ALST) and the Content Specialty Tests (CST) are revised versions of earlier tests. According to many of our faculty members and candidates, the most difficult of the four state certification exams is the ALST, which is purportedly designed to assess candidates' reading comprehension of complex informational and narrative text and their argumentative and evidence-based writing skills. It consists of multiple-choice questions as well as two written essays. Candidates have 210 minutes in which to complete the exam, and the cost is $131.

The CST are discipline-specific exams; the candidates in the elementary education program take the multiple subjects version that consists of three parts (English language arts, mathematics, and arts and sciences). The CST is designed to assess proficiency in content knowledge and the pedagogical skills in literacy and English language arts, mathematics, and arts and sciences required for planning, implementing, and assessing. Candidates can take all three parts back-to-back or take each part independently, and they are allotted six hours to complete it in its entirety. Each section of the CST has both multiple-choice items and a written essay. The cost is $179 if taken together in one administration or $199 if taken separately.

The Educating All Students (EAS) and Teacher Performance Assessment (edTPA) are new exams for teacher candidates in New York State. The EAS exam is designed to assess "the professional and pedagogical knowledge and skills necessary to teach all students—diverse student populations, English-language learners, and students with disabilities" (City University of New York 2016). Both multiple-response items and short-answer items are related to a scenario, which is usually accompanied by a chart or figure. Candidates receive 135 minutes to complete the exam, and the cost is $102.

Finally, candidates complete the edTPA performance exam during their student teaching experience. Candidates in the elementary education program in New York State complete four tasks (as opposed to three that most other certification areas require). Three focus on the teaching of literacy, and one focuses on the teaching of mathematics. The literacy tasks require candidates to demonstrate their ability to plan a connected sequence of three to five lessons, teach these lessons, and assess students' learning. The math task requires candidates to analyze students' work and describe a reengagement experience based on an area of need identified through assessment for growth. They discuss the process and their thinking through a series of commentaries. Candidates also submit artifacts (e.g., lesson plans, video clips of instruction, examples of feedback, student work samples) to illustrate their work with students. The portfolio is then uploaded and sent to Pearson Education, Inc., who is in charge of administration and logistics for the edTPA. At a cost of $300, an outside evaluator scores each candidate's completed work.

The district introduced all of the exams almost simultaneously and without much lead-time for programs to prepare teacher candidates within courses or from their entry to the program. It was surprising that the district required our spring 2014 teacher candidates to pass all of the new state certification exams before they could be granted their initial teaching certification by the state, even though all the certification exams were not available for them to take before they graduated in the spring with their degrees. Possibly more problematic, candidates from fall 2013 who had not passed all the old exams by April 30, 2014, were required to take and pass all the new exams before they could receive their initial teaching certification.

The haste of high-stakes implementation has meant that several teacher candidates who earned their degrees but did not pass one or more of the old tests (sometimes by only a two-point margin) have to pay for, take, and pass all the new exams before they can be certified to teach. This is a financial hardship. Moreover, this latter group is also experiencing logistical hurdles to certification; because they should complete the edTPA during the student teaching capstone experience, which these candidates have already completed, they are thus left without a classroom or children with whom to work for this exam.

It seems that New York State has heard our concerns as teacher educators about the impetuous implementation of these exams. Two years after the changes to the exams, the state announced safety nets for all the certification exams. While the state implemented an edTPA safety net (passing an old certification exam, the Assessment of Teaching Skills—Written) toward the end of the first semester of high-stakes implementation, concerns about the low passing rates for the other exams seem to have prompted similar state policies. The ALST safety net requires candidates to have the dean attest that the candidate either has comparable skills and a grade point average of 3.0 or higher in related coursework at the university or successfully retakes the exam. This safety net was initiated and set to sunset one year after its implementation. For the Content Specialty Test—Multiple Subject (CST-MS), the safety net requires candidates to take and receive a satisfactory score on the predecessor to the current CST exam. In the case of the CST-MS and the edTPA, the cost remains significant to candidates because they must pay to take other exams.

## Context of Preparation: City College of New York

Our work as teacher educators aligns with CCNY's commitments to both access and excellence, where excellence is defined, in part, by its inclusion of the great diversity of individuals living in and around New York City. We work to support our candidates in having access to a rich and challenging curriculum and other opportunities, and this encompasses our work around certification exams. Yet, we are aware of the importance of our role as gatekeepers and our responsibility to ensure that the candidates we support are ready and capable individuals who can meet the diverse needs of children in schools. With the knowledge that many of our teacher candidates work in the highest-need schools in the city, it is imperative that we do not allow our advocacy to trump capacity.

There are approximately two thousand teacher candidates in the School of Education at CCNY, and undergraduates make up about one-third of that group. We educate a population of ethnically, culturally, religiously, linguistically, and socioeconomically diverse teacher candidates who often work part-time or full-time in addition to pursuing their coursework (see table 5.1). Candidates often report that they attended low-resource, high-accountability K–12 schools that struggled to meet their learning needs. They describe learning from old and outdated textbooks, lacking access to computers or internet at their high schools, missing fieldtrips in elementary, middle, or high school, and feeling unsafe at their schools despite security guards and metal detectors. On an exit survey, 43 percent of undergraduates and 29 percent of master's students reported that they were the first in their family to earn such a degree. Although we do not

TABLE 5.1

**Diversity of School of Education Teacher Candidates**
**(Graduate and Undergraduate)**

| Candidate Characteristics | Percentage (%) |
|---|---|
| Racial/cultural self-identification | |
| African American | 16 |
| Middle Eastern | 2 |
| Asian; Pacific Islander | 13 |
| Latin@; Hispanic | 38 |
| White (European) | 24 |
| Mixed | 7 |
| Age | |
| 18–23 | 17 |
| 24–29 | 47 |
| 30–35 | 20 |
| 36–40 | 9 |
| 41+ | 7 |
| Hours worked while completing program | |
| 0–10 | 12 |
| 11–20 | 14 |
| 21–30 | 22 |
| 31–40 | 29 |
| 41+ | 23 |

have definitive statistics on the languages spoken by our candidate population, our experiences suggest that many candidates speak one of eight languages other than English: Bengali, Hindi, Spanish, Russian, French, Mandarin Chinese, Arabic, and Korean. More than 50 percent of our undergraduate and graduate population worked more than thirty hours per week while completing the program, with half these candidates holding the equivalent of a full-time job. Moreover, the majority of candidates applied for and received financial aid for the 2014–2015 school year, and approximately two-thirds of those individuals were awarded needs-based grants and scholarships. The diversity of our candidate population provides not only richness to our programs but also challenges.

## Challenges Experienced by Teacher Candidates

Our discussion focuses on three of the four exams—the ALST, CST, and the edTPA—because both candidates and faculty report these as most challenging. Although the EAS is challenging, our candidates have been largely successful on this exam, probably because it directly reflects the kind of work they are doing in classrooms and learning about through their coursework. To provide texture and nuance to understandings, we draw on the voices of teacher candidates and teacher educators to illustrate the hurdles they are experiencing with passing these exams. We gathered these anecdotes through e-mail and in-person communication with faculty members as part of their workshops and coursework and from internal qualitative research projects focused on certification exams and clinical experiences. We use pseudonyms for all student names.

### Cost of the Exams

The economic literature suggests that occupational entry regulations often change the face of a profession, which results in increased wages and restricted entry (Law and Kim 2005; Shapiro, Slutsky, and Watt 1989); such findings hold true for teaching as well (Angrist and Guryan 2008; Berger and Toma 1994; Cochran-Smith and Fries 2005; Hanushek and Pace 1995). The wage increases for those who can afford to take, subsequently pass the certification exams, and gain employment are beneficial. These wage increases can be an equity game-changer. Many of our teacher candidates at CCNY are first-generation college students and, on occasion, first-generation high school graduates. Consequently, their ability, or inability, to enter into the teaching profession can change not only their lives but also the lives of their family members because it provides for a professional track and the accompanying benefits and salary.

We, thus, find particularly concerning the candidates' and faculty's reports that cost is a barrier to even taking the certification exams. Roberta, a biracial, nontraditional undergraduate student, discussed how she very carefully budgets and forgoes other expenses in order to afford the exams. She was concerned about juggling the expenses for retakes; at the time she wrote to us she had just learned that she failed the ALST. Dalia, a graduate student in her mid-thirties, reported failing the ALST twice and was grateful for a voucher from the state so she did not have to pay for the exam a third time. Throughout her student teaching experience, the cost of the exams was an enduring concern, particularly because she was working only part time to allow time for her student teaching. During advisement and courses, candidates are eager to discuss cost and the ways in which the college might support them with these expenses.

### Academic Literacy Skills Test (ALST)

The ALST has been a contested exam, even in its previous iterations. The original basic skills test, the Liberal Arts and Sciences Test (LAST), was found to be "discriminatory and not job related" by a New York State court (*Gulino v. New York State Education Department*). African American and Latin@ teachers brought the case and argued that the tests were biased. Although all had earned master's degrees, passed their content specialty tests, and received satisfactory evaluations, their inability to pass the LAST resulted in loss of their permanent teaching licenses and seniority, reduction in salaries, and, for some, loss of their tenured teaching positions. Although the LAST was revised and the next iteration was used for many years, concerns endure, particularly because the ALST is considered significantly more difficult than the revised LAST.

Our discussions with faculty and teacher candidates highlight the challenges and complexity of the ALST. The test has specific requirements: candidates must be able to efficiently read and write in high-pressure situations and effectively read and write across a number of genres; they must show evidence of a large English vocabulary; they must be familiar with all essential elements of the test (e.g., argumentative writing, multiple choice); they must demonstrate strong computer-usage skills; they must display efficient note-taking skills; and they must sustain their attention for a long period of time. All the required skills and knowledge, except the sustained attention span, are particularly challenging for candidates who speak English as an additional language. As Layla, a graduate student and Arabic speaker, explained, "Reading complex texts in English requires more time because I constantly have to reread and decipher unfamiliar vocabulary. I can do it, but it takes me much longer than I am given on the test."

Both faculty and teacher candidates consistently raised the issue of time. One faculty member reported that the questions on the ALST are difficult, with a very thin line between two potentially correct answers, and the candidates were struggling to make decisions against a very short timeline. Dalia also discussed time as her greatest barrier to completing the test. At the time of our conversation, she had just taken the ALST for the third time. When asked about her challenges, she wrote, "I couldn't get through the whole exam in time the first two times, even with thorough preparation. I just do not write well quickly." Roberta reported similar challenges with her initial attempt at the ALST: "Given the time pressure, I wasn't confident that I could write efficiently and make sure I was being very clear with what I was trying to say."

Two faculty members hypothesize that many of our teacher candidates' struggles are related to their prior educational experiences that provided them with little, if any, formative feedback on their reading and writing. Such prior experiences make it difficult for candidates either to gauge where their writing goes wrong or to glean important information from complex text in genres with which they are unfamiliar. These challenges appear exacerbated by the time constraints. Jennifer, a nontraditional, African American undergraduate candidate, expressed such concerns: "The passages were very complex, and I needed more time to ensure I was paying close attention when reading." Roberta concurred: "The complexity of passages meant that I had to go back and reread constantly. This was particularly challenging because the passages were generally outside a genre with which I was familiar." The very challenging ALST requires close reading and time management skills. Some candidates, particularly those who were not educated in technology-oriented K–12 environments, might also find the computer-based format to be difficult.

### Content Specialty Test—Multiple Subject (CST-MS)

Subject matter knowledge is notably integral to the Highly Qualified Teacher provision of the No Child Left Behind Act (2001) and has been considered a marker of teacher quality for decades (Goodwin and Oyler 2008). The threshold for sufficient subject matter knowledge for effective teaching and the sources of that knowledge, however, remain the subjects of much debate (Wilson, Floden, and Ferrini-Mundy 2001). There is a dearth of research documenting whether these content knowledge certification exams are predictors of good teaching. Indeed, the vast majority of research focuses on the relationships between subject matter majors and student outcomes on standardized tests (e.g., Floden and Meniketti 2005; Rowan, Correnti, and Miller 2002), particularly with mathematics majors at the secondary level (e.g., Hill, Rowan, and Ball 2005). Questions remain about the value of such exams.

Given time constraints or misinformation about the breadth of content knowledge to be tested, many candidates take the CST-MS with little preparation. Those who prepare by studying materials available online through the state often comment about the lack of clarity regarding the potential topics covered on the exam and the overwhelming feelings that follow such vague information. In part, the anxiety results from the limited scope of the sample questions available through the state—approximately six multiple-choice questions and one constructed response per section. Candidates feel both apprehensive because there is little specific information about the precise coverage and unnerved by blanket statements that suggest successful candidates display "knowing everything from first to sixth grade." Although they may have reviewed the material available online from New York State, when the candidates get to the test they often find the mathematics content particularly beyond their grasp and report, as they do with the ALST, that they run out of time for the written response and the forty selected response questions. One student who failed the CST the first time described the math questions as exceptionally complicated, as if "they were trying to trick us."

On the math portion of the CST, the selected response questions are not quick traditional computation problems; instead, they tend to be problems that assess a deeper understanding or multistep thinking. Additionally, for the elementary education candidates, the mathematics content on the CST covers more advanced topics, such as algebra, geometry, probability, and function analysis. Preparation for secondary teachers addresses these more complicated computations, but candidates at the elementary level may not have worked substantially with such problem sets in many years. Candidates may, for instance, be familiar with the commutative property, but they may not immediately think of it as a possibility for writing an equivalent expression when presented with 8x—4y. For the written response, the integration of three pieces of evidence to support the writer's statements is challenging because students are unsure about pertinent evidence, and their experiences with evidence-based writing are often more limited because they were not educated in the era of the Common Core. In 2010, New York introduced Common Core Standards, which emphasize such skills beginning in the primary grades; however, the K-12 education of our candidates rarely considered this approach to writing, which makes it time consuming to communicate in this manner.

Moreover, the cost of the different options for completing the CST (in one sitting versus in three different sittings) is a source of tension for our candidates. Seraphina's comments on this issue are typical of candidates with these concerns: "The cost is a huge issue for me. I really wish that I could take the three subtests separately, but it costs $20 more to do that. There are times that I have to choose between lights and eating, so $20 is a big deal for me." The reality is, however, that candidates who took all three in one sitting found the experience exhausting and performed much better on the first of the three exams; they often had to retake one or more portions, and that pattern ultimately cost them even more. Candidates who have completed the CST all in one sitting recommend to their peers that, despite the additional costs, they should take the three sections individually.

As with the ALST, candidates have found the time constraints and the computer-based structure of the exam limiting. Maya, who speaks English as an additional language, reports that pacing was challenging for her on her first attempt at the CST. She "spent too much time writing the essay and ended up having to put down all Cs on the select response items." Julie, a nontraditional undergraduate teacher candidate, had never taken a test on a computer before; in fact, despite the inefficiency of the approach, she still handwrites her essays before typing them Julie ran out of time while typing the essay on the CST, and she, though frustrated, is trying to learn how to type essays directly onto the computer.

### Teacher Performance Assessment (edTPA)

The edTPA has created nationwide tensions. Some concerns relate to its relationship to Pearson Education, Inc. (the for-profit company that distributes and manages the assessment), while other concerns object to the test's broad claims about measuring teacher readiness without sufficient outside research (Au 2013). Our candidates and faculty have reported both logistical and structural barriers to success on the edTPA. The most common logistical concern raised, beyond cost, is completing the edTPA during the one-semester capstone student teaching experience. The edTPA requires extensive time for preparation and coordination with the cooperating teacher, a challenging requirement in the best of situations. The single semester becomes a more profound challenge when student teaching overlaps with the intensive preparation of K–12 pupils for completing state standardized tests (in the spring semester). Because the high-accountability elementary schools in which we place many of our candidates focus on ensuring pupils perform well, teachers might devote as much as half the school day to test preparation during the weeks leading up to the test. The candidates also lose two full weeks in the middle of the semester when the K–12 pupils actually take the tests. Moreover, candidates report tension between the requirements of the edTPA and the expectations of cooperating teachers. Roberta, for instance, described a discussion with her cooperating teacher concerning the requirement to teach an "essential strategy," which differed from his usual pedagogical approach to literacy. Thus, she had to shape her edTPA lessons to meet the requirements of both the exam and her cooperating teacher—no easy feat.

Beyond the work in the classroom, many candidates and faculty members describe struggling with understanding the requirements laid out in the handbook. As one faculty member noted: "The edTPA is authoritative, intimidating, and unnecessarily verbose, making it inaccessible to many candidates." Layla, a talented candidate who speaks English as an additional language, described struggling with the "confusing language in prompts and rubrics" because it made the "expectations obscure." Although she "calibrated to the Level 4 and 5 on the rubrics," she ultimately passed by mere points. She was particularly frustrated because the scorer's feedback was "unclear" and did not allow her to understand the points of weakness. She suspected that her low scores are likely related to her English writing skills, even though she worked extensively with a writing tutor. The edTPA materials suggest that writing difficulties are not taken into account in scoring, but the extent to which scorers are prepared to ignore these differences is unclear. Others concur with the confusing language of the prompts and rubrics, which results in misunderstanding tasks and many hours of translation during office hours and class time.

Both time for writing and stamina with writing the extensive commentaries required for the edTPA are also barriers to completion for candidates. Given that candidates spend full days in K–12 classrooms and occasionally work part-time, finding the time to sit and write is challenging. Roberta discusses at length trying to schedule time during nights and weekends. Faculty report that many traditional (aged eighteen to twenty-two) undergraduate candidates struggle with writing stamina, likely because they have never written a forty-page document prior to this experience (particularly one with so many complex critical thinking tasks).

Negotiating these demands has proven tricky and prompted discussions of a longer capstone experience, yet the experience is currently a single semester because many candidates require salaried employment and more than one unpaid semester may lead to financial hardships. Despite these challenges, candidates consistently feel that the edTPA is a powerful educative assessment and the most valuable of the certification exams.

## Social/Psychological Aspects of the Exams

We would be remiss to ignore the ways in which social/psychological and affective dimensions of test taking profoundly impact our candidates. Previous research on African American and Latin@ experiences with teacher certification exams demonstrates how several factors can influence the actual test-taking experience: stereotype threat (Bennett, McWhorter, and Kuykendall 2006; Graham 2013; Petchauer 2015; Steele and Aronson 1995), identity contingencies (Bennett, McWhorter, and Kuykendall 2006; Petchauer 2014), and perceived bias (Graham 2013; Petchauer 2015). Our candidates raised some of the same concerns when going to take the ALST, CST-MS, and EAS at testing centers outside the university. Although fellow test takers were often taking different tests, many candidates described their rigid and foreign experiences when entering the testing centers and during the actual test taking; they found announcing the rules around coming in and leaving the testing center and the clicking of other test takers' computer mice to be particularly disconcerting. These aspects seemed to raise their anxiety. Moreover, for those candidates who were retaking an exam, self-efficacy beliefs seemed to inform the test-taking experience; many believe they failed a second or third time because of lacking confidence.

In terms of the edTPA, the social and psychological aspects of completing the test came into play when the students had to ask their cooperating teachers for the time, space, and guidance to do their edTPA work. Several faculty members report that candidates were hesitant to ask cooperating teachers to share their curriculum plans, provide time for implementation, or help them make choices with lesson plan sequencing. Indeed, one teacher educator described her elementary teacher candidates as "not feeling entitled to learn in the classroom space."

## Responding to the Needs of Teacher Candidates

We designed our work with teacher candidates around the certification exams to ensure that our candidates are experiencing both access and excellence in their teacher preparation. Thus, the School of Education at CCNY historically provides flexibility for candidates. For instance, courses are offered at different times of the day to accommodate candidates' work schedules, and students do not have to take the classes in the same order and with the same cohort. We similarly applied this flexibility to taking certification exams by providing a space for candidates to consult with their advisors while deciding about the best timing for the exams. With the addition of the edTPA and the EAS and the changes in the other exams, our School of Education faculty has, in addition, been working to ensure that candidates take the exams when they are most ready academically, avoid retakes, and take and pass exams prior to student teaching, when the edTPA will dominate much of their time. For instance, we encourage candidates to take the CST-MS after passing the math content and methods courses (three for undergraduate and two for graduate candidates), the inclusive practices course, and all of the other methods courses. This kind of advising seems to encourage candidates to complete the exams in a more timely manner. We are also paying much closer attention to certain materials used in admissions decisions, particularly the in-house essay and interview, to help us gauge the kinds of supports potentially necessary not only to graduate from the program but also to pass the exams.

### Addressing the Cost of Certification Exams

The concerns about cost have been on the forefront of faculty and administrators' agendas since the tests began coming down the pike, and they have actively sought vouchers to help our students defray the costs. The state has provided vouchers for both first-time takers and those candidates who are retaking exams. There are certainly not enough vouchers to cover the costs of all tests, and it is unlikely the state in the long run will sustain this level of support (provided through Race to the Top funds). We are currently pursuing how to include the cost of exams in financial aid packages.

Because the cost increases exponentially when retakes are required, faculty members provide targeted preparation for candidates prior to taking these exams. Workshops for the ALST, CST, and the edTPA offer considerable opportunities for preparation. We invite all current students and alumni from programs across the School of Education to attend the ALST and CST workshops, which are usually held in the evening or on the weekend at no cost to the candidates. The elementary education program also developed a workshop, offered prior to student teaching, to familiarize our candidates with the four important elements of the edTPA: unfamiliar vocabulary, critical writing, technological test taking, and sustained analytical demands.

### Addressing the Academic Literacy Skills Test (ALST)

The ALST workshops are designed to provide scaffolded experiences with the different required tasks, including developing their test-wiseness (McPhail

1981; Millman, Bishop, and Ebel 1965)—how test takers might leverage "the characteristics and format of the test and/or test-taking situation to receive a high score" (Millman, Bishop, and Ebel 1965, 707). Faculty simply support candidates through targeted practice: for instance, they dissect complex texts in various genres, eliminate choices on multiple selection tasks, manage their time, read and understand graphs and charts, and construct coherent argumentative writing. Jennifer found the workshops to be extremely beneficial. She noted that she "learned strategies to make her reading of passages more efficient." She also appreciated opportunities to examine strong writing samples because they gave her a "better sense of the structure of good essays." She passed the exam on her third try and exceeded the passing score by thirty points. Roberta also found the workshops to be helpful, particularly in developing her time management skills and familiarizing herself with the exam tasks: "When I walked into the test, I didn't need to read the directions—I knew what it was asking me to do, so I could use that extra time to calm myself and get right to work." José, a Latino English-language learner graduate student, passed the ALST after two failed attempts. He exclaimed after the workshops, "I finally understand what these kinds of tests have been asking me to do my whole life! The structure is so much clearer!" Dalia felt she benefited most from learning how to be a more efficient writer and strategizing about her initial task—the reading or writing. While she tried taking the test in each sequence, she ultimately passed it the third time by developing more efficient reading skills to accommodate the slow speed at which she writes.

The ALST also inspired faculty members to attend more to teaching the skills and knowledge the ALST requires in coursework. Many faculty members with whom we spoke noted that candidates often received piecemeal K–12 education so the instructors make sure to expose them to a wide variety of writing genres, give targeted formative feedback on argumentative writing, provide experiences with reading graphs and charts, and teach strategies for close reading of unfamiliar and complex texts. Though these types of educational experiences occurred in the coursework prior to the exams, the faculty purposefully makes connections for the candidates. José thought that the strategies he was learning in his courses to teach English-language learners promoted his success on the ALST. As a native Spanish speaker, whose education was unresponsive to his needs, he felt that his professor's ability to make those strategies visible as a tool for his own test taking was invaluable.

### Addressing the Content Specialty Test—Multiple Subject (CST-MS)

While the coursework integrates much of the content knowledge required to pass the CST-MS, many skills and some content knowledge continues to challenge our teacher candidates, particularly those whose K–12 education occurred many years prior to entering college. Similar to the ALST workshops, we designed the CST-MS workshops to develop the students' test-wiseness. In addition, the workshops seek to bolster the knowledge of content that candidates may only superficially recall. Candidates specifically report that they benefited from learning how to manage their time on the selected response questions to allow enough minutes for planning and writing the essays. For the math portion, we teach the candidates to break down the three major components—strengths, needs, and instructional interventions—and then give them strategies, which they practice, to support their writing.

Mathematics is a particular challenge for the candidates on the CST-MS. Therefore, we design the math methods courses to help nurture the skills and knowledge candidates need for the exam. The teacher candidates explain student understanding by describing both a strength and a need of a student they have assessed; the candidates then design an instruction intervention aligned with the Common Core standards. Additionally, the writing assessment for the math methods courses is quite similar in requirements to the written response for the CST-MS. The mathematics courses incorporate problem solving and conceptual understandings at higher levels, including algebra, linear functions, and geometry—not what one would expect to teach an elementary school student.

### Addressing the Teacher Performance Assessment (edTPA)

Although the ALST seems to have raised the most anxiety for our teacher candidates and faculty, the edTPA had a broad-scale impact on our teacher education programs. Schools of education were given only a single semester to pilot the edTPA before it became consequential for candidates. This was not enough time to ensure that we integrate the required skills and knowledge into coursework and prepare candidates who were entering student teaching for the complexity of the task. The major challenges that candidates experience with the edTPA lie in the handbook's lack of clarity, the single-semester timeline, and the writing demands.

The elementary education program developed mandatory zero-credit courses for candidates to take the semester before student teaching to support them in understanding the four tasks they must complete, interpret the unique language of the handbook, and practice the required evidence-based writing. Race to the Top grant funding, which lasted for three semesters, provided funding for these courses. Candidates reported finding the workshops helpful, particularly in understanding what was being asked of them and exposing them to the tasks. Faculty reported that those who completed the workshops seem to have an easier time getting started during their student teaching semester than those who did not.

Although the preparation was not as beneficial to the first two groups of student teachers completing the edTPA (because they had mostly completed their courses), the professors integrated into coursework the skills and knowledge required to effectively complete the edTPA. For example, candidates are now videotaping themselves teaching and analyzing their practice in literacy to further their understandings for the edTPA. Layla found this very helpful because it allowed her to "get feedback from professors on what elements make for strong lesson implementation" and to choose her edTPA clips more wisely. In addition, faculty now requires candidates to draw on the theories of teaching and learning from their courses and integrate them with practice into evidence-based writing.

The student teaching seminar ultimately become the space where supports are most useful because candidates are actively developing the lessons, videotaping, and analyzing student work during that time. In the seminar, faculty members revisit the language of the edTPA, clarify the prompts, help candidates understand the rubrics, and provide logistical supports. This includes negotiating time for teaching the edTPA lessons amid testing and the demands of schools that can sometimes be quite rigid. Candidates like Roberta, who struggled with time management around the edTPA, found it particularly helpful when the seminar leader helped her build and sustain a writing group, which not only supported her emotionally but also increased her productivity. Acknowledging the tremendous writing demands of the edTPA, faculty also helped candidates schedule blocks of writing time into their schedules and required that they produce a minimum number of written commentary pages prior to the end of the semester.

Faculty members have worked more closely with schools, cooperating teachers, and university supervisors to support the completion of the edTPA. New York City public schools were delayed in getting information to administrators about the exam so candidates often experienced resistance until faculty entered the schools to provide further information. Moreover, helping cooperating teachers understand the demands was imperative, a priority communicated by both faculty and university supervisors in the field. This meant that university supervisors needed to understand the requirements of the edTPA and the candidates' potential barriers to completion. We provided professional development to all university supervisors, with follow-up meetings via e-mail, phone, and in person.

Our current model of fieldwork and student teaching continues to be in tension with what many of our candidates need to complete the edTPA prior to graduation. Although the single-semester capstone experience accommodates the candidates' financial needs, our experiences suggest that most candidates are not in the position to submit a strong edTPA portfolio by the end of their student teaching, which thus prolongs the time to state certification. Our elementary education program is considering a very structured practicum experience in the same school during the semester prior to student teaching; this could not only give candidates many experiences of a yearlong student teaching experience without the time and financial burdens but also allow them to begin their edTPA sooner and submit it during the last semester before they graduate.

### Addressing the Social/Psychological Aspects of the Exams

Much of the work addressing the social and psychological aspects of test taking happens in workshops and student teaching seminars. Faculty describe the test-taking situation (the testing centers, signing in, using the restrooms, asking questions) in workshops in an effort to make the experience less foreign for the candidates who have not yet taken an exam. They bolster this experience by conversations in the student teaching seminars where peers who have taken the exams describe their experiences (positive, foreign, and unnerving) and the strategies they used. Conversations with faculty suggest that candidates have vastly different experiences even within the same test-taking center—depending upon the day, the proctor, the exam, and their identity—so having multiple perspectives is particularly helpful in easing anxieties. More could be done to explicitly address the roles that stereotype threat, identity, and bias play in the test-taking experience. For the edTPA, faculty report working with candidates on the language to speak with cooperating teachers about their needs to complete the exam. This has largely happened through mock conversations, and some candidates feel much more prepared by having an unstructured script as a guide. University supervisors in the elementary education program and cooperating teachers have also discussed the requirements at length so that candidates experience less resistance when entering these conversations.

## Conclusions and Recommendations

We have presented some barriers that diverse candidates encounter in passing certification exams and some ways the faculty in the School of Education at CCNY have attempted to address these obstacles. Our processes and approaches continue to evolve as we learn from candidates and as the state changes requirements. Our main concern, however, remains: some of our capable and knowledgeable graduates continue to struggle with passing these exams. Once our candidates leave CCNY, they often get full-time jobs in other industries and find it difficult to find the time to prepare for the exams, attend workshops, and complete their commentaries. This increases the likelihood that they may never earn their certification.

Although we do believe that candidates require skills and professional knowledge to be capable teachers of children, we are concerned that these exams are not fair indicators, particularly because New York State developed and implements them. We wonder if we would have needed such robust safety nets had the state developed and implemented these exams at a more deliberate pace. We also wonder why the state introduced the tests almost simultaneously, instead of allowing a staggered introduction to allow preparation programs time to make adjustments. We believe that these decisions caused some of our capable teacher candidates to leave the profession even before they truly entered it.

The New York State Education Department proposed regulations to accompany the introduction of these new exams that render these exams high stakes for not only teacher candidates but also the institutions that prepare them. Andrew Cuomo, the governor of New York, proposed that the state take the following actions: "Deregister and suspend the operation of any teacher education program that has more than 50 percent of its graduates failing to pass any state certification exam in a given year, in three consecutive years" (King 2014). Do those in power believe that teacher educators have the capacity to make reasoned judgments about teacher candidate readiness?

By presenting the ways in which our teacher education program has navigated the implementation of new teacher certification exams, we acknowledge that this work is still in process. To ensure that our candidates are prepared not only to teach but also to pass the teacher certification exams, we have chosen to support them in the areas of content, process, social/psychological, and cost. The content covered on the exams is important for future educators, and our program's coursework meets the content preparation. Highlighting the ways in which the content connects directly to the exams scaffolds the candidates' learning that much more.

For many candidates—particularly those whose dominant language is not English, those whose K–12 education poorly prepared them for college-level work, and those who are slow readers and writers—the efficiency of their reading and writing and the exposure to different genres are important areas in which to build skills. Beyond efficiency with reading and writing, time management for the edTPA is a large hurdle for our candidates. By helping them to schedule blocks of time for writing and working directly with the schools to help remove barriers to implementation, we as faculty are supportive of such processes.

Our findings here, while largely anecdotal, suggest that we must also address the cost of the exams, which is a huge burden for candidates, and provide them with a clear picture of the cost from the outset of their programs, which might help them budget more effectively. Finding ways to have financial aid go toward the cost of these exams seems like an important step. For our candidates, the cost of retaking the exams weighed heavily. Prior to taking the exams, preparation and support are critical steps to avoid unnecessary retakes. The introduction of workshops and explicit integration of assignments into courses readies the candidates so the certification exams become familiar. Freed from the burden of the unknown, candidates can thus focus on the tasks at hand.

We must also address the social/psychological aspects of test taking. Many of our candidates feel extreme anxiety around test taking. Rarely are they aware of the ways in which the actual testing situation, beliefs about self-efficacy, and their mindset about test taking shape their success. We have found that providing some familiarity with the test-taking situation and sharing stories around test taking is helpful for the computer-based tests. For the edTPA, it is important that candidates feel they have permission to request the necessary time and assistance to complete it in classrooms. Faculty members and university supervisors can bolster candidates' confidence by working with them on the language used in discussions with cooperating teachers.

Some states, such as our own New York, have added an extra layer of concern because we are working under very real threats to shut down teacher education programs when candidates have neither taken nor passed the exams. Teacher education programs must address another burden—tracking data. Our experiences suggest that the state's data on who has taken and passed exams is highly inaccurate; such inaccuracies are unacceptable, given not only the high stakes for both candidates and programs but also the importance of correct tracking of individuals and their test results.

These exams are daunting for many of our candidates, but we have seen many of them thrive with targeted preparation that addresses gaps in their skills, knowledge, familiarity, and concerns. As teacher educators, we have a responsibility to be both gatekeepers of the profession and guards who lift the gates that prevent able candidates from entering the field. Further empirical research is needed on the barriers to candidates' successes, and this chapter also serves as a call for more of these investigations. Our commitments to access, excellence, and the diversification of the teacher workforce drive our work, and we continue to respond to the new challenges that arise in our approach to equity-minded teacher education.

REFERENCES

Angrist, Joshua D., and Jonathan Guryan. 2008. "Does Teacher Testing Raise Teacher Quality? Evidence from State Certification Requirements." *Economic of Education Review* 27: 483–503.

Angus, David L. 2001. "Professionalism and the Public Good: A Brief History of Teacher Certification." Washington, DC: Thomas B. Fordham Foundation. http://files.eric. ed.gov/fulltext/ED449149.pdf.

Au, Wayne. 2013. "What's a Nice Test Like You Doing in a Place Like This? The edTPA and Corporate Education 'Reform.'" *Rethinking Schools* 27: 22–27.

Bennett, Christine I., Lynne McWhorter, and John A. Kuykendall. 2006. "Will I Ever Teach? Latino and African American Students' Perspectives on Praxis I." *American Education Research Journal* 43: 531–575.

Berger, Mark C., and Eugenia T. Toma. 1994. "Variation in State Education Policies and Effects on Student Performance." *Journal of Policy Analysis and Management* 13: 477–491.

Cochran-Smith, Marilyn, and Kim Fries. 2005. "Researching Teacher Education in Changing Times: Politics and Paradigms." In *Studying Teacher Education: The Report of*

the *AERA Panel on Research and Teacher Education*, edited by Marilyn Cochran-Smith
and Ken Zeichner, 69–109. Mahwah, NJ: Lawrence Erlbaum Associates.

D'Agati, John L., and Ken Wagner. 2015. "Creation of Safety Nets for Candidates Who Take
the New Teacher Certification Examinations (ALST, EAS, and the Redeveloped CSTs)
and an Extension of the Safety Net for the edTPA." https://www.regents.nysed.gov/
common/regents/files/meetings/Sep%202015/915brca2.pdf.

Darling-Hammond, Linda. 2000. "Teacher Quality and Student Achievement: A Review of
State Policy Evidence." *Education Policy Analysis Archives* 8: 1–44.

Darling-Hammond, Linda, and Jon Snyder. 2000. "Authentic Assessment of Teaching in
Context." *Teaching and Teacher Education* 16: 523–545.

Dilworth, Mary E. 1990. "Reading between the Lines: Teachers and Their Racial/Ethnic
Cultures." Washington, DC: ERIC Clearinghouse on Teacher Education and American
Association of Colleges for Teacher Education. http://files.eric.ed.gov/fulltext/
ED322148.pdf.

Dilworth, Mary E., and Anthony L. Brown. 2008. "Teachers of Color: Quality and Effective
Teachers One Way or Another." In *The Handbook of Research on Teacher Education:
Enduring Questions in Changing Contexts*, edited by Marilyn Cochran-Smith, Sharon
Feiman-Nemser, and D. John McIntyre, 424–444. New York: Routledge.

Floden, Robert, and Marco Meniketti. 2005. "Research on the Effects of Coursework in the
Arts and Sciences and in the Foundations of Education." In *Studying Teacher Education:
The Report of the AERA Panel on Research and Teacher Education*, edited by Marilyn
Cochran-Smith and Ken Zeichner, 261–308. Mahwah, NJ: Lawrence Erlbaum
Associates.

Gay, Geneva. 2000. *Culturally Responsive Teaching: Theory, Research, and Practice*. New York:
Teachers College Press.

Gitomer, Drew H. 2007. *Teacher Quality in a Changing Policy Landscape: Improvements in the
Teaching Pool*. Princeton, NJ: Educational Testing Service. http://www.ets.org/Media/
Education_Topics/pdf/TQ_full_report.pdf.

Gitomer, Drew H., Andrew S. Latham, and Robert Ziomek. 1999. *The Academic Quality of
Prospective Teachers: The Impact of Admissions and Licensure Testing*. Princeton, NJ:
Educational Testing Service.

Goodwin, Anne L., and Celia Oyler. 2008. "Teacher Educators as Gatekeepers: Making
Decisions about Who Should/Can Teach." In *Handbook of Research on Teacher Education:
Enduring issues in Changing Contexts*, edited by Marilyn Cochran-Smith, Sharon
Feiman-Nemser, and D. John McIntyre, 395–546. New York: Routledge/Taylor and
Francis/Association of Teacher Educators.

Graham, Anthony. 2013. "Black Teacher Education Candidates' Performance on Praxis I:
What Test Results Do Not Tell Us." *Negro Educational Review* 64: 9–35.

*Gulino v. N.Y. State Education Department.* 2006.

Hanushek, Eric A., and Richard A. Pace. 1995. "Who Chooses to Teach and Why?" *Economics
of Education Review* 14: 101–117.

Hess, Frederick M. 2003. "Tear Down this Wall: The Case for a Radical Overhaul of Teacher
Certification." Presented at White House Conference on Preparing Tomorrow's
Teachers, Washington, DC, August 23.

Hill, Heather C., Brian Rowan, and Deborah Loewenberg Ball. 2005. "Effects on Teachers'
Mathematical Knowledge for Teaching on Student Achievement." *American Educational
Research Journal* 42: 371–406.

Ingersoll, Richard M. 2004. "Why do High-Poverty Schools Have Difficulty Staffing
Their Classrooms with Qualified Teachers?" Center for American Progress.

https://www.americanprogress.org/issues/education/news/2004/11/19/1205/why-do-high-poverty-schools-have-difficulty-staffing-their-classrooms-with-qualified-teachers/.

King, John B. 2014. *Statement from Commissioner John. B. King Jr. Regarding the edTPA Teacher Certification Exam*. http://www.nysed.gov/news/2015/statement-commissioner-john-b-king-jr-regarding-edtpa-teacher-certification-exam.

Law, Marc T., and Sukkoo Kim. 2005. "Specialization and Regulation: The Rise of Professionals and the Emergence of Occupational Licensing Regulation." *Journal of Economic History* 65: 723–756.

Margolis, Jason, and Anne Doring. 2013. "National Assessments for Student Teachers: Documenting Teaching Readiness to the Tipping Point." *Action in Teacher Education* 35: 212–219.

McPhail, Irving P. 1981. "Why Teach Test Wiseness?" *Journal of Reading* 25: 32–38.

Millman, Jason, Carol H. Bishop, and Robert Ebel. 1965. "An Analysis of Test Wiseness." *Educational and Psychological Measurement* 25: 707–726.

Mitchell, Karen J., David Z. Robinson, Barbara S. Plake, and Kaeli T. Knowles, eds. 2001. *Testing Teacher Candidates: The Role of Licensure Tests in Improving Teacher Quality*. Washington, DC: National Academy Press.

Nettles, Michael T., Linda H. Scatton, Jonathan H. Steinberg, and, Linda L. Tyler. 2011. *Performance and Passing Rate Differences of African American and White Prospective Teachers on PRAXIS Examinations*. Princeton, NJ: Educational Testing Service. http://www.ets.org/Media/Research/pdf/RR-11–08.pdf.

Pecheone, Raymond L., and Ruth R. Chung. 2006. "Evidence in Teacher Education: The Performance Assessment for California Teachers." *Journal of Teacher Education* 57: 22–36.

Petchauer, Emery. 2014. "'Slaying Ghosts in the Room': Identity Contingencies, Teacher Licensure Testing Events, and African American Preservice Teachers." *Teachers College Record* 116: 1–40.

———. 2015. "Passing as White: Race, Shame, and Success in Teacher Licensure Testing Events for Black Preservice Teachers." *Race, Ethnicity, and Education* 18: 834–857.

Ravitch, Diane. 2003. "A Brief History of Teacher Professionalism." Presented at White House Conference on Preparing Tomorrow's Teachers, Washington, DC, August 23.

Rowan, Brian, Richard Correnti, and Robert J. Miller. 2002. "What Large-Scale Survey Research Tells Us about Teacher Effects on Student Achievement." *Sociology of Education* 75: 256–284.

Shapiro, Martin M., Michael H. Slutsky, and Richard F. Watt. 1989. "Minimizing Unnecessary Differences in Occupational Testing." *Valparaiso University Law Review* 23: 213–265. http://scholar.valpo.edu/cgi/viewcontent.cgi?article=2048&context=vulr.

Steele, Claude M., and Joshua Aronson. 1995. "Stereotype Threat and the Intellectual Test Performance of African Americans." *Journal of Personality and Social Psychology* 69: 797–811.

Taylor, Kate. 2015. "Questions of Bias Are Raised about a Teachers' Exam in New York." *New York Times*, April 7. http://www.nytimes.com/2015/04/08/nyregion/questions-of-bias-are-raised-about-a-teachers-exam-in-new-york.html?_r=0.

Wilson, Suzanne M., Robert E. Floden, and Joan Ferrini-Mundy. 2001. *Teacher Preparation Research: Current Knowledge, Gaps, and Recommendations*. Seattle: University of Washington, Center for the Study of Teaching and Policy.

Wilson, Suzanne M., and Peter Youngs. 2005. "Accountability processes in teacher education." In *Studying Teacher Education: The Report of the American Educational*

*Research Association Panel on Research and Teacher Education*, edited by Marilyn Cochran-Smith and Ken Zeichner, 591–643. Mahwah, NJ: Lawrence Erlbaum Associates.

Wilson, Mark, P. J. Hallam, Ray Pecheone, and Pamela Moss. 2007. "Using Student Achievement Test Scores as Evidence of External Validity for Indicators of Teacher Quality: Connecticut's Beginning Educator Support and Training Program." Berkeley, CA: Berkeley Evaluation and Research Center.

Zumwalt, Karen K., and Elizabeth Craig. 2008. "Who Is Teaching: Does It Matter?" In *Handbook of Research on Teacher Education: Enduring Issues in Changing Contexts*, edited by Marilyn Cochran-Smith, Sharon Feiman-Nemser, and D. John McIntyre, 404–423. New York: Routledge and Association of Teacher Educators.

# 6

## Special Education Teacher Preparation Reform in Context

### Lessons from a Decade of Program Support

MARY BAY

NORMA A. LOPEZ-REYNA

ROSANNE WARD

$M$ost would agree that the reform of teacher preparation programs is not done in a vacuum. It is done in a particular context, and factors in that context play a key role in the nature of the reform work (Cochran-Smith et al. 2008; Cochran-Smith and Villegas 2015; Delandshere and Petrosky 2004; Elmore 2004; Kennedy 2010; Wang et al. 2010). In our experience working with hundreds of teacher educators who were engaged in teacher preparation program reform, we often heard comments, stories, and descriptions of dilemmas that exemplified how an array of contextual factors surfaced that either facilitated or impeded reform outcomes. These contextual factors came in many forms: for example, expectations, directives, requirements, distractions, and barriers. After years of working with teacher educators engaged in reform efforts and after listening carefully to their voices, we learned to pay careful attention to their ideas about the contexts in which they worked and the impact of those contexts. In chapter 6, we discuss the relationship between contextual factors and the design and implementation of teacher preparation reform initiatives.

Our work in providing technical assistance to more than 175 faculty teams from Minority-Serving Institutions (MSIs) that sought to improve their programs, as well as our reading of the literature, suggests that we can frame contextual influences in various ways. Discussions that analyze dominant reforms within the teacher preparation policy arena are keenly aware of the influence of context on reform outcomes. Sometimes referred to as "situational constraints," examples include the short duration available to teacher educators to prepare candidates and the modest resourcing of teacher preparation program design (for a discussion, see Sykes, Bird, and Kennedy 2010). We can also frame contextual influences as mandates to which programs must align; for example, consider the program accreditation process, alignment with state-level teacher preparation standards, and the impact of high-stakes standardized accountability measures on program curriculum and assessments (Brown 2010; DeLuca and Bellara 2013; Freeman et al. 2014). Of course, less restrictive dimensions of contextual factors often come in the form of supports (e.g., cooperative faculty colleagues, a stable institutional environment, a strong project leader). Finally, our experiences with faculty teams working to improve their programs suggest yet another category: reform of programs to address specific demands, such as using a culturally responsive framework to reconceptualize a program that prepares candidates to meet the interests and needs of a changing PreK–12 student demographic and graduating increased numbers of candidates in a shorter period of time to meet local market demands. Whether framed as situational constraints, mandates, supports, or demands, there is a growing consensus that understanding the relationship between context and reform initiatives is important. With a deeper understanding of the factors influencing the outcomes of reform initiatives, our conceptions of reform can be reconsidered and better understood.

Except for a few isolated cases (e.g., Brown 2010; Peck, Gallucci, and Sloan 2010; Sayeski and Higgins 2014), the existing literature on teacher preparation reform offers few detailed descriptions of the design and implementation process and the ways in which the work is influenced by contextual factors. In an effort to fill this void, we present the work of seventeen faculty teams involved in a Data-Based Problem-Solving (DBPS) program improvement endeavor. Each team represented an MSI that aimed to improve its special education teacher preparation program. We begin with background information that provides the setting for the DBPS endeavor, followed by a brief description of the technical assistance model in which these teams participated. We then present a description of the teams' reform initiatives and how those initiatives were influenced by contextual factors. Drawing from the teams' experiences, we offer suggestions for how a reform initiative may result in successful outcomes and conclude with our suggestions for needed research.

Although the insights and recommendations reported in this chapter come from work done with special education teacher preparation programs, our reading of the literature and experiences with general teacher education reform suggest that these ideas are relevant to improving all types of teacher preparation programs. We think that teacher educators at both MSIs and predominately white institutions (PWIs) will recognize and perhaps identify with many of the contextual factors presented. Likewise, they will also recognize aspects of the initiatives because they will likely apply to their own experiences. As a result, we think teacher educators from all types of institutions will benefit from the work discussed here.

## Background: The Monarch Center

From 2002 to 2014, the Office of Special Education Programs (OSEP) in the US Department of Education funded a center located at the University of Illinois at Chicago (Project Number H325R080002). The Monarch Center provided technical assistance to faculty members at MSIs. The technical assistance focused on providing professional development in two domains: (1) developing OSEP-funded grant proposals and (2) improving the quality of preparation programs. First, the center provided technical assistance pertaining to grant proposal development, training, and mentoring to faculty members who sought to write successful grant proposals. A funded grant provided scholarships for university students preparing to be special education teachers or related services professionals (e.g., speech pathologists), afforded opportunities to reconfigure course and fieldwork for unique specializations, or provided funds for specified program improvement projects. Second, the center provided technical assistance pertaining to preparation program reform, evidence-based knowledge, mentoring, and support to faculty teams who aimed to enhance the quality of their programs, or design and offer new programs. An enhanced program often resulted in such successes as producing an improved curriculum, gaining accreditation, or meeting particular market needs (e.g., preparing candidates with a better understanding of local needs).

The action of OSEP to create a center that provided this type of technical assistance to MSIs originated when the US Congress passed a law in 1990 based on strong advocacy for Historically Black Colleges and Universities (HBCUs) and other MSIs that were not receiving a proportionate amount of the funds available through OSEP grant competitions. The proposed bill, aimed at supplying annual funding to provide technical assistance to HBCUs, actually included all institutions of higher education that enrolled at least 25 percent students of color. OSEP subsequently requested proposals to establish a center that would strive to reach the law's intended goals of providing technical assistance that focused on grant proposal development and program improvement. In response to the call, Mary Bay and Norma Lopez-Reyna (chapter 6's first two authors) submitted the grant proposal selected for funding; hence, OSEP established the Monarch Center at the University of Illinois at Chicago—classified as both a Hispanic-Serving Institution (HSI) and an Asian American and Native American Pacific Islander Serving Institution (AANAPISI).

Each MSI that received service from the Monarch Center met the federal government's definition for this classification and had programs in special education and/or related services. Examples of MSIs with which the Monarch Center worked were HBCUs, AANAPISIs, HSIs, Tribal Colleges and Universities (TCUs), and those institutions serving multiple groups of minority students.

While it varied across the years, the total number of MSIs eligible for services, on a yearly basis, was approximately 350.

The Monarch Center's specific focus was to provide the type of technical assistance described above so that MSIs could prepare and graduate outstanding professionals to serve children and youth with disabilities, particularly those children and adolescents from diverse racial, ethnic, and linguistic backgrounds. During the years leading up to the work described in this chapter, the Monarch Center had provided technical assistance to nearly three hundred institutions and to more than one thousand participants. Evaluation data overwhelmingly revealed that participants were highly satisfied with the center's services. Moreover, the data indicated that with grant proposal development support, participants had a 51 percent greater chance of securing a grant, and, of those receiving program improvement support, approximately 70 percent (150 institutions) showed significantly positive change in the quality of their programs; twelve institutions designed and started new programs.

## The Technical Assistance Approach

To explore the relationship between contextual factors and teacher preparation reform, we examine the work done with seventeen MSI teams who were committed to special education teacher preparation program reform. The DBPS endeavor began with the Monarch Center's announcement that it would provide technical assistance to teams of faculty members from MSIs with a focus on using data for problem solving toward improvement of the teams' programs on two levels. First, we guided and supported teacher educators as they collected, analyzed, and used data to improve their programs. Second, we assisted teams in ensuring that their teacher candidates graduated with the abilities to collect, analyze, and use data to inform their decisions about classroom instruction and behavior management, a quality that new teachers were (and still are) expected to demonstrate (American Association of Colleges of Teacher Education 2011; 2012; US Department of Education 2011).

Armed with the general goal of improving their programs by using data to solve problems and determine actions, the Monarch staff worked with seventeen teams that represented fifteen MSIs. (Two institutions sent two teams, one to work on their undergraduate program and the other to work on their graduate program.) The teams were grouped into three cohorts, each with five to six teams. The teams represented six HBCUs, four HSIs, four AANAPISIs, and three multiples; each team included three or four persons for a total of fifty-two participants.

All participants were members of their institutions' education faculty. From documents and comments, we discovered that the participant group ranged from those who had just started in their positions to those who were seasoned veterans. Moreover, at least seven participants also held administrative positions at their institutions: one interim dean, four directors/coordinators of programs, and two department chairs.

The teams were working with programs that enrolled a wide range of students—from twelve to more than six hundred—with the typical team working to improve a program that consisted of approximately one hundred teacher candidates. Teams often described their teacher candidates as older and nontraditional: representing racially and ethnically diverse communities, struggling financially, changing careers, and/or speaking English as a second language. In addition, some teacher candidates were described as strong advocates for social justice and as individuals who worked relentlessly for equitable educational opportunities.

### The Technical Assistance Model

The technical assistance model used for this project required that the teams engage with the Monarch Center across a twelve-month period. During this time, the teams worked with three professors from MSIs who were experts on data-based problem solving and strategic personnel preparation as well as with the Monarch staff.

The work began with a three-day conference to learn about the specific data-based problem solving approach, the supporting relevant research, and standards. Team members engaged in deep discussions with each other, presenters, Monarch staff, and other teams as they shaped ideas into plans that reflected each program's unique cultural and institutional needs.

As participants explored the topic of data-based problem solving throughout the three-day conference, we introduced teams to each step in the process. While there are many versions, the Monarch Center staff chose to use the five-step approach to structure the work around level-one DBPS: (1) identify your problem, (2) collect and analyze data, (3) propose a solution, (4) respond and revisit, (5) and disseminate. We presented guiding questions for each step. See table 6.1 for a description of the action plan process. During the conference, the teams completed step one (problem identification) and brainstormed data sources and collection and analysis methods (step two). They completed step two and the remaining steps on their home campuses. (Presentations and guided discussions about preparing candidates to use DBPS to inform their teaching (level two) were woven throughout the conference.)

At the end of the conference, each team presented its plan and received feedback from the other participants, facilitators, and the Monarch staff. We assigned each team a mentor (one of the three experts), and we reminded them that the Monarch Center could provide additional, individualized supports (beyond mentoring), if the team needed assistance when it returned to its home campus. For example, we could supply funds to offer a retreat for a

TABLE 6.1

**Action Plan Process**

| Steps | Guiding questions |
|---|---|
| Identify your problem | What problems do you have? How would you prioritize them? How can you frame them in observable and measurable terms? What problem will you work on? How do you know it is a problem? If approved to address this problem (or a revised version of this problem), then how will you attain the approval? Who will be responsible for attaining this approval? |
| Collect and analyze data | What do you need to know to tackle the problem? What data sources do you currently have and what are they telling you? What else do you need to know? What other data sources do you need? How will you collect and analyze these data? What are the data saying? |
| Propose a solution | What are you going to do about it? Who shares responsibility for the solution? Who are the stakeholders? Does the proposed solution truly address the identified problem? What supports will you need to implement the solution? Of the above needed supports, which ones are already in place? How will you gather those supports that you don't have? Are there barriers that might impact your team's work (e.g., power struggles, lack of leadership, hoarding-colleagues keeping their expertise to themselves)? How can you prevent these barriers from surfacing? How can you respond to the barriers that do surface in such a way as to be able to continue with your work? Do you have to revise your program because of state mandates (e.g., new standards, new teacher candidate assessment system) or because of changes in your department? College? Could you embed this solution into this required change process? |
| Respond and revisit | What anticipated and unanticipated consequences resulted from your solution? Did your solution work? If not, where did the process break down? how will you sustain your success? If so, |
| Disseminate | Who needs to know? What do they need to know? How will you tell them? How will you use feedback from stakeholders to continue to shape the process? |

*Note*: The Action Plan steps and guiding questions were developed in collaboration with Drs. Mary Little, Patricia Alvarez McHatton, and Elizabeth Cramer.

team's departmental colleagues and assist with on-site meetings with department or college level administrators to describe the identified problem and the proposed solutions.

Throughout the year following the conference, a team's mentor was available for assistance via email, phone call, and face-to-face meetings. Each team worked with its assigned mentor in some fashion. Cohort group discussions took place via four- and eight-month conference calls for the purpose of monitoring progress, exchanging successful strategies, seeking advice regarding challenges, nudging each other to keep going, and holding each other accountable to attain goals. Mentors and Monarch staff members, who took detailed notes, participated in these conference calls as well.

The twelve-month period concluded with a face-to-face Comeback Session in which one member from each team came together and reported on the extent to which its team was able to solve its targeted programmatic problem(s). We allocated time to discuss strategies and approaches, contextual facilitators, and (equally emphasized by Monarch staff) barriers that they encountered.

## Artifact Review

Throughout the twelve-month period, Monarch Center staff gathered and systematically catalogued a variety of artifacts and products for later review. These included each team's preconference needs-assessment survey, its action plan created during the conference, and its final Comeback Session presentation. In additional, we gathered notes taken during the initial conference, phone conferences, final presentations, and the teams' final oral and written reports. The authors completed a detailed analysis of these artifacts to better understand the types of reforms the teams sought, the impetus for these desired changes, the barriers encountered, and their resolutions. In short, we were interested in understanding the relationship between program reform and contextual factors.

## Reform Embedded in Context

Participants based their reform effort on a problem that they needed to address to improve the program. Five types of problems surfaced.

A frequent type of reform work focused on the lack of teacher candidates' subject matter knowledge (often referred to as content knowledge). Each of five teams, who planned to address their teacher candidates' lack of content knowledge, framed the problem in various ways. For example, one team concluded that their program was "out of date" because their program graduates were not considered highly qualified in a subject area by the state and, therefore, had difficulty securing teaching positions upon graduation. This team revised their program so that teacher candidates received their degrees in the content area and an endorsement in special education. Their program design was constrained by the need for the new program to maintain the same total number of credit hours as the current program.

Another team identified the problem as lack of content knowledge based on teacher candidates' poor performance on state exams that measured content knowledge, particularly science, technology, literacy, and math. Additionally, this team had collected observation data that documented the teacher candidates' difficulty in teaching these subjects to their students. Similar to the first team, this team revised their program so that graduates could be eligible to teach in general education and inclusion classes, with a specialty in the above subject areas. From a review of data and informal interviews with their teacher candidates, two teams identified low scores on state required exams that measured content knowledge. An analysis of the scores informed subsequent reform work for one team, but the other team, while recognizing the need for change, chose to work on another program area that needed improvement.

Finally, a third team expressed concern about the extent to which their teacher candidates were not passing the required state exam that measured content knowledge. Because the state based its exam on the state's competencies for a new teacher, this team made considerable progress in ensuring that its preparation program's curricular content aligned with the state's competencies. The team explained, however, that they could not keep pace with the frequent state competency revisions. For example, during the team's work with the Monarch Center, the state had recently issued its nineteenth edition of the competencies.

The influence of contextual factors on such work is obvious. A federal mandate (a teacher must be highly qualified) and state-level requirements to pass exams that measure content knowledge greatly impacted this work. In fact, the mandates were often the impetus for the reform work. Teacher candidates having difficulty passing state exams in content knowledge was a common problem for the MSI teams with which we worked throughout the twelve years of the Monarch Center. Teams often generated various reasons for the poor performance: older students sometimes had not studied the subject matter since the early years of their undergraduate education; teacher candidates occasionally discontinued enrollment for a period of time to earn tuition funds, which resulted in a disjointed education; some candidates suffered from test anxiety; other candidates contended with unidentified and undocumented disabilities; and some candidates' primary language was not English.

Taking the exam multiple times created a hardship for many because the exams, in general, were expensive. Those teacher educators with whom we worked clearly understood the obvious need for teachers to know the subject matter they were teaching. Too frequently, however, those same teacher educators observed candidates who could not pass the exam but who could still teach an excellent lesson and demonstrate more than sufficient knowledge of the subject matter.

A second identified type of reform pertained to the idea of collaboration at the levels of teacher candidate, teacher educator, and MSI-school partner. Five teams described issues of collaboration in their problem statements and developed plans to address them. First, they considered the lack of collaboration among higher education faculty to be a problem. Candidates could not observe collaboration in action, and a program's curricular content often overlapped or contained gaps because faculty members were reluctant to jointly examine content, assignments, and experiences. Second, lack of collaboration among professional candidates was also considered a problem. Because the programs existed in silos, the candidates lacked opportunities either to work collaboratively—a much needed ability in the workplace—or to conduct cross-program analyses to identify places where candidates could come together to study and hear each other's ideas. A third form of necessary collaboration aimed for MSI faculty to cooperate more effectively with PreK–12 school-based partners.

In general, the teams that decided to improve the collaboration dimension of their programs were quite successful. The teams devised numerous strategies that fostered collaboration: securing grant funds to allow for such options as course buyouts to provide time; ensuring opportunities for voices to be heard; reforming work in transparent ways; establishing structures to bring people together (e.g., professional work teams, brown bag lunches, professional learning communities); conducting cross-program analyses to identify courses where content was similar and candidates could study together; and continually informing those involved in teacher preparation of outside pertinent policy mandates. It appeared that the ongoing communication of issues, especially when coupled with relevant program data, assisted faculty in taking ownership of the program, which led to a greater interest in collaboration.

With regard to the influence of contextual factors, much of this work seemed to be grounded in internal situational constraints. For example, problems often existed because of persistent deficiencies: lack of time, lack of understanding of a colleague's area of expertise, lack of interest, and lack of awareness that a teacher needs to know how to work collaboratively. From our observations, we include issues with administrators, who, when making major decisions such as those pertaining to tenure, promotion, and salary increases, demonstrated a lack of professional recognition for collaborative work; this administrative outlook thus deterred collaborative work. Finally, we noticed how often working collaboratively became an unexpected positive outcome of a program reform initiative. We observed that the work may have begun under a sense of obligation and duty, but when well executed, the collaboration morphed into an opportunity for professional growth, cooperation, and development of an expanding sense of program ownership.

A third type of reform pertained to the problem of offering a program that was not competitive in the marketplace. The major reason for the uncompetitive status pertained to the program requirements—too many credit hours when compared to other programs in the institution's geographical area. One graduate level program, which initially required 46 credit hours, was reduced to 34 while maintaining the program's integrity. The team revised the program structure to offer a dual certification program (i.e., certification in either K–6 or in 6–12) and integrated the content of six courses into three. The new program needed new syllabi to ensure that candidates studied important content and practiced and demonstrated significant skills. To examine the program's curricular content, assignments, and teacher candidates' experiences, the MSI faculty had to work collaboratively. At another institution, the team reduced an undergraduate program, initially requiring 135 to 140 semester hours, to 120 hours. Again, this reduction acknowledged the program's lack of competitiveness in the local market. Apparently, the lack of competitive status was affecting other programs on campus because, during the twelve-month period, this team's university president mandated that no undergraduate program could require more than 120 credit hours. The team reviewed other programs in the area for content, structure, and format and analyzed their own program for redundancy and possible co-teaching arrangements.

In MSIs, enrollment is critical for the program to stay alive. During the years of operation, the Monarch Center, in more than one instance, assisted program faculty when called upon to help keep a program in existence. Typically, this advocacy meant reviewing the competition's programs to better understand their offerings, revising or restructuring the team's program to reduce the total required credit hours, developing a marketing plan to identify and inform prospective students, and providing a mentor to guide the team through the various approval levels. At times, it also included conversations with administrators to encourage them to maintain a special education teacher preparation program.

A fourth area that needed reform pertained to developing and using a data system to determine program effectiveness. Two teams focused specifically on this dimension. The first team indicated that a program-level assessment system was in place but poorly managed. The team developed steps to better manage the data and use it to inform program improvements; that is, the team determined when the data would be collected, to whom the data would be submitted, who would analyze the data, and where they would house the data. In addition, the team clarified roles and responsibilities and provided staff development to train both adjunct and regular faculty members in the new system. By the end of the twelve-month period, the dean had approved the data management system. The second team similarly had collected a considerable amount of data on their candidates' performance and satisfaction with the program but had not managed it well. The team was unsatisfied with the extent to which the data had not informed the program improvement process. They completed the initial steps in creating a management system to use the data for meaningful decision making and to present the system to their candidates so that they could see how the data prompted program reform.

In considering how contextual factors influenced this program improvement, it is noteworthy that the teams, at times, indicated how such a management system required the alignment of course objectives with state standards and state teacher candidate assessment systems. Teams also commented that the management systems would make writing reports for state and professional accreditation much easier.

A final reform area pertained to teacher candidates' difficulty with applying what they had learned in their campus courses to the real world of the classroom. Teacher educators observed this while instructing their candidates in the field and analyzing teacher candidates' work samples. Their teacher candidates had difficulty linking data to the instructional and behavioral decisions they had to make regarding teaching approaches. This difficulty was especially evident as it pertained to incorporating district and state mandates and working in inclusive classrooms. The complexity of teaching became evident in the candidates' required field projects. To improve the program in this area, the teams adopted several approaches, including creating a handbook for candidates that displayed courses and their competencies as well as the aligned assessment measures. To create the handbook, the team met with field supervisors, advisory board members, and multiple subject instructors to align key assignments with competencies and assessments. The team created rubrics for the assessments and trained supervisors and key faculty to use the assessments and aggregate the data, steps that informed the program curricular revisions. Another team led an initiative, which resulted in transforming the program. Candidates were prepared to teach both general and special education students, but they could not practice their teaching strategies and approaches because the school district lacked inclusive classrooms. Team members and their colleagues worked with key stakeholders in both the school district and the university to create inclusive settings, to prepare university and school-based mentors to co-teach, to guide everyone toward working collaboratively, and to train teacher candidates to teach all students.

### Working Simultaneously in Multiple, Shifting Contexts

A review of these seventeen teams' experiences revealed an overarching contextual factor that seemed to impact their reform efforts. Teacher educators carried out their initiatives in multiple contexts, not just one, and worked in these multiple contexts simultaneously. Adding to this challenge, these contexts often shifted or changed. Hence, our participants were simultaneously working in multiple contexts that were frequently changing.

Threaded throughout the teams' reform work was a concrete example of the need to work in multiple contexts simultaneously. For instance, teams had to address a number of sets of standards, ranging from one to nine, when reforming their programs; most teams listed three sets from their state and two from professional accreditation organizations. Typically, these standards described knowledge, skills, and dispositions, or competencies that teacher candidates were expected to demonstrate before earning their certificates or licenses; moreover, the program itself had to demonstrate adherence to standards describing its qualities and accomplishments. Program standards, characteristically, addressed state and professional organization standards to ensure accreditation by both bodies. Typically, when a program did not meet these various sets of standards, accreditation was postponed or denied, and the life of the program was called into question., The very nature of a standard provides a major impact on the design and content of the program. Standards and competencies strongly influence and, at times, dictate content, which often drives the teacher candidates' experiences and assessments of their abilities. Standards pertaining to the clinical component of a program have the potential to impact the program's structure, including hours in the field, location of fieldwork, and the candidate's activities. For these reasons, the need to meet teacher candidate and program-level standards looms large in a teacher educator's professional life.

Whereas the sets of standards played critical roles, some teams' written comments were reminders of the additional frameworks to which their programs had to adhere. For example, teams had to be mindful of maintaining alignment with Charlotte Danielson's teacher evaluation framework (Danielson 2007), addressing the national Common Core Standards (Achieve 2013), as well as incorporating the edTPA teacher certification assessment (Sawchuck 2013) into the program; in addition, depending on their institutions' selected teacher preparation approach, local PreK–12 school systems' curricular content, and their states' decision about teacher candidate assessment, teams' reform decisions often had additional requirements to meet. In other words, teams' reform decisions often had to adhere to not only several sets of standards but also additional requirements. Donna Wiseman (2012) offered her insights about this phenomenon.

> Policy affecting teacher education evolves from a wide range of sources, including public perceptions and attitudes, federal initiatives, current trends in public schools and higher education, the visions and whims of politicians, and the profession's own initiatives. No matter how it emerges, it is not unusual for policy ebbs and flows to result in major reforms or restructuring of programs and curriculum as the teacher education community attempts to respond to federal and state political wishes and to the attitudes and perspectives of legislators and the public. (87)

Our experiences with teams engaged in reform suggest that there are layers of mandates with little regard for who must implement them.

The hundreds of teacher educators with whom the Monarch Center has worked identified the challenges of working in several different contexts simultaneously while remaining flexible to accommodate shifting agendas and requirements. Teacher educators engaged in a reform effort indicated that working in shifting contexts simultaneously could either present a barrier to accomplishing program improvement goals or result in a major shift in the nature of the goals (Bay, Lopez-Reyna, and Guillory 2011; Lopez-Reyna et al. 2011). Two teams provided examples. One team struggled to keep pace with the state's frequent changes in teacher competencies with all the associated consequences (e.g., change in the content of the licensure exam). Thus, state-level changes required revision of the preparation program's curricular content to align with the state change. Another team reported that they were told to defer their plan until the myriad of changes in their institution's administration was resolved. Changes in a university's high-level administrators often meant frequent changes in priorities and the allocation of resources. Jian Wang and colleagues (2010) comment on this shifting context phenomenon:

> Not only are the contextual challenges that teacher education programs face in reform efforts related to the nature of teaching professionals, school systems, and their students, but these contextual factors are constantly changing, which also influences approaches to reform work. We lack a deeper understanding of how this dynamic of constant change affects the relationship between reform efforts and contextual factors. (399)

Thus, this notion of "tidal shifts of change" is significant, and the special education community (and perhaps all teacher preparation communities) should consider factors of reform as shifting targets while they engage in program improvement initiatives.

Working in multiple contexts simultaneously raises critical questions that the teacher education reform community must address: At what point does monitoring progress and ensuring accountability become overreach? Do these requirements and mandates actually become restrictive? Do they create settings that stifle creativity and innovation? In group discussions, our team members frequently described the difficulty of adhering to all the mandates and discussed the negative impact of those mandates on piloting innovative ideas, especially as those ideas pertained to the preparation of nontraditional students to be special education teachers. Conversely, are there instances when requirements and mandates are the impetus for creativity and innovation? When this occurs, what does the reform work look like? How did the requirements and/or mandates act as incentives? What are the contextual factors influencing this situation?

In addition to navigating multiple contexts and adjusting to frequent changes, our teacher educators frequently described factors that fell into the domain of situational constraints, of which the most frequently mentioned was lack of time. Teaching courses, instructing teacher candidates in the field, advising students, coordinating the daily functioning of the preparation program, responding to programmatic issues, serving on committees, conducting research, writing, presenting, and other responsibilities dominated the teacher educator's professional life. They had to squeeze program reform work into extremely busy schedules. Rarely did we hear a member of a team say that he or she had release time to do the reform work; if release time was given, it reflected the individual's ability to secure a grant, and funds were available for buy-out purposes.

In addition to lack of time, team members also described some of their colleagues' qualities or disposition that resulted in making program changes more difficult. For example, these qualities included lack of buy-in and commitment to the reform work, territorial behavior regarding a program component or dimension, an unwillingness to share expertise, and a preference for maintaining the status quo.

Another frequently discussed situational constraint pertained to the lack of resources available for team members' work. Lack of resources surfaced as a shortage of funds to purchase needed materials and necessary technology, to employ individuals to complete specific tasks, to compensate faculty members for their hours of work, and/or to train adjunct faculty and staff on the use of new practices and procedures. The modest resourcing given to teacher preparation was evident.

The last constraint replicates an outcome of the Teachers for a New Era project (Carnegie Corporation 2006). Teams often had difficulty establishing and maintaining communication about the initiative and related topics. Team members discussed the challenge of establishing a process for collaboration and shared responsibility, creating a process in which all voices could be heard, and ensuring that the process was transparent enough to foster trust.

Taken together, these situational constraints highlight the complexity and consequences of reform efforts in teacher preparation. Working within these contextual challenges underscored the significance of the teams' accomplishments.

## Successful Reform Outcomes: How Did They Do It?

Even with the requirements, mandates, shifting contexts, and situational constraints crowding the teacher preparation reform environment, most of our teams were successful in their efforts. Eleven teams solved problems and made fundamental changes in their programs, and five teams accomplished significant tasks that advanced their work and moved them closer to their long-term goals. One team did not make any progress toward solving their identified problem because a university mandate to revise all curricula required their attention.

What did those who solved their problem(s) and significantly improved their programs do to obtain a successful outcome? How did this happen? We propose four strategies that may assist a team to attain its reform goals: (1) using data, (2) crossing boundaries, (3) implementing work-arounds, and (4) bringing the right people into the loop.

### Using Data

Each team's work was grounded on sound evidence. The team members and their colleagues gathered program-level data and aggregated teacher candidate-level data to identify and better understand problem areas. They then examined the evidence available in the research and professional literature and their work settings to design solutions to improve their programs. While these solutions often had to be shaped or molded to meet a team's unique institutional culture and needs, the critical feature is that data continually informed the teams' decision making.

In their work on teacher preparation programs, Charles A. Peck, Chrysan Gallucci, and Tine Sloan (2010) support the investment in data: "We came to see the way in which data were regularly collected, analyzed by the leadership team, and presented to program faculty and staff as an essential process through which important new meanings of the policies, and the program's response to them, were negotiated collaboratively" (460). Similar to this observation, we noticed the value of the team collecting and analyzing data and then presenting it to other program faculty so that they could collectively consider the meaning, better understand significant program issues, and think through the various factors influencing the issues and their responses. In this way, program colleagues and other stakeholders seemed to take greater ownership of the program and its effectiveness.

### Crossing Boundaries

A feature of the reform initiative designed by five teams who made transformational changes in their programs was the necessity to cross boundaries. That is, these teams stepped outside their usual ways of working and reached out to a different group of people. While challenging, crossing boundaries may have contributed to making significant, positive changes when improving a program. The teams to which we refer crossed disciplinary lines (e.g., communication disorders and education candidates enrolled in a seminar to exchange ideas and learn from each other), crossed program boundaries (elementary education and special education candidates were required to work together in a joint seminar), and crossed institutional lines (school districts and the university worked collaboratively to identify inclusive classrooms and educate teacher candidates in those classrooms). These five teams aimed to prepare future teachers to work collaboratively with other school-based professionals as an approach to developing the skills and abilities needed to effectively educate all students. They embraced the idea that they could accomplish more when working together. Crossing boundaries afforded the opportunity to design a preparation program where those with diverse expertise promoted a culture of collective learning and joint work on shared educational problems for both professors preparing individuals to be school-based professionals and candidates preparing to work in schools.

### Work-Arounds

As each team's reform work unfolded, factors surfaced that either impeded or facilitated the team's progress. Although some of these factors could have been barriers to the completion of the initiative, team members were not stymied; they remained focused on solving the problem, working around that barrier, and continuing to move forward. When one team was directed to stop working on the initiative because of impending administrative changes, the team worked around the directive by collecting survey data from key stakeholders to better understand the dimensions of the problem. Another team worked around resistant colleagues by collaborating with administrators from the university who saw the need for change and for inviting an outside person to begin the difficult conversation. In other words, teams who knew how to turn barriers into nothing more than distractions were successful at maintaining momentum and eventually reaching their targeted outcomes.

### Bringing the Right People into the Loop

Knowing who to include and at what level (i.e., an active participant as opposed to an individual to merely keep informed) was critical to a team's success. Using multiple data sources (teacher candidates, school based mentors, teacher educators in the program), one team developed better understandings of their teacher candidates' abilities, or lack thereof, to teach in an inclusive classroom. Working with key stakeholders, the team designed and implemented a solution that involved creating more inclusive classrooms by merging special and elementary education. These classrooms were then available for clinical experiences. Collaborations/co-teaching arrangements within the university and among the merged field placements (teacher candidates/mentors) became a hallmark of the program. We think that this success could not have occurred without the active participation of those involved and without informing those in administrative positions of this transformational program change.

Research in teacher education has demonstrated that changing a program is a difficult and complex process (e.g., Cochran-Smith 2005; Zeichner 2010) that moves slowly (Hökkä and Eteläpelto 2014; Peck, Gallucci, and Sloan 2010). Local values, concerns, and reform goals make this process even more challenging (Wang et al. 2010). The discussion of our teams' experiences reveals some reasons why program change can be so difficult and complex and how contextual factors contribute to the challenges that are present. Research on higher education program improvement efforts and the context in which they occur has not been a priority in the past, but that must change (Peck, Gallucci, and Sloan 2010; Sykes, Bird, and Kennedy 2010). Jian Wang and colleagues (2010) underscore this point: "the systematic and long-term monitoring of the relationship between reform efforts and their contexts is important and necessary for continuously adjusting teacher education reform across time" (399).

Although the work presented here contributes to our growing understandings, we recognize its limitations. In particular, we cannot compare MSIs and PWIs because we conducted all of our work with MSIs; we did not provide technical assistance to PWIs. Nonetheless, our reading of the literature and our work in teacher education reform, more generally, suggest that teacher educators across institutional types tend to be influenced by, and confronted with, similar contextual issues. All institutions must adhere to their university's requirements, meet state standards, fulfill accreditation criteria, and consider their local market demands. We have, however, observed one exception. Within the groups of MSIs with whom we worked, we observed a wide range of available resources between those who were underresourced (based on faculty perceptions) to those who were quite stable and adequately resourced (again, based on faculty perceptions). Clearly, the interplay of resources and reform efforts needs further study within both MSIs and PWIs.

The education community is just beginning to explore relationships among contextual factors and program reform. Our work suggests the need for careful study of topics in a few areas: the impact of layering mandates on teacher preparation program design, the long-term consequences of reform within the multiple contexts in which it occurs, the unanticipated outcomes of reform as contexts shift and change, the strategies or approaches successful teacher educators use, and a close examination of situational constraints across program and institutional types. Examination of the relationship between the program reform process and contextual factors can advance our understandings of the complexities of designing and implementing a change initiative, and such study can help us envision how we might improve the process of building outstanding teacher preparation programs to better serve beginning teachers and their students.

NOTE

From 2002 to 2014, the Office of Special Education Programs (OSEP) in the US Department of Education funded a center located at the University of Illinois at Chicago

(Project Number H325R080002). The views expressed in this chapter do not necessarily represent the views and opinions of the Office of Special Education Programs in the Department of Education.

## REFERENCES

Achieve. 2013. "Closing the Expectations Gap: 2013 Annual Report on the Alignment of State K–12 Policies and Practice with the Demands of Colleges and Careers." http://www.achieve.org/2013annualreport.

American Association of Colleges of Teacher Education. 2011. "Transformations in Educator Preparation: Effectiveness and Accountability." https://aacte.org/pdf/Publications/Reports_Studies/Transformations%20in%20Educator%20Preparation%20-%20Effectiveness%20and%20Accountability%20-%20June%2022,%202011.pdf.

———. 2012. "Statement on Teacher Preparation and K–12 Assessment Report." https://aacte.org/news-room/press-releases-statements/126-aacte-statement-on-teacher-preparation-and-k-12-assessment-report.

Bay, Mary, Norma A. Lopez-Reyna, and Barbara Guillory. 2011. "Advancing Culturally Responsive Personnel Preparation: A Technical Assistance Model." In *Knowledge, Skills, and Dispositions for Culturally Competent and Interculturally Sensitive Leaders in Education*, edited by Erica D. McCray, Patricia Alvarez McHatton, and Cheryl L. Beverly, 81–103. Gainesville, FL: CreateSpace Independent Publishing Platform.

Brown, P. Christopher. 2010. "Children of Reform: The Impact of High-Stakes Education Reform on Pre-service Teachers." *Journal of Teacher Education* 61: 477–491.

Carnegie Corporation. 2006. *Teachers for a New Era: Transforming Teacher Education.* New York: Carnegie Corporation of New York.

Cochran-Smith, Marilyn. 2005. "Studying Teacher Education: What We Know and Need to Know." *Journal of Teacher Education* 56: 301–306.

Cochran-Smith, Marilyn, Sharon Feiman-Nemser, D. John McIntyre, and Kelly E. Demers. 2008. *Handbook of Research on Teacher Education: Enduring Questions in Changing Contexts.* New York: Routledge.

Cochran-Smith, Marilyn, and Ana Maria Villegas. 2015. "Framing Teacher Preparation Research: An Overview of the Field, Part 1." *Journal of Teacher Education* 66: 7–20.

Danielson, Charlotte. 2007. *Enhancing Professional Practice: A Framework for Teaching.* 2nd ed. Alexandria, VA: Association for Supervision and Curriculum Development.

Delandshere, Ginette, and Anthony Petrosky. 2004. "Political Rationales and Ideological Stances of the Standards-Based Reforms of Teacher Education in the US." *Teaching and Teacher Education* 20: 1–15.

DeLuca, Christopher, and Aarti Bellara. 2013. "The Current State of Assessment Education: Aligning Policy, Standards, and Teacher Education Curriculum." *Journal of Teacher Education* 64: 356–372.

Elmore, Richard F. 2004. *School Reform from the Inside Out: Policy, Practice, and Performance.* Cambridge, MA: Harvard University Press.

Freeman, Jennifer, Brandi Simonsen, Donald E. Briere, and Ashley S. MacSuga-Gage. 2014. "Pre-service Teacher Training in Classroom Management: A Review of State Accreditation Policy and Teacher Preparation Programs." *Teacher Education and Special Education* 37: 106–120.

Hökkä, Päivi, and Anneli Eteläpelto. 2014. "Seeking New Perspectives on the Development of Teacher Education: A Study of the Finnish Context." *Journal of Teacher Education* 65: 39–52. doi: 10.1177/0022487113135042.

Kennedy, Mary. 2010. "Against Boldness." *Journal of Teacher Education* 61: 16–20. doi: 10.1177/0022487109347876.

Lopez-Reyna, Norma A., Mary Bay, Dianne Zazycki, and Peggy A. Snowden. 2011. "Advancing Culturally Responsive Personnel Preparation in Special Education: Barriers and Supports for Change." In *Knowledge, Skills, and Dispositions for Culturally Competent and Interculturally Sensitive Leaders in Education*, edited by Erica D. McCray, Patricia Alvarez McHatton, and Cheryl L. Beverly, 104–121. Gainesville, FL: CreateSpace Independent Publishing Platform.

Peck, Charles A., Chrysan Gallucci, and Tine Sloan. 2010. "Negotiating Implementation of High-Stakes Performance Assessment Policies in Teacher Education: From Compliance to Inquiry." *Journal of Teacher Education* 61: 451–463.

Sawchuck, Stephen. 2013. "Performance-Based Test for Teachers Rolls Out." *Education Week* 33: 1–22. http://www.edweek.org/ew/articles/2013/12/04/13assess_ep.h33.html.

Sayeski, Kristin L., and Kyle Higgins. 2014. "Redesigning Special Education Teacher Preparation Programs with a Focus on Outcomes." *Teacher Education and Special Education* 37: 91–105.

Sykes, Gary, Tom Bird, and Mary Kennedy. 2010. "Teacher Education: Its Problems and Some Prospects." *Journal of Teacher Education* 61: 464–476.

US Department of Education. 2011. *Preparing and Credentialing the Nation's Teachers: 8th Annual Report to Congress on Teacher Quality.* Washington, DC: Office of Postsecondary Education.

Wang, Jian, Sandra J. Odell, Cari L. Klecka, Elizabeth Spalding, and Emily Lin. 2010. "Understanding Teacher Education Reform." *Journal of Teacher Education* 61: 395–402.

Wiseman, Donna. 2012. "The Intersection of Policy, Reform, and Teacher Education." *Journal of Teacher Education* 63: 87–91. doi: 10.1177/0022487111429128.

Zeichner, Ken. 2010. "Rethinking the Connections between Campus Courses and Field Experiences in College- and University-Based Teacher Education." *Journal of Teacher Education* 61: 89–99.

# 7

# Becoming a Black Institution

## Challenges and Changes for Teacher Education Programs at Emerging Minority-Serving Institutions

BYUNG-IN SEO
DEWITT SCOTT
EMERY PETCHAUER

Many colleges and universities now designated as Minority-Serving Institutions (MSIs) were formed specifically to educate certain segments of the population. For example, philanthropists, government agencies, and communities formed Historically Black Colleges and Universities (HBCUs) to educate African Americans because most higher education institutions would not accept students of color or other minority groups (Abelman and Dalessandro 2009; Brown and Davis 2001). Some institutions, however, began as predominately white institutions and through demographic and policy changes became MSIs. This has been the case with many Hispanic-Serving Institutions and Asian American and Native American Pacific Islander Serving Institutions. Another type of institution that fits this model is Predominantly Black Institutions (PBIs). Often mistakenly grouped with HBCUs, PBIs are not institutions that were founded for the purpose of educating African Americans; instead, over time they grew to serve significant percentages of African American students. Consequently, PBIs, given their different origins than HBCUs, have had to adapt and change over time in order to serve a majority Black student population, including students who wish to become teachers.

One such institution is Chicago State University (CSU). From its founding in 1867 as Cook County Normal School, the institution focused on educating teachers for the region's schools. Over the course of 140 years, the institution changed names, moved locations, and added other fields, but its backbone continued to be teacher education. Prior to 1950, African American students made up less than 10 percent of institutional enrollment (Kearney 1969). Between 1960 and 1980, however, the student racial demographics of the institution changed significantly, and it emerged in the latter half of the twentieth century as a Predominately Black Institution. Within its current enrollment of approximately 4,500 students, 86 percent identify as African American/Black (CSU 2015). In 2015, CSU ranked first in awarding all bachelor degrees, including education degrees, to Black students in Illinois, and it ranked fourth in awarding education degrees to Latinos in Illinois (CSU 2015). Because approximately two thirds of its students come from the south side of Chicago, the institution also serves mostly working-class and low-income students.

Chapter 7 uses the journey of CSU as a platform to outline challenges and opportunities that emerging MSIs will likely face in their teacher education programs. By emerging MSIs, we mean institutions like CSU that have come to enroll a more racially and economically diverse student population over the past decades but were not founded directly on such a mission. These institutions are well positioned to help create a more racially diverse teaching profession if they anticipate and respond to the challenges that accompany an emerging MSI. These challenges relate to anticipating and supporting student needs, making programs more relevant to what motivates preservice teachers of color into the profession, and attending to some pitfalls of field experiences. We discuss these challenges, highlight CSU's responses, and outline ways that emerging MSIs can respond proactively. Furthermore, we offer a set of questions that emerging MSI teacher education departments can use to consider the degree to which they are prepared to educate a more diverse teaching profession.

## Chicago State University and the Black Belt

Segregation in Chicago has always been a way of life. African Americans in Chicago have endured de jure and de facto segregation almost from the moment they arrived from the South in large numbers (Travis 1981). The availability of jobs brought African Americans and other immigrants to Chicago, particularly the south side, where meat-packing plants, factories, railroad work, and other industries were primarily situated. As African American migrants came to Chicago, they were corralled into a subsection of the south side known as the Black Belt (Cutler 2006). Redlining, housing discrimination, and "restrictive covenants" (Lemann 1991, 63) became regular barriers for Black families who attempted to live in other parts of the city. As more African Americans migrated from the South in the early twentieth century, the neighborhoods in the Black Belt became denser and consequently formed urban slums. Throughout the twentieth century, as the Black middle class in Chicago grew and de facto segregation in housing ended, Black families began to spread to other neighborhoods across the south side.

In 1965, leaders decided to move Chicago State College from its home at Sixty-third and Stewart in the Englewood neighborhood to Ninety-fifth and King Drive, thus placing the college in the Roseland neighborhood on the city's far south side. They chose this new location for several reasons, none more paramount than the large amount of land at that locale. Executing its vision of significant physical expansion, Chicago State College transformed from a campus of one building the size of one city block to 161 acres of wooded land on the far south side. In this new location, the surrounding all-Black community became a source of recruiting and enrolling students. At a time when most Black high school graduates did not have college as a legitimate opportunity, Chicago State College positioned itself as a postsecondary option for Chicago's Black south side population. In addition, the college offered programs beyond education, and it became clear that Chicago State College was expanding beyond the bounds of a college and becoming a university.

Over time, the Roseland neighborhood started to deteriorate, similar to the fate of the Englewood neighborhood when the college was located at Sixty-third and Stewart. Poverty levels began to increase in Roseland, along with crime and incarceration rates. While the surrounding neighborhood continued to decay, the college realized the strong need for education reform efforts and serious, trained, high-quality educators in the neighborhood's elementary and high schools. Consequently, Chicago State College became an institution that served Chicago's Black south side students who aspired to become certified teachers in the area's predominantly Black schools. An unintended outcome of this location was the increase in the number of students of color who considered teaching as a career after they encountered many other education majors on campus.

When it relocated to Ninety-fifth and King Drive at the height of its enrollment, Chicago State College had approximately 8,500 students, some of whom attended classes at satellite sites. In 2016, the student population is 5,211. According to CSU's Office of Institutional Research, in fall 2014, 72 percent of the student population was Black, 7 percent was Latino/a, 5 percent was Asian, and 6 percent was white (CSU 2015).

### Race and Socioeconomic Class: On Campus and in the Field

Minority-Serving Institutions typically serve higher percentages of students who are underrepresented in higher education (Gasman and Conrad 2013). Therefore, one finds more low-income, first-generation students of color at MSIs when compared to predominantly and historically white institutions. CSU represents this trend. At every graduation ceremony, graduates who are the first people in their families to graduate from college are asked to stand, and every year more than half of the graduates rise from their seats. Often, these students are more likely to have been on the short end of K–12 opportunity gaps because they attended underfunded schools staffed by greater proportions of inexperienced teachers. As a result, students frequently enter institutions like CSU in need of academic supports en route to becoming teachers. These are supports that students from more privileged academic backgrounds require less often. Enrollment changes with regard to academic preparation do not mean that academic standards of an institution are declining; rather, these changes mean that students overall represent a wider range of academic preparation levels, and to maximize student success the institution must provide necessary support services at both institutional and departmental levels.

CSU has responded to these needs at the institutional level with resources and support centers that leverage ethnic identity as a source of academic and social strength. For example, the Latino Resource Center, established in 1988 under the Department of Student Affairs, provides mentoring, tutoring, scholarship opportunities, cultural activities, and outreach initiatives for Latino/a students on campus and in the surrounding community. Similarly, the African American Male Resource center, established in 2008, receives federal funding through Predominately Black Institution initiatives. Like the Latino Resource Center, it provides a range of academic and social supports in addition to seminars and discussions rooted in research on Black male success in college. In 2015, the Women's Resource Center opened to provide support, promote education, raise awareness of gender and women's issues, and increase the visibility and diversity of women at the institution.

MSIs extend initiatives like these particularly well (Conrad and Gasman 2015; Gasman, Baez, and Turner, 2008), and such programs have been successfully emulated by predominantly and historically white institutions (e.g., Guiffrida 2003; Harper and Quaye 2007). Campus centers and initiatives, however, are often far removed from schools of education and teacher education programs, and the division of departments on campus often hinders faculty members' awareness of these programs. Moreover, the applied nature of education programs, directing faculty members toward schools and other field locations, tends to focus attention away from these larger resources on campus. Although centers such as these provide important supports that extend beyond the reach, resources, and staffing capacities of education departments, particularly in smaller, under-resourced institutions, education faculty members should prioritize awareness of these programs and leverage the resources for students.

An additional institutional support is a solid and comprehensive developmental program that addresses core skills—reading, writing, and mathematical computation. Attention to this support is particularly important for emerging MSIs because of the possibly changing academic profile of students. A proactive, comprehensive developmental program, requiring time and resources to build, is essential when admitting classes of students who require additional assistance for success. These supports are particularly important when preparing prospective teachers to pass basic skills licensure exams before their admission into teacher education programs. Education departments would benefit by advocating for these support systems at the institutional level and aligning these developmental courses to the content of the licensure exams that prospective teachers must take.

The cost of a college education places on immense financial stress on low-income and working-class students. With an in-state tuition of $5,805 (CSU 2015), CSU has the lowest tuition cost of any public institution in Illinois. This comparatively low figure, however, is still incredibly high for students in the surrounding area. The 2010 mean income for a household in Grand Crossing, a neighboring community, was $30,241, where 40 percent of households were living at or below the poverty line (Urban Mapping 2015). This financial strain is often greater for preservice teachers because the major requires additional costs for fingerprints, criminal background checks, and child abuse clearances necessary before entering schools for field internships; in most states students must also fulfill medical requirements, like a tuberculosis test, which are necessary before entering schools. Moreover, some states and school districts require preservice teachers to annually renew these clearances. Additional costs derive from licensure exams required for entry to programs and exit to the profession. Scholarships and financial aid typically cannot cover these costs. At CSU, every dean receives additional monies in the college's budget to help cover these incidental costs. In the College of Education, students must complete an application to explain the expenses with which they need help, and the dean's office evaluates the request. Expenses can range from state licensure fees to covering the cost of books to buying baby formula. Of all students at CSU, 70 percent are women, and 45 percent of all CSU students care for at least one dependent (CSU 2015). As a result, CSU's administration acknowledges that many nonacademic reasons may prevent students from completing their program and provides supports accordingly.

The process associated with field placements and internships often presents low-income students with additional barriers. This process is most often decentralized wherein students receive what seems like an arbitrary placement location and are expected to transport themselves to and from the school. Low-income students, however, seldom own cars and rarely have access to cars for reliable transportation. The public transportation system around an urban campus like CSU helps ameliorate this problem, but few institutions are surrounded by such a system. Education departments should thus be mindful of the field location radius as their student demographics change and consider policies that reduce these challenges. Students without their own transportation should have priority to field locations closest to campus. For larger institutions that have an internal or regional bus systems, education departments should advocate that the routes include the locations of students' field placements. On smaller campuses without these internal systems, education departments can share transportation with other programs, including athletic teams that typically have or use a small fleet of vans for travel to local competitions. Getting a group of education majors approved to drive campus vehicles not only facilitates this process but also earns them income because institutions often pay for these student jobs.

Preservice teachers who enter college from low-income backgrounds can also receive pushback from their families about their choice of major and profession. This pushback, often more intense for first-generation college students, comes from perceptions about the low economic standing of the profession, however accurate or inaccurate. Because of the economic mobility a college degree can bring, family and friends might look at this career choice as a waste of a college degree. Departments should be aware of this possible resistance and craft responses to these critiques into introductory courses. Such responses include knowing pathways for career advancement and growth, attending to job security, and promoting professional value beyond income.

Emerging MSIs must also confront the difficult truth that their preservice teachers of color may be subject to racism and unfair treatment in surrounding schools from cooperating teachers, administrators, staff, parents, and students. We sense that CSU preservice teachers have experienced less of this racism because the institution has been nested within a Black community for decades, and community members from multiple generations have gone through the institution. Emerging MSIs, however, cannot be naïve about what their students will experience when they step into schools that normalize whiteness or operate by colorblind ideologies.

This hostility toward students of color can range from explicit to subtle. One of the more subtle forms of racism makes assumptions about preservice teachers' abilities. Administrators commonly assume that teachers of color hold a natural ability to either "reach" students of the same ethnic background or keep them in line through punitive discipline. Black teachers can certainly leverage shared ethnic affiliation for caring and educative purposes, and doing so is often an important aspect of their pedagogy (Irvine 2002; Mawhinney 2014). This assumption, particularly for Black preservice teachers, deskills them by ignoring the professional practices necessary to develop as a teacher and expects uniformity in the experiences of Black students and teachers. These assumptions can also play into subject matter. For example, cooperating teachers may believe that Asian American preservice teachers are predispositioned to teach mathematics or African American preservice teachers are perfect for Black History Month presentations. Cooperating teachers may be genuinely excited to have more racial diversity in their classroom, but assumptions such as these, regardless of intentions, subject preservice teachers of color to microaggressions (Sue 2010), stereotype threats (Steele 2010), tokenism, and other hostilities. In the early stages of a preservice teacher's career, racist experiences during field placements detract from professional growth.

Perhaps most damaging to the development of preservice teachers is presumed incompetence, a phenomenon that has received much attention with regard to race and gender in higher education (Guiterrez y Muhs et al. 2012). Accordingly, cooperating teachers and supervisors in the field can view the areas of need that preservice teachers of color show as confirmation of incompetence, rather than as opportunities for support and growth. This treatment, based upon not only race but also the heritage language of preservice teachers if it is not white normative English, is particularly damaging in this early stage of professional growth because experts in the field should be supporting preservice teachers while they develop competence in their teaching negative views about the emerging MSI that the preservice teachers attend can fuel these assumptions and judgments. Despite the range of institutions across more than one hundred HBCUs, news coverage often focuses on the most troubled institutions and generalizes them across all HBCUs (Gasman and Bowman 2011). Institutions that are emerging as MSIs may be subject to a similar stigma in the surrounding community, and this stigma may transfer unfairly onto its preservice teachers.

Responses to these challenges are more complex than simply partnering with schools that hold firm antiracist and equitable stances. Education departments are often hard pressed to secure field internships so they typically take whatever they can get, especially where rural institutions reach few schools in the immediate area. In the midst of this challenge, education departments have a responsibility to place their preservice teachers into settings that facilitate their growth and do not undermine morale. Microaggressions, stereotype threats, presumed incompetence, and other hostilities add to the cognitive and affective load of field internships and will deter preservice teachers from entering the profession. In response, departments should be in tune with the racial climate at field internship schools before placing students.

Despite these proactive efforts, preservice teachers of color may still have these experiences in the field. When they do, departments should affirm the validity of the experience; that is, departments should *neither* appeal to the presumed good intentions of the offender *nor* suggest that perhaps the preservice teacher is reading too much into a situation or taking it too seriously. Responses like these blame the preservice teacher for being the victim of racism instead of identifying the cause and fighting against it. Instead, the department should more appropriately affirm its solidarity with the preservice teacher and advocate for them at the school level. This response requires faculty members on the ground to have the language and tools to confront colorblind racism, white supremacy, and white fragility (DiAngelo 2011). If the department cannot make progress at the school level, then it should responsibly place the preservice teacher into a new location.

## Called to Teach: Different Motivations into the Field

Emerging MSIs must also understand the reasons why preservice teachers of color enter the profession and how these reasons often differ from those of white preservice teachers. From this view, life experiences related to race, socioeconomic class, educational opportunities, and other influential factors are intimately related to what draws young adults into the profession. These experiences can be stronger influences upon preservice teachers than the training they receive in a teacher education program (Bramald, Hardman, and Leat 1995). Teacher education departments at an emerging MSI cannot assume that incoming college students of color will choose education as a major if the conceptual framework guiding the program remains built around the motivations of white preservice teachers. Departments must understand how life experiences that vary by race, socioeconomic class, and other factors shape what students decide to study in college.

Zhixin Su (1997) studies motivations into the profession and outlines some commonalities and differences by race. Through surveys and interviews, Su explored the perspectives of more than two hundred preservice teachers in California on several areas, in particular conceptualizations of good teaching, reasons for choosing teaching as a career, and perceptions on the role of teachers in school reform and social change. Half of the participants were preservice teachers of color. All participants agreed that good teaching was progressive and child-centered; they loved children and loved learning. Approximately one-third of the preservice teachers of color, however, saw good teaching as expanding beyond these child-centered ideals. For them, good teaching included challenging the culturally narrow curriculum of schools and developing critical social consciousness in their students. Good teaching also entailed developing racial and ethnic knowledge, promoting agency for social change, and other items that fit into asset-based and culturally responsive frameworks (e.g., Gay 2000; Ladson-Billings 1994). No white preservice teachers discussed ideas such as these as qualities of good teaching. Similar differences existed with regard to participants' ideas about the function of school for their future students. Preservice teachers of color were more likely to believe that schools should have a critical educative function by teaching students how to challenge injustice and help build a more equitable society.

Su (1997) also found common reasons across white and preservice teachers of color for why they chose teaching as a profession. Like the findings of other large-scale studies (e.g., King 1993), the most common reasons were altruistic and pragmatic, such as choosing a career that gives them personal satisfaction, enables them to contribute to society, and positions them to help others. As with ideas about what constitutes good teaching, however, approximately one-third of the preservice teachers of color also held justice-oriented reasons for becoming teachers. This subgroup was acutely aware of educational inequalities that poorer students and students of color more often experience; many of them experienced these very inequalities directly throughout their own schooling experiences. Because of these experiences, their motivation to teach included attention to educational opportunity gaps, bilingual language rights, and culturally inclusive curriculum. In contrast, "none of the white candidates expressed concerns for the conditions of education for the poor and minority children and what they would do for them as teachers" (Su 1997, 331).

The justice-oriented reasons that drew many preservice teachers of color into the profession also shaped how they saw their roles in schools. They saw it as their duty to supplement and change culturally narrow curriculum and remedy education opportunity gaps rather than wait for larger systems to bring about this kind of change. They more often saw themselves as teacher activists who should be involved in the political and social struggles related to and beyond schools, often in the same communities where they grew up. White preservice teachers also thought about being change agents as teachers, but they often articulated an abstract and depoliticized idea that revolved around changing teaching methods, perceptions from the community, students' habits, and students' abilities to be successful. White preservice teachers usually rooted their ideas about change at the classroom level without much attention to the larger systems in society that create these classroom conditions and restrict students' life choices. Overall, "none of them mentioned the dire experiences that children from the poor and minority backgrounds have in urban schools and what they could do to help these children" (Su 1997, 335).

In-depth research on teacher life histories adds further detail to these findings by Su (1997). In a study of forty preservice teachers from three institutions, Lynnette Mawhinney, Carol R. Rinke, and Gloria Park (2012) found advocacy as a salient theme among twenty African American participants (ten men and ten women), one Latina participant, and five white male participants, but advocacy was less important among the fourteen white female participants. Between the white male and Black preservice teachers, the researchers found differences in their conceptualizations of advocacy in the classroom. Black teachers focused on who they *are* as teachers, whereas white preservice teachers focused on what they could *do* as teachers. Black preservice teachers understood that their mere presence in schools was a political act because so few students (of all races) ever have a teacher of color. They understood that their presence as competent and committed Black teachers challenged the underrepresentation of teachers of color in the profession and the systemic reasons for this. Their presence in schools was particularly important for their future Black students who seldom see themselves reflected in the adults responsible for teaching them (Foster 1997; Irvine 2002). White male preservice teachers' ideas of advocacy centered on their actions—making decisions about curriculum that might challenge the school authority, responding to students' personal needs, and creating safe spaces for students. Though important, their ideas about advocacy, unrelated to who they were as teachers, pertained to actions within the walls of their classroom.

Other life history studies on Black preservice teachers further illustrate some differences along these lines. Mawhinney (2014) found that Black preservice teachers are often motivated to be the great teacher they never had. Similar to the findings of Su (1997), this source of motivation connects to experiences with uncaring and racist teachers, underresourced schools, lack of academic rigor, and educational opportunity gaps. Although these negative experiences can be motivators for some Black preservice teachers, they may also deter many others from viewing teaching as a desirable career (Graham and Erwin 2011). Sometimes a single influential teacher whose support went far beyond professional obligations—paying for college application fees, providing extensive feedback on college essays and application materials, securing resources inaccessible to students, and attending to emotional and nonacademic needs—motivated Black preservice teachers. The depth of this support, well outside the bounds of advocacy conceptualized by white male teachers in the findings of Mawhinney, Rinke, and Park (2012), inspired Black preservice teachers to be supportive in similar ways for their future students.

Understanding the deeper reasons that draw students of color into the teaching profession should lead emerging MSIs to reconsider key aspects of their programs. Such reconsideration should begin with recruiting college students into the major once they are on campus. Programs across all different academic departments typically take a passive approach to recruitment: they wait for students to choose them. For teacher education departments, this approach often brings them particular college students: they enjoy working with children, know teachers in their families, report positive schooling experiences, speak only English, and sought to become teachers since they were young. In most cases, these students are white. This passive approach to campus recruiting will not effectively attract college students who choose a major at least in part by a desire for service and social change. Teacher education departments at emerging MSIs will attract more students of color if they conceptualize and present teaching as a tool of social change rather than simply an altruistic pursuit.

Likewise, we should reconsider field placements. At CSU, preservice teachers desired different locations for field experiences. Motivated by their desire to be racial role models, both Black preservice teachers and graduate students in school administration programs wanted to have experiences in schools with high percentages of students of color, both within and outside Chicago. They did not limit their requests to racial demographics of schools; instead, they looked for service in high-need schools, similar to the school settings that many of them experienced. Many outer-ring suburban districts are becoming more racially diverse while they undergo the very transitions that changed many Chicago neighborhoods during the 1970s. Ultimately, CSU graduates with a record of successful field experiences in racially diverse and high-need settings are more desirable as potential employees in a range of employment settings within these districts. Teacher education departments at emerging MSIs must be prepared to meet the desires that attract many young adults of color to the profession, whether these center on race, language, or socioeconomic class.

Finally curricular changes are also necessary in the midst of a more diverse student population. In teacher education programs at CSU, professors must include readings and classroom activities relevant to culturally and linguistically diverse student populations. At the graduate level, faculty developed an urban education seminar course that focuses on current issues occurring in urban educational environments. In addition, the course Educational Issues in the Black Community covers topics such as the control of schools, relevance of curriculum, teacher qualifications, and Black self-concept, achievement, and intelligence. Institutions of all types have diversity threads through their teacher education curricula. In many instances, however, these diversity course and requirements go no further than emphasizing holidays, historical figures, and a select few authors of color; such minimal exposure often fails to equip preservice teachers with the understanding of systemic oppression in schools and practical tools for combatting it. To be clear, having preservice teachers of color in a program is not the sole reason for a robust, equity-centered program. White preservice teachers also need these threads through their program. The absence of such elements, however, will deter preservice teachers of color from choosing the classroom as the space in which they serve their communities. Emerging MSIs must proactively institute an equity-centered curriculum in their program even before they admit preservice teachers of color.

## Conclusion: Questions for the Future

As the United States continues to experience national racial and cultural shifts, many other institutions will experience a journey similar to that of CSU. This is particularly true as more institutions in urban centers, the West, and Southwest shift to becoming Hispanic-Serving Institutions and Asian American and Native American Pacific Islander Serving Institutions. It is thus important to pose some pertinent questions and related points of discussion for teacher education programs to consider, especially at the emerging MSIs.

- How can departments assist students with the extra costs of becoming a teacher?

This question derives from the various extracurricular costs associated with majoring in education. The exact costs of these requirements vary by state, and specific background checks and forms vary by partnering district and state as well. Departments should consider ways to ameliorate the burden of these costs. By incorporating some of these costs, wherever possible, into course-related fees, students can pay for them through student grants, scholarship, or financial aid (a method that prevents students from paying out of pocket).

Occasionally, districts voluntarily require preservice teachers to renew certain clearances each year; thus students incur even more costs. Departments should discuss with partnering districts the unnecessary burden this may place upon preservice teachers with few economic resources. In addition, if departments are mindful of these costs, they might be able to pursue other institution-specific solutions. States and institutions that require a full-year internship during a fifth year of coursework should consider avenues to waive tuition for low-income preservice teachers.

- How will departments assist preservice teachers who struggle to pass licensure exams?

Departments should ask themselves this question because preservice teachers of color are more likely to struggle to pass licensure exams than are white preservice teachers (Nettles et al. 2011). The struggles are not somehow linked in an essentialist way to race, but they do reflect different K–12 educational opportunities that map out along racial lines. This question can also play out differently depending upon the size of an institution and department. Teacher education departments at large institutions typically do not have their students in class until these students have passed their basic skills exam, completed other requirements, and received admission into the major. This arrangement means that departments are less aware of the struggles their prospective students have with licensure exams. Smaller institutions with equally small departments have greater contact with students intending to major in education before they are formally admitted to programs. These smaller departments, however, typically have fewer resources for support structures so support often means that faculty members commit time to help prepare students to pass. These size differentials mean that institutions should be conscious of how their size creates both opportunities and challenges to supporting their students through licensure exam success.

- How are departments leveraging support services at the institutional level?

This question is particularly important for education departments that operate more independently from other bodies of an institution because they run the risk of duplicating efforts to support students that already exist at the institutional level. Rather than doing this, departments should seek to understand what systems already exist for students at the institutional level, such as first-year advising and academic support centers, but simply directing students to these supports is not enough. Departments should more sensibly collaborate with institutional offices to ensure that they offer supports calibrated to the precise needs of preservice teachers, such as tutoring for licensure exams. In these cases, an academic support or writing center should understand the writing exam and align support with its exact content. This kind of coordination ensures that the support students receive outside of the department aligns with the needs in the department.

- How are programs oriented toward equity and justice?

Research on what draws preservice teachers of color into the profession suggests that focusing on equity and justice is important (Irvine 2002; Mawhinney, Rinke, and Park 2012; Su 1997). For MSIs that were founded as such, principles like equity and justice are woven into their mission. Those institutions that are emerging as MSIs must, however, consider this question from multiple perspectives, including the conceptual framework driving the programs, specific course offerings, the content of individual courses, and the commitment that individual faculty members bring with them into the classrooms. How do justice and equity run through the program at these scales? Typically an institution responds to this question by creating a course within the program that focuses on diversity as defined by race/ethnicity, gender, socioeconomic class, or sexual orientation. Although a course is valuable, requiring a single course on diversity or equity often suggests to preservice teachers that this material is merely an addendum to the real material that comprises the rest of the program. In a better approach (albeit more labor-intensive) the program weaves equity and justice throughout multiple courses.

Large programs with high volumes of part-time instructors face additional challenges because adjuncts are typically less connected to the central workings of a department. As a result, there is more variation in terms of content across the course sections that part-time instructors teach. A reference to diversity in a course objective can be translated into anything from diversity in learning preferences to critical race theory, depending upon an instructor's area of comfort and expertise. This variation creates an unbalanced program. Larger institutions might assign multiple sections of a course to an anchor section taught by a full-time faculty member, an approach that should emphasize nonnegotiable equity threads fixed across sections yet stop short of rigid uniformity.

- How prepared are faculty members to engage in equity-conscious dialogue?

This very important and most difficult question cuts across a number of ideas presented in chapter 7. Effective justice-oriented programs and curricular changes hinge upon the abilities of faculty members to understand and discuss colorblind ideologies, power, white supremacy, and intersecting systems of oppression. These topics plunge much deeper than the simple "diversity" that is often the beginning and the end of equity work in higher education. Broaching these topics relates not only to program offerings and the preparation of teachers but also to field placements. Preservice teachers of color and preservice teachers whose heritage language is not white normative English can be subject to different forms of racism in classrooms, and their faculty members must assume the responsibility to advocate for them in such instances. Likewise, the ability to advocate for preservice teachers who want justice-oriented curricular changes hinges upon how effectively faculty members can engage in equity-conscious dialogue. Teacher education departments should judge for themselves how prepared they are to engage their field partnership schools along these lines. If departments feel unprepared, they should form readings groups, attend conferences, and pursue development activities that will push them forward in these ways.

## REFERENCES

Abelman, Robert, and Amy Dalessandro. 2009. "The Institutional Vision of Historically Black Colleges and Universities." *Journal of Black Studies* 40: 105–134.

Bramald, Rod, Frank Hardman, and David Leat. 1995. "Initial Teacher Trainees and Their Views of Teaching and Learning." *Teaching and Teacher Education* 11: 23–31.

Brown, M. Christopher, and James Earl Davis. 2001. "The Historically Black College as Social Contract, Social Capital, and Social Equalizer." *Peabody Journal of Education* 76: 31–49.

Chicago State University. 2012. "Undergraduate Catalog: 2012–2014." http://www.csu.edu/catalogs/pdf/catalog201214undergrad.pdf.

———. 2015. "2014–2015 Fact Book." https://www.csu.edu/IER/documents/factBook2014–2015.pdf.

Chicago State University, College of Education. 2015. "About the College: History." www.csu.edu/collegeofedcuation/history.htm.

Conrad, Clifton, and Marybeth Gasman. 2015. *Educating a Diverse Nation: Lessons from Minority Serving Institutions*. Cambridge, MA: Harvard University Press.

Cutler, Irving. 2006. *Chicago: Metropolis of the Mid-Continent*. Carbondale: Southern Illinois University Press.

DiAngelo, Robin. 2011. "White Fragility." *International Journal of Critical Pedagogy* 3 (3): 54–70.

Foster, Michele. 1997. *Black Teacher on Teaching*. New York: The New Press.

Gasman, Marybeth, Benjamin Baez, and Caroline Sotello Viernes Turner, eds. 2008. *Understanding Minority-Serving Institutions*. Albany: State University of New York Press.

Gasman, Marybeth, and Nelson Bowman. 2011. "How to Paint a Better Portrait of HBCUs." *American Association of University Professors*. http://www.aaup.org/article/how-paint-better-portrait-hbcus#.VjvocxNViko.

Gasman, Marybeth, and Clifton Conrad. 2013. *Minority Serving Institutions: Educating All Students*. Report from the Center of Minority Serving Institutions. http://www.gse.upenn.edu/pdf/cmsi/msis_educating_all_students.pdf.

Gay, Geneva. 2000. *Culturally Responsive Teaching: Theory, Research, and Practice*. New York: Teachers College Press.

Graham, Anthony, and Kimberly D Erwin. 2011. "'I Don't Think Black Men Teach Because How They Get Treated as Students': High-Achieving African American Boys' Perceptions of Teaching as a Career Option." *Journal of Negro Education* 80 (3): 398–416.

Guiffrida, Douglas A. 2003. "African American Student Organizations as Agents of Social Integration." *Journal of College Student Development* 44: 304–319.

Guiterrez y Muhs, Gabriella, Yolanda Flores Niemann, Carmen G. Gonzalez, and Angela P. Harris, eds. 2012. *Presumed Incompetent: Intersections of Race and Class for Women in Academia*. Boulder: University Press of Colorado.

Harper, Shaun R., and Stephen John Quaye. 2007. "Student Organizations as Venues for Black Identity Expression and Development among African American Male Student Leaders." *Journal of College Student Development* 48: 127–144.

Irvine, Jacqueline Joyner. 2002. *In Search of Wholeness: African American Teachers and Their Culturally Specific Classroom Practices.* New York: Palgrave.

Kearney, Edmund W. 1969. *Chicago State College 1869–1969: A Centennial Retrospective.* Chicago: Chicago Teachers College.

King, Sabrina Hope. 1993. "Why Did We Choose Teaching Careers and What Will Enable Us to Stay? Insights from One Cohort of the African American Teaching Pool." *Journal of Negro Education* 62 (4): 475–492.

Ladson-Billings, Gloria. 1994. *The Dream Keepers: Successful Teachers of African American Children.* San Francisco: Jossey-Bass.

Lemann, Nicholas. 1991. *The Promised Land.* New York: Alfred A. Knopf.

Mawhinney, Lynnette. 2014. *We Got Next: Urban Education and the Next Generation of Black Teachers.* New York: Peter Lang.

Mawhinney, Lynnette, Carol R. Rinke, and Gloria Park. 2012. "Being and Becoming a Teacher: How African American and White Preservice Teachers Envision Their Future Roles." *The New Educator* 8: 321–344.

Nettles, Michael T., Linda H. Scatton, Jonathan H. Steinberg, and Linda L. Tyler. 2011. *Performance and Passing Rate Differences of African American and White Prospective Teachers on PRAXIS Examinations.* Princeton, NJ: Educational Testing Service. http://www.ets.org/Media/Research/pdf/RR-11-08.pdf.

Steele, Claude M. 2010. *Whistling Vivaldi: How Stereotypes Affect Us and What We Can Do About It.* New York: W. W. Norton.

Su, Zhixin. 1997. "Teaching as a Profession and as a Career: Minority Candidates' Perspectives." *Teaching and Teacher Education* 13 (3): 325–304.

Sue, Derald W. 2010. *Microaggressions in Everyday Life: Race, Gender, and Sexual Orientation.* Hoboken, NJ: John Wiley and Sons.

Travis, Dempsey. 1981. *An Autobiography of Black Chicago.* Chicago: Urban Research Institute.

Urban Mapping. 2015. "Greater Grand Crossing Neighborhood in Chicago, IL." www.city-data.com.

# 8

## The Future of Teacher Education at Tribal Colleges and Universities

### A Talking Circle of Education Warriors

CARMELITA LAMB

The American Indian self-determination movement of the 1960s gave birth to the concept of Tribal Colleges and Universities (TCUs). During this time, tribal leaders began considering alternative ways to provide opportunities in higher education for their people in a place-based reservation environment. Instead of Indian people leaving the reservation for an education, which had been the history of Indian education since the early nineteenth century (with very limited success), postsecondary opportunity needed to be part of the Native community in which Indian students lived. Thus, in 1968, the Navajo Nation established the first tribally controlled college: Diné College, located on the 26,000-square-mile Navajo Nation, includes a land-base in the states of Utah, Arizona, and New Mexico. Establishing this first American Indian–controlled college set the benchmark for other tribal communities, both on and off the reservation, to begin the path of self-determination through higher education. Since Diné's founding, thirty-eight tribal colleges have been chartered. Thirty-seven are in the United States, and one is in Canada. According to the American Indian Higher Education Consortium (AIHEC 2015), tribal colleges operate on seventy-five unique campuses reaching across sixteen states: from the farthest northern reaches of the United States Iḷisaġvik College in Barrow, Alaska; to the south, Tohono O'odham Community College in Sells, Arizona; to the east, Saginaw Chippewa in Mount Pleasant, Michigan; and on the western edge of the lower forty-eight states, Northwest Indian College in Bellingham, Washington. Tribal colleges serve approximately 27,000 students from more than 250 tribal nations (AIHEC 2015).

The American Indian Higher Education Consortium serves as an advocate of public policy in support of all TCUs in the United States and Canada. Its board of directors consists of the presidents from the accredited US-based TCUs.

AIHEC promotes a multipronged mission: (1) maintain commonly held standards of quality in American Indian education; (2) assure participation in the foundation and administration of educational legislation, policy, rules, regulations, and budgets; (3) assist Tribal Colleges in establishing a secure financial base; and (4) encourage greater participation by American Indians in the development of higher education policy (AIHEC 2015). Existing as a 501c (3) organization, AIHEC is funded through memberships, dues, grants, and contracts.

Teacher education began within the tribal college and university system in 1979. In the first bachelor's degree programs, tribal nations partnered with state colleges/universities. Today, tribal colleges themselves directly confer bachelor's and master's degrees. It has been challenging for some institutions to reach the level of academic and programmatic accountability for accreditation by state and national agencies. Through intertribal college collaboration, institutions have achieved success and empowered more Native students with the opportunity to earn education degrees while remaining in their communities. This success has further transformed how TCUs have implemented Indian higher education to meet the uniquely Indigenous understanding of knowledge sharing and exchange. Taking the lead in the effort to bring this vitally important plan of study to Indian Country was South Dakota's Sinte Gleska University (SGU), offering a four-year bachelor's degree in human services and elementary education in 1979. Since that time, nine other tribal colleges have joined the ranks in teacher preparation programming: Turtle Mountain Community College (TMMC), United Tribes Technical College (UTTC), Nueta Hidatsa Sahnish College (NHSC), and Sitting Bull College (SBC) all in North Dakota; Salish Kootenai College (SKC), Montana; College of Menominee Nation (CMN), Wisconsin; Diné College (DC), Arizona; Haskell Indian Nations University (HINU), Kansas; and Oglala Lakota College (OLC), South Dakota. In the 2013–2014 academic year (AIHEC 2014), these ten tribal colleges conferred bachelor's degrees in education on eighty-one students. The success of these students is no small feat in view of the formidable challenges inextricably associated with higher education in Indian Country.

This chapter describes the extreme challenge and struggle of American Indian higher education—through stories of joy, hope, and sheer determination to make a better life for future Native generations—with particular attention to teacher education. I approach my discussion, in Indigenous research methodology terms, as a literary Talking Circle. Within Native communities, the Talking Circle gives all participants an opportunity to express themselves on a topic or matter relating to a subject. Normally in an American Indian setting, participants first take part in a smudge bath of cleansing smoke to help them get centered. After a smudge, the initiator gives the ground rules for the Talking Circle. An eagle feather or talking stick is used to designate who is allowed to talk. They share the topic, and the Talking Circle begins. The eagle feather or stick goes around once or twice, and the person who initiates the Talking Circle gives wisdom to the group at the end (Personal communication, JT Shining Oneside, 2015).

As a group, the participants in this literary Talking Circle hope to collaborate to make their programs stronger, more effective, and more culturally centered. Many outside the TCU system argue that collaboration does not require face-to-face interaction and that effective team work can happen through digitalized meetings via Skype, Go-to-Meeting, and other formats. These methods, however, are not the Indian way. Meetings from an Indigenous perspective focus on building close relationships and allowing a forum in which everyone has an opportunity to be seen and heard. The Talking Circle serves as the most traditional way in which Native people share ideas.

By way of oral tradition transcribed, this chapter speaks to the history and the future of American Indian teacher preparation. It contains heartfelt testimony from the most remote reservation communities to the bustling urban city centers—all from a deeply Indigenous perspective. The storytellers are the education warriors (department chairs) in these tribal colleges who work tirelessly to ensure the future of these precious teacher education programs. Department chairs of teacher education in the tribal college system are not only administrators in the field of higher education, but they also participate as grant writers, program directors, leaders in the attainment of program and institutional accreditation, assessment coordinators, budget officers, curriculum planners, community leaders, student advocates, and faculty and student recruiters. Most noble of all positions, they are also instructors within their own early childhood, elementary, and secondary teacher education programs. What these truly dedicated individuals offer to the current state of teacher education in Indian Country can only be matched by the steadfast faculty who stand alongside them to further the educational opportunities for their Native students. The ultimate outcome of these efforts is student academic success and the transformation of Indian education in their homeland communities. In equal partnership are the TCU faculty and staff outside teacher education who provide support in course instruction, student advising, financial aid, enrollment services, academic/career student support services, cultural immersion, and language revitalization. Among all personnel within the tribal college system, the unique collective effort promoting student success is one key feature that distinguishes tribal colleges from mainstream postsecondary institutions. The registrar, instructors, financial aid officers, counselors, and numerous other support staff are all part of the family in which the tribal college student exists on a daily basis. The relationships between students and TCU employees are deeply personal, and they share family histories in a way that has been in place from time immemorial. Thus, tribal college faculty and staff see each student as a vested interest in the future of their tribe.

For years, I was a member of this family. I began my career at Turtle Mountain Community College (TMCC) as an adjunct faculty for a US Department of Agriculture equity grant that provided undergraduate adult education coursework in agriculture in partnership with the state land grant university, North Dakota State University, and the Turtle Mountain Indian Reservation Extension Service. From that appointment, I was recruited from my full-time position as a secondary science teacher at a Title IX high school adjacent to the Turtle Mountain reservation to TMCC to become a project director for the National Science Foundation–sponsored Native Ways of Knowing grant. TMCC designed this grant to train and prepare Native American secondary science teachers on the Turtle Mountain and Fort Berthold Indian reservations (Lamb 2013, 2014; Martin and Lamb 2008). This program graduated twenty students with bachelor's degrees in secondary science. Over the next four years, I served as the director, advisor, and support faculty for this program. In the fifth year, I moved to the teacher education department as chair at TMCC. The department had two bachelor's degree programs: elementary education and secondary science education. During my five-year tenure as chair, we added early childhood education, and I worked with other department chairs within the tribal college system to support their efforts in accreditation and program development. Collectively, we supported one another in many ways to ensure the excellence of our education programs across Indian Country. I know intimately the extent to which all participants in this story engage in their profession and passion on a day-to-day basis.

While conducting the literary Talking Circle necessary to create this chapter, many department chairs expressed thanks to me for taking the initiative to recount their stories. The unfortunate truth is that both the pace at which these individuals must engage in their work and the numerous roles carried within the tribal college environment prevent these educators from taking precious time away from their duties to share their knowledge in a public way. I am honored to have been trusted enough to bring their thoughts and dreams forward in this format. It takes years to earn the relationship capital necessary to unfold a story as remarkable and sacred. The relationship between non-Native researcher and Indigenous communities has been fraught with generations of misunderstanding, piracy, betrayal, and disrespect for Indigenous traditional knowledge systems and culture. Indigenous scholars such as Gregory Cajete (2015), Lori Lambert (2014), Margaret Kovach (2010), and Bagele Chilisa (2012), to name a few, have contributed to the body of knowledge describing ethical Indigenous research methodologies that honor and respect Indigenous traditional knowledge, epistemologies, oral language patterns and interpretations, and responsibilities to tribal communities to bring forward research questions and solutions that ultimately benefit the Native community in tangible ways. As a former colleague of tribal college teacher education faculty, staff, and administrators, I feel a sisterhood and kinship of sorts to the leaders I interviewed for this chapter (see table 8.1).

TABLE 8.1

**Talking Circle Participants**

| Department chair | Institution | Location | Affiliated tribes | Programs |
|---|---|---|---|---|
| Lisa Azure | United Tribes Technical College | Bismarck, ND | Seventy or more tribes from the United States; predominately: Cheyenne River Sioux, Standing Rock Dakota and Lakota, Mandan, Hidatsa, Arikara, Pine Ridge Oglala and Lakota | Elementary and early childhood education |
| Constance Frankenbery | Nueta Hidatsa Sahnish College | Ft. Berthold Indian Reservation—New Town, ND | Mandan, Hidatsa, Arikara | Elementary education |
| Cindy O'Dell | Salish Kootenai College | Flathead Indian Reservation—Pablo, MT | Salish Kootenai, Pend d'Oreille | Elementary and early childhood education |
| Regina Sievert | Salish Kootenai College | Flathead Indian Reservation—Pablo, MT | Salish, Kootenai, Pend d'Orelle | Secondary science education |
| Cheryl Medaris | Sinte Gleska University | Rosebud Sioux Reservation—Mission, SD | Sicangu Oyate (Lakota) | Elementary, early childhood, and secondary history education; master's in education |
| Chris Fried | Sitting Bull College | Standing Rock Sioux Reservation—Fort Yates, ND | Dakota and Lakota | Early childhood, elementary, secondary science, and special education |
| Cyndi Pyatskowit | College of Menominee Nation | Menominee Indian Reservation—Keshena, WI | Menominee | Elementary education |
| Teresa Delorme | Turtle Mountain Community College | Turtle Mountain Indian Reservation—Belcourt, ND | Turtle Mountain Band of Chippewa | Elementary, early childhood, and secondary science education |
| Geraldine Garrity | Diné College | Navajo Nation—Tsaile, AZ | Navajo | Elementary education |

Over the course of five months, I conducted telephone interviews and follow-up conversations by e-mail with the above leaders. Given the extensive distances between tribal college campuses (more than 1,800 miles between Diné College and College of Menominee Nation), face-to-face interviews were not possible. This was unfortunate because it had been years since I had seen many of these individuals, and a true visit would have been quite meaningful and more in line with Indigenous research methodology. My intention was to conduct short interviews focused on the current status of their respective education programs, the challenges that have been navigated while they engaged in administration of the programs, and, most important, their vision of the future of teacher education across Indian Country.

As expected, what began as a short interview focusing on these topics expanded to much more than answers to the original set of questions. Dialogue with the leaders flowed from some of the deepest places of the heart. Their contributions have been instrumental in conveying to the general higher education constituency what a tribal college is, in what manner it operates, and how curricula uniquely grounded in the Indigenous ways of understanding knowledge, which is acquired and shared, serves Native students.

These interviews create a picture of the tribal college system, the cooperative participants in Indigenous higher educational programming, and the future of tribally controlled colleges and universities in the United States and Canada. The state of teacher education in tribal colleges today involves a number of important challenges that include enrollment, funding, accreditation, and high stakes examinations for licensure. In the face of these challenges, however, are true successes: the development of new bachelor's degree programs in education; sustaining the master's degree programs currently offered; establishing meaningful partnerships between tribal colleges and local communities; reaffirming dedication to Indian culture, heritage, and language; and promoting longstanding relationships between students and faculty. Most important, the interpersonal student relationships in teacher education cohorts will last their entire professional careers.

Still, the department chairs at these tribal colleges all feel compelled to speak of a critical set of needs: a forum for collaboration across all ten institutions, greater resources in technology, and more faculty to support high-quality instruction. In some instances, the conversation moved into areas of deep concern: questions about the viability of their programs, employment opportunities for graduates, social disadvantages, and federal regulations that threaten the very existence of teacher education in all tribal colleges. Ever hopeful, these department chairs have courageously elected to press on in the face of these pressures. Their support of the students in teacher education is beyond what may be expected at a mainstream institution in many respects because it is the very fabric of the tribal college, indeed the strength of Indian higher education.

## Enrollment and Location

Declining enrollment in teacher education has been a common theme at several of the tribal colleges interviewed. At some institutions, such as Sitting Bull College, there have been modest gains in numbers of students seeking a bachelor's degree in education, but most programs are making strong efforts to recruit more students into the teaching profession. Lisa Azure at United Tribes Technical College cited the current economy in North Dakota as a major reason for the low numbers in her program: "Our students are typically families with children, so they are taking advantage of the economic opportunities of the state and delaying college." North Dakota is home to four tribal college teacher preparation programs. Nueta Hidatsa Sahnish College is in the heart of the Bakken oil formation on the Fort Berthold Indian Reservation, home to the Three Affiliated Tribes: Mandan, Hidatsa, and Arikara. Constance Frankenbery noted that, while their numbers in the bachelor's program are not where she would like them, the two-year early childhood education program has served as a pipeline for future growth in the bachelor's program. The early childhood graduates provide much-needed support for the Head Start programs on the Fort Berthold Reservation. Thus, the two-year degree serves as a stepping stone for these students to meet the academic rigor of the bachelor's in elementary education. By contrast, student enrollment in teacher education continues to be strong at Sinte Gleska University. Cheryl Medaris maintains that these numbers directly reflect their allegiance to the mission, which she offered in her own words: "To prepare our teachers to look forward to Seven Generations and to be able to instill in themselves and others the Lakota values." The Seven Generations philosophy refers to the responsibility of Indigenous leaders to consider the consequences of their decisions for seven generations into the future as expressed in the Rosebud Sioux Tribe Constitution.

At Diné College, Geraldine Garrity attributed low enrollment to the remote location of the college: "Even with the residential nature of the college, students still struggle to get to the campus." Online instruction has not been a viable option for potential Diné students, owing to either the variability in Internet access at their homes and/or lack of Internet sites within their communities. Garrity also mentioned Diné College's efforts to support distance education students through off-campus branches. The college designed these sites to allow students an opportunity to complete and submit their work to their course instructors; however, students still must travel to submit their work digitally, which she said can, in itself, present a hardship.

Chris Fried at Sitting Bull College on the Standing Rock Reservation further substantiated the hardship that remote location and distance places on the teacher education students. The Standing Rock Reservation covers more than 3,500 square miles. On campus, Sitting Bull College offers limited housing options for an enrollment of slightly less than 300 students: twenty family units and five dormitory rooms, which can serve four students each. Consequently, transportation becomes an important part of acquiring postsecondary education on Standing Rock Reservation. According to Chris Fried, "Students on average drive between twenty and thirty-five miles one way to attend classes. We do have a few students who drive forty miles one way for classes Monday through Thursday." Sitting Bull College has two satellite campuses in McLaughlin and Mobridge, South Dakota, but their course offerings are limited to the general education curriculum. In an effort to meet the daily challenges of transportation for students, a bus service has been operating between the campus and local reservation communities. Again, the restricted availability meets the needs of only a small demographic of student. "If students have night classes, then riding the bus is not an option," said Fried. Barriers to attending college classes can even include lack of funds for gasoline to drive the distance to and from the main campus at Fort Yates. These types of physical challenges to attend college are a grim reality for many Native students living on reservations. Although the price of gasoline fluctuates, it is not unusual to pay more than $4.00 per gallon in these locations. North Dakota is also known for severe winter weather and life-threatening blizzard conditions. In 2014, record snowfall hit the Standing Rock Reservation area numerous times and caused school closures across several southwestern North Dakota counties within the reservation territory.

Fort Berthold Reservation has the added physical barrier of Lake Sakakawea, which covers 155,000 acres of reservation land and about 600 miles of reservation shoreline. There is only one bridge (Four Bears) across this body of water; thus, travel from one location of the reservation to another involves going around the lake. The Nueta Hidatsa Sahnish campus is located in New Town, North Dakota, which is the location of the tribal agency. According to Frankenbery, there are six main reservation communities on the Fort Berthold Reservation with proximities to main campus that range from four to ninety-eight miles: "The roads across Fort Berthold range from dirt to gravel to paved and present distance, winter-weather-based challenges, and trailer-truck traffic dangers." Frankenbery also added that there are plans for the construction of a four-plex of student housing to add to the current dorm space that houses fifteen to eighteen students on the main campus, an addition that will reduce the travel requirement for students who can live there.

Housing shortages are not only a challenge in rural remote reservation communities but are equally persistent in urban settings such as Bismarck, North Dakota, home of United Tribes Technical College. The North Dakota tribe transformed the campus, formerly a military post, for the purpose of educating and training American Indian students and their families for their economic, social, and cultural advancement (United Tribes Technical College 2015). Family housing is available on campus, but the demand far exceeds the

availability. The influx of oil workers has inflated the rental rates for apart-
ments and homes in Bismarck ; for example, modest two-bedroom apartments/
homes rent for a minimum of $1,200 per month or higher, which computes to
$10,800 per academic year. The current maximum Federal Pell grant award for
2015–2016 is $5,775, based on academic plan and student need. Some tribes
offer scholarships of $1,000 per semester. Most tribal colleges do not offer
other federal financial aid loan packages to their students because that often
places students at a high risk of incurring significant debt. Although tuition at
tribal colleges ($1,200 to $1,700 per semester) is considered some of the most
reasonable in the country, lack of resources presents real obstacles for Native
students in reaching their professional goals through higher education studies.
Consequently, tribal college students in Bismarck seeking affordable housing
struggle to meet this basic need.

## Institutional Funding

Common to all institutions of higher education in the United States today are
inadequate funding resources to maintain and continue established programs
of study. Public and state land grant institutions are supported with state-
legislated dollars; however, many tribal colleges do not receive state support
because of their location on reservation lands. The Tribally Controlled College
and University Assistance Act of 1978 mandated federal support of all tribal colleges, and all tribal colleges are highly dependent upon these federal dollars for
basic operational costs. As expected, though, the need far outweighs the federal
revenue stream. As a result, tribal colleges must rely upon funding through
their respective tribes, public/private grants, and ancillary federal dollars that
are currently insufficient to meet rising costs. Geraldine Garrity described her
needs at Diné College as they related to preparing teachers to be career ready:
"I feel it is mostly in the areas of instructional resources, and of course technology. If we could have the same kind of technology resources here in our
division [as in the area K–12 schools], we could better train our students to be
able to step into a classroom." In many tribal colleges with teacher education
programs, the current funding streams from the Office of Indian Education or
Department of Education are reaching maturity or have closed. Cindy O'Dell at
Salish Kootenai College acknowledged this deficit: "Funding is so important for
our students and right now we have no funding for next year. We have one grant
we are finishing up with the Office of Indian Education and we are hoping for a
carryover year, but last year we lost 90K of carryover."

   According to a report by the National Education Association (2010), recommendations from the American Indian and Alaska Native communities in
the reauthorization of the Elementary and Secondary Education Act included
funding tribal education agencies. This effort would work both to strengthen

tribal control of education and to provide a source of support for tribal colleges with accredited teacher education programs through scholarships and pay incentives. The US Department of Education recognizes tribal colleges as unique institutions in their ability not only to train culturally competent Native educators to enter the PreK–12 classroom, but also to create pipelines of skilled and qualified Native instructors through Title II (Preparing, Training, and Recruiting High-Quality Instructors and Principals).

Most troubling, however, is the disparity in equity for funding opportunities available to tribal college teacher education programs. The current status of this necessary support across the ten tribal institutions with education programs ranges from full funding to no funding at all. Full funding represents a total support system through which the college provides students with tuition, fees, books, laptop computers, professional development, examination fees for licensure, and a small monthly stipend to assist with living expenses. Generally, these types of grants keep an account of all financial support provided to the students during the time they are participating in the program. Students are expected to maintain a minimum GPA, attend at least 90 percent of classes, and develop other dispositions befitting the profession of educator. Once the student has graduated and entered into the teaching workforce, the granting institution expects them to provide as many months in the classroom teaching as they were given in grant support. Students who do not fulfill this commitment must repay the funding agency for all support received. Moreover, this type of grant, similar to a federal student loan, is available only to Native Americans or direct descendants of Native Americans.

Tribal colleges who do not receive any funding are the unsuccessful applicants for these grant opportunities. The lack of equity stems from the fact that federal resources are limited, which leads to tribal colleges competing against one another in the grant application process directed by the US Department of Indian Education. In rare instances where tribal college teacher education faculty and administrators convene for collaborative purposes, they share a common feeling of dismay because this funding system means that, in essence, they are not working together as one but are directly competing against one another. Cheryl Medaris at Sinte Gleska University lamented that the environment has changed from what she once knew: "In early days of the tribal college movement, everyone worked together to get the work done, everyone shared all they knew in order to support each other." In today's tribal college environment, it is not a lost trust but rather a survival strategy to hold close to the vest anything that might be seen as an edge in the competitive grant writing field. Open sharing of knowledge is more guarded.

Tribal college students are also highly dependent upon Pell grants through the federal Title IV program. In recent years, however, the funding policies for this source of student financial aid have changed. For instance, Pell grants no longer include summers in the number of semesters students are eligible for support. According to Medaris, "Our students [are recognizing the financial aid changes] and are successfully getting through our program in a timely manner." This will be increasingly important for future teacher education students in tribal colleges as resources become more subject to federally mandated budgetary changes.

## Recruiting and Retaining Faculty

Another area of significant need in tribal college teacher education programs is faculty. Since most tribal colleges are located on reservations, the rural, remote location can present challenges in recruiting and retaining high-quality faculty. Teresa Delorme of Turtle Mountain Community College commented on this issue: "We have such a tiny, tiny staff here, and they have to do the work of an entire department anywhere else. Our greatest need right now is to attract diverse faculty, who really want to come in and work here because they have a sense of community, [are looking to] work with tribal people, and just want to do good work." Regina Sievert of Salish Kootenai College added that candidate expectations for career advancement do not always match the structure of tribal institutions:

> It is almost impossible to find one [faculty]. I did a national search, spent thousands of dollars advertising and couldn't attract anyone [who was] qualified. So many are looking for tenure to move through the system and that does not happen here. So you have to have a different type of person, who is not a ladder climber, and who is willing to live in a rural area. There are those kinds of people that enjoy this kind of life, but we have not been able to find one.

Finally, no one seemed to know for certain why opportunities for tenure are not available to faculty in tribal colleges. Frankenbery stated, "Nueta Hidatsa Sahnish College (formerly Fort Berthold Community College) is considering implementing a tenure track for our faculty, but I am not sure why it has not occurred prior to this consideration." Joe McDonald, former president of Salish Kootenai College, offered several reasons why tenure was not implemented in the tribal colleges:

> One was that our funding was not stable enough to offer tenure. Another reason is that we wanted to be different from mainstream universities. At least I felt that way. I and other SKC people didn't want to use professor, associate professor, and other titles used in academia. In the university system, when I was there (forty-seven years ago) when granted professor, you earned tenure upon your third contract, associate professor earned tenure after ten years. [Also], I didn't want the college to get stuck with some ineffective instructor with tenure.

Most department chairs collectively agreed that the subject of tenure was something that had never entered the academic conversation at their institution. In view of the current financial climate at TCUs, the idea of developing a tenure policy is nearly impossible. The greatest percentage of revenue for TCUs comes from grants and private funding sources that are highly competitive and of short duration.

## High-Stakes Licensure Exams

While institutional support, student financial aid, and faculty shortages present challenges to tribal college teacher education programs, these pale in comparison to the real threat to program success for future Native educators— high-stakes licensure exams. A majority of the institutions interviewed voiced grave concerns about the Praxis Core (Educational Testing Service) and edTPA (Pearson) exams, intended to assess preservice teachers' basic skill competencies in reading, writing, and mathematics. Graduates of teacher education programs are required to pass either of these exams in order to become licensed in their state (Wentworth et al. 2009), with the exception of Salish Kootenai College, Pablo, Montana. Students from Montana are only required to take the Praxis content examinations (Curriculum Instruction and Assessment, Practices of Teaching and Learning, and/or General Science) for licensure. Each state has a measure of latitude in authorizing which exam (and cut score) is necessary for licensure. In some cases, the Praxis Core has completely stalled the progression of Native teacher education students in their programs of study. Some students find themselves taking the exam over and over only to see their score become worse. Chris Fried from Sitting Bull College spoke to this point directly: "What we need to do better is prepare our students for the Praxis Core." The problem, however, is greater than simply preparing the students to take the test. Lisa Azure at United Tribes Technical College agreed that students need to be prepared for the Praxis Core tests, but she also touched on how time is of the essence: "The challenge is helping the students prepare for these tests, learn the content, pedagogy, and theory necessary to be effective teachers, and do it all in a shorter period of time because of the reduced number of semesters they are able to get funded." The frustration was clearly evident in her voice.

The College of Menominee Nation is exploring a new bachelor's degree program that would allow teacher education graduates who have neither passed the Praxis Core nor intended to become a licensed teacher in Wisconsin to seek other options for a career in the field of education. With this in mind, faculty members at the college have looked at this licensure exam challenge as an opportunity for innovation and program development. The new bachelor's degree at College of Menominee Nation would have a greater emphasis in the language and culture of the Menominee Nation with the target being

PreK children in early learning facilities. The degree, including a certificate in American Indian studies and possibly some courses in business, would prepare those individuals who may be considering an administrative role in Head Start or similar facilities because those qualified employees must hold a bachelor's degree in education.

Some tribal institutions such as Diné College, Turtle Mountain Community College, Sinte Gleska University, and United Tribes Technical College have begun aggressive tutoring programs to assist their students in meeting the skill level necessary to pass these career changing exams. The most ironic part of this scenario is, however, that preservice students are able to successfully pass the education content exams in curriculum, instruction, and assessment as well as the exams in principles of teaching and learning—truly the heart and soul of every effective K–12 educator—yet the Praxis Core and the edTPA remain serious obstacles to licensure. The soulful words of Cheryl Medaris affirm this point: "A test does not a teacher make."

## Meaningful Partnerships and Relationships

It is widely acknowledged that teacher education programs must provide meaningful field experiences in classrooms for their students in order to ensure student success and longevity in the profession (Darling-Hammond 2014; Ralph and Walker 2012; Spooner et al. 2008). Through these clinical experiences, preservice teachers gain much needed mentoring and support from the greater community of educators in their school districts. Placement of Native students in classrooms requires tremendous effort by tribal college department chairs and faculty. Prior to student placement in the schools, department chairs and faculty host meetings between community leaders, K–12 administrators, and mentor teachers who in many instances are non-Native. In predominately non-Native communities, these meetings provide Native preservice teachers with an opportunity to experience what an interview with a non-Native administrator might entail, understand how non-Native school systems operate professionally as well as interpersonally, and become familiar with a predominately non-Native parent constituency. These experiences are pivotal in the development of a professional self-concept for new Native American teachers. Naturally for those tribal college teacher education graduates who stay within their home community, the transition to the workplace is much more fluid. Family, friends, and Native mentors who have supported these students in their pursuit of a bachelor's degree in education from the beginning surround the candidates. Native professionals overwhelmingly staff K–12 administration in Bureau of Indian Education (BIE) school systems, as is the case on the Turtle Mountain Indian Reservation. Graduates from Turtle Mountain Community College seek employment in the BIE schools in order to further their commitment to stay in their community and serve their own people. It is unfortunate that not all tribal college teacher education graduates experience this same level of cultural acceptance. In some instances, fully licensed Native teachers from tribal college programs are employed as teacher aides, positions that pay little above minimum wage and require neither more than a few college credits nor skill competency assessments through professional exams.

Other strategies practiced in tribal college teacher preparation programs involve organization of professional development opportunities for students to enhance their pedagogical skills and provide purposeful supervision and constructive feedback during the clinical placement portion of the curriculum. At United Tribes Technical College, for example, students must present at colloquia and state teacher conferences in order to build public speaking skills and develop a level of comfort in standing in front of peers who are not of their cultural or social background. Because Native students struggle to overcome years, even generations, of intimidation and diminished self-worth, standing in front of an audience can present some significant challenges. Dr. Azure noted that the transformation in the demeanor of the students who have participated in this program requirement is remarkable. They develop the self-confidence to navigate within professional circles and take upon themselves the role of leader within their communities: "We see huge gains from the time that they come here, in their first year, and then the confidence and level of professionalism that they develop over the five years they are typically here."

The overreaching objective is building relationships based on trust and mutual understanding of the goals sought on both sides, Native and non-Native. Cyndi Pyatskowit at College of Menominee Nation recounted the following about these relationships:

> [It's about] the *whole* relationship . . . we are a new teacher education program, and have built a strong relationship with the school districts. Not only the reservation schools but the surrounding schools that serve high numbers of Native students are really starting to look at the tribal college as a partner who can help them serve their Native children better. It should be this way as our focus within our college classes is built under tribal clan structure.

The prevailing message, particularly within Indigenous communities, emphasizes building and sustaining trusting relationships. In the context of tribal colleges, building partnerships means developing relationships with those who are most closely impacted by the mission and vision of American Indian higher education.

An extension of these partnerships occurs between tribal colleges and mainstream state institutions as well. Turtle Mountain Community College has engaged in a diversity experience exchange with a state college in North Dakota.

Salish Kootenai College has had a longstanding relationship with Montana State University, and the longest of histories exists between Diné College and Arizona State University, which led to Diné College's bachelor's degree in teacher education. Whether longstanding or newly developed, the mutual understanding of building crosscultural relationships in order to bring benefit to the community is so important for the future success of all tribal colleges.

Higher education can no longer afford to be socially identified as Euro-centered mainstream, but rather it must seek to embrace a wide range of cultural perspectives, which include MSIs. Tribal colleges are being recognized as a true force in the goal of providing high-quality postsecondary education opportunities for students of all nations, Native and non-Native alike. Dr. Frankenbery of Nueta Hidatsa Sahnish College explained this force eloquently:

> Our motto here is "Tribally educated, globally prepared," whether you are from one of the Three Affiliated Tribes [Mandan, Hidatsa, Arikara] or not, Native or non-Native, you need to know. You need to know about some of the trauma that has taken place throughout the years. You need to understand where families and people are operating from. You need to be sensitive to that.

Dr. Frankenbery is referring to the context from which tribal colleges address higher education. When Indigenous students walk through the door of a tribal college, they enter into a space of learning that honors their personal Native history and the historical trauma that has been endured by and inflicted upon all of their people. Their story does not have to be retold because it is already known, and thus, from this moment in their lives, they can begin to build a new story, a new life that is not only valued in their communities but also allows for their own success in broader environments. The decisions of this generation will light the fires for the next Seven Generations. This ideal, though never spoken, is understood by all. What happens today will be the future of the next Seven Generations of tribal members.

## Conclusion

In the final analysis, what tribal colleges do best is support their students and preservice teachers in a way that cannot be matched by typical mainstream institutions. Although other colleges and universities may talk about building relationships and being culturally relevant to Indigenous student populations on their campuses, tribal colleges actually build upon the cultural heritage that has always been a part of the tribal nations represented by their student body. Within the walls of the tribal college exists a spirit of collectivism that fosters the future of Native self-determination. The shared Indigenous history is an integral ingredient in how knowledge is communicated from instructor to student. I found impressive examples of how the educational programs incorporate Native cultural relevance in the tribal college classrooms where instructors recount American history from the perspective of the Native people who were present and contributed to the story. US geography references the original tribal territories and the current reservation systems. Botany and ecology note the ancient plants that have served as food, medicine, and sources of spirituality. These colleges approach nursing from the context of Native healing and wellness. A tribal college infuses Native language and culture across entire curricula; the smudge and drum are neither far away nor left to idle for very long. According to Geraldine Garrity, "I think one thing that we will continue to make sure of is to support Navajo children both in the Navajo language and culture. I feel like that is our greatest strength in this whole institution."

Each tribal college gives honor to the tribe(s) served by the institution, as articulated through the mission statement and vision. What is not written but is understood and felt by all who enter into this space is something of equal importance: the Native understanding of family, connectedness, respect, and validation. Within the walls of tribal colleges all across Indian Country, students have a level of cultural mindfulness that they cannot always experience in a mainstream university or college.

To fully understand the passion and commitment of the Education Warriors across the tribal college system, one has to hear their voices as they speak of the victories their programs have witnessed. For these faculty and administrators, each graduate represents years of significant challenge and much welcomed success. Whether the struggle is financial, basic housing and transportation, licensure or professional marginalization, these students have prevailed due to the efforts of their tribal college family. The following testimonies speak to the essence of a tribal college:

> "We help them see that college is not as scary as they thought, that we are their support system." (Constance Frankenbery)

> "We have been their biggest cheerleaders and their toughest coaches." (Cyndi Pyatstowit)

> "We are best in how we help the student through the program. It is a unique benefit of the tribal college system that students will not find at other universities. We are able to take the time to figure out what works best for the adult learner and apply that to the curriculum to render success. Being a small institution, we can do that." (Chris Fried)

> "There is a great deal of pride [at TMCC] from where we pick the students up and where we take them to." (Teresa Delorme)

> "Every student is precious, we do everything we can to make sure that [our] student has every opportunity to prove themselves. They say,

'I can't believe I got all the way through school!' . . . they come to my office and cry . . . I mean . . . that's life changing." (Cindy Odell)

"A student told me, 'You don't know how many times I wanted to quit, but the people at Sinte . . . they encouraged me, I'm here where I am today because other people believed in me.' I thought that speaks volumes because in a large system, she would have just disappeared." (Cheryl Medaris)

"[Our] strengths are that the students are very supportive of each other. Most of them either grew up on a reservation or went to schools with a lot of tribal members. They have a frame of reference for culturally competent teaching. Also, they are very cohesive as a group. They understand not only pedagogical techniques, but cultural norms, it's just part of their lives." (Regina Sievert)

Today the obstacles are formidable, and these department chairs certainly have their worries. They are asking for help, but thus far their college presidents, tribal governments, federal funding agencies, and national teacher licensure regulatory bodies have not heard their queries. One of the greatest needs expressed by all department chairs during the interviews was the opportunity to be able to communicate with others in their position about the future of teacher education in the tribal college. This vital conversation must take place because it could influence whether other tribal colleges will join in the effort to prepare future educators in their tribal communities. Across the United States, a change is taking place in how educators are held accountable. The exchange of No Child Left Behind for the Every Student Succeeds Act brings yet another political shift in how teachers teach and students learn. Teacher education in the tribal colleges must now face the added implications of these changes. The future is uncertain for teacher preparation in mainstream colleges and universities as well as tribal colleges. In fact, all schools of education struggle with many of the challenges presented here. But the difference in the level of institutional resources available to state and private schools as compared to tribal colleges is significant.

While it has been a great victory to feature ten tribal colleges with teacher preparation programs, some are hanging on by only the slimmest of margins. The rigor necessary to design and develop a program, meet accreditation standards, recruit students and faculty, and support students toward program completion appear insurmountable to other tribal colleges that are considering teacher education. In hindsight, as I look back upon the years I was directly involved in these efforts, they may be right. Many of the warriors in this story are becoming elders. Like me, they are looking for new Native leaders to take the reins and bring forth the strong leadership so desperately needed in Indian Country. Perhaps the answers are in training Native educational leaders who will continue the efforts of those now in service and greater collaboration rather than competition among the tribal colleges with existing teacher education programs. No one can predict where the future will lead us in this endeavor; the only certainty is that Native children will continue to need competent instructors in the classroom in order to further the efforts of their ancestors to pursue a better future for all Native people.

### REFERENCES

American Indian Higher Education Consortium (AIHEC). 2014. "American Indian Measures of Success." Unpublished Data Set, American Indican Higher Education Consortium, 2013–2014.

———. 2015. "American Indian Higher Education Consortium." http://www.aihec.org/index.cfml.

Cajete, Gregory. 2015. *Indigenous Community: Rekindling the Teachings of the Seventh Fire.* St. Paul: Living Justice Press.

Chilisa, Bagele. 2012. *Indigenous Research Methodologies.* Los Angeles: Sage Publications.

Darling-Hammond, Linda. 2014. "Strengthening Clinical Preparation: The Holy Grail of Teacher Education." *Peabody Journal of Education* 89: 547–561.

Kovach, Margaret. 2010. *Indigenous Methodologies: Characteristics, Conversations, and Contexts.* Toronto: University of Toronto Press.

Lamb, Carmelita. 2013. "Cohort Model Learning Communities: The Tribal College Perspective of Best Practices in Teacher Education." *Mellon Tribal College Journal* 1: 28–76.

———. 2014. "Growing Our Own: A Sustainable Approach to Teacher Education at Turtle Mountain Community College." *Tribal College Journal* 26: 30–31.

Lambert, Lori. 2014. *Research for Indigenous Survival: Indigenous Research Methodologies in the Behavioral Sciences.* Pablo, MT: Salish Kootenai College Press.

Martin, Tibi, and Carmelita Lamb. 2008. "From Turtle Mountains to the Badlands: Learning to Teach Native Ways of Knowing." *Tribal College Journal* 19: 38–40.

National Education Association. 2010. "Focus on American Indians and Alaska Natives: Charting a New Course for Native Education." http://www.nea.org/home/53291.htm.

Ralph, Edwin G., and Keith D. Walker. 2012. "Internships in Rural Schools: Post Interns' Views." *Journal of Cooperative Education and Internships* 46: 44–57.

Spooner, Melba, Claudia Flowers, Richard Lambert, and Bob Algozzine. 2008. "Is More Really Better? Examining Perceived Benefits of an Extended Student Teaching Experience." *The Clearing House: A Journal of Educational Strategies, Issues and Ideas* 81: 263–270.

United Tribes Technical College. 2015. "History of United Tribes and Fort Lincoln." http://www.uttc.edu/about/site_ft_lincoln/site.asp.

Wentworth, Nancy, Lynnette B. Erickson, Barbara Lawrence, J. Aaron Popham, and Bryan Korth. 2009. "A Paradigm Shift toward Evidence-Based Clinical Practice: Developing a Performance Assessment." *Studies in Educational Evaluation* 35: 16–20.

# 9

# Teacher Preparation at Historically Black Colleges and Universities

## Remaining Relevant in a Climate of Accountability

BRIAN HARPER

LYNNETTE MAWHINNEY

The specific contribution of Historically Black Colleges and Universities (HBCUs) to the field of higher education is undeniable (Harper 2007). Historically Black Colleges and Universities were founded on principles of service, activism, and identity tied to the larger movement of racial uplift in Black communities (Anderson 1988). These tenets continue to inform the ways they conceptualize, design, and implement teacher preparation. Beginning in 1837 with Cheyney University, which was closely followed by Lincoln University, the first degree-granting Black institution, the 105 HBCUs in this country make up only 3 percent of the total population of postsecondary institutions in the United States, but they have produced more than 30 percent of all African Americans earning bachelor's degrees and 50 percent of African American teachers currently employed in the United States (Irvine and Fenwick 2011).

Although these statistics certainly reinforce the efficacy of these institutions, they by no means capture the totality of their impact. From their inception, many HBCUs uniquely served as normal schools responsible for training teachers; during their more than 150 years of existence, they have developed unique institutional advantages in the preparation of teachers (Robinson and Albert 2008). Specifically, these institutions emphasize the development of a healthy self-concept, commitment to community, the principles of human freedom, and the legacy of African American achievement as foundational tools to guide pedagogical development. These experiences contribute to educating a cadre of teachers who perform at a level superior to that of many peers (Robinson and Albert 2008).

To assure their viability in the twenty-first century and beyond, HBCUs must demonstrate that they remain capable of preparing a new generation of students (more specifically, highly qualified PK–12 teachers), while simultaneously providing the type of supportive, nurturing environment for students of color that is characteristic of their institutional mission. Chapter 9 describes the efforts of HBCUs to reconcile these two aims by describing current criticisms of the relevance of HBCUs and examining specific policy-implemented challenges to teacher education programs, especially those policies based on contemporary pressures of accreditation and program evaluation. Finally, the chapter outlines some of the tangible ways that HBCU teacher education programs can enact the principles of service, activism, and social justice in the midst of this contemporary climate of accountability.

## Institutional Challenges

Historically Black Colleges and Universities are no strangers to criticism. Public commentary related to them most frequently centers on financial mismanagement, leadership scandals, and irrelevance in the twenty-first century landscape of higher education (e.g., Nazaryan 2015; Riley 2010). These criticisms can be traced through numerous decades (Roebuck and Murty 1993). Moreover, these commentaries most often fail to acknowledge that HBCUs, like any institutional type, are diverse institutions that vary by size, fiscal resources, admission standards, and other factors. Instead of beginning from this stance, commentaries focus on a small group of the most troubled and underresourced institutions and generalize across the 105 HBCUs (Gasman, Samayoa, and Commodore 2015).

Many Predominantly White Institutions (PWIs) and their proponents claim that HBCUs, though appropriate and necessary in the twentieth century, have outlived their usefulness in the twenty-first century. These individuals point to the abundant resources, extensive influence, and tradition of academic excellence provided by PWIs, which, they argue, are in position to offer opportunities for Black students that cannot be matched by HBCUs (e.g., Riley 2010). Proponents of PWIs further point to declining enrollments, dilapidated facilities, and shrinking endowments as reasons to remove federal and state funding from HBCUs. The cornerstone of this argument is based on the premise that more opportunities—for both white *and* Black students—are available at PWIs than could ever present themselves at HBCUs.

Public criticisms, however, often ignore the ways that PWIs still struggle to create healthy and equitable campus climates for students of color. Although there are certainly increased opportunities for Black students at PWIs, compared to those of previous generations, matriculating at PWIs is not without problems. Many PWIs still struggle to create healthy, humanizing, inclusive, and supportive campus climates for students of color (Allen and Jewel 2002; Fleming 2001; Harper 2009; McGee and Martin 2011). That is, while African

American students may gain from the available resources of PWIs, that gain often comes at a high price.

Philosophical challenges to the mission and purpose of HBCUs may be quite insidious, but legislative challenges prove to be equally harmful to the existence of these institutions. In 2011, the Obama administration introduced changes to the eligibility requirements for Parent PLUS loans, a federal low-interest loan program that allows parents to offset the cost of higher education. As a result of this new policy, prospective borrowers were deemed ineligible, a determination that left tens of thousands of HBCU students unable to meet tuition costs (Gasman and Collins 2014). Although Secretary of Education Arne Duncan later revised this policy in response to criticism from current HBCU presidents, less than one-third of applications for the Parent PLUS loan were approved for the 2013–2014 academic year, a change that affected more than 35,000 additional HBCU families (Gasman and Collins 2014).

On the heels of changes to this federal loan program, the Obama administration introduced the Postsecondary Institution Ranking System, the first step in a federal plan to enhance institutional quality. This system seeks to publicize tuition cost, average student loan debt, graduation rates, and other measures as indicators of institutional quality to promote consumer awareness among families who are considering particular institutions. In the effort to establish objective criteria to promote comparisons among accredited institutions, the proposed ranking system does not consider the issue of diversity among institutions. As a consequence, the system disadvantages many HBCUs because traditional measures of success like graduation rates do not consider the remediation that many HBCUs must take on to address academic deficiencies that present themselves among many enrolled students (American Council on Education 2014; Perry and Toldson 2014).

To counter these criticisms, HBCU advocates must consistently communicate not only their relevance but also the ways their stated purpose is pertinent to that of the US Department of Education. With respect to changes in the way higher education costs may be subsidized, Marybeth Gasman (2013) suggests a number of remedies for HBCUs that focus on the philanthropic efforts of successful alumni. For example, increasing outreach initiatives and making connections to public and private sector agendas can motivate partnerships between institutions and funders. In addition, with respect to the proposed use of quantitative metrics to establish institutional quality, individual HBCUs—especially public institutions that work with similar student populations—would benefit from maintaining open lines of communication to share ideas and resources about best practices (Gasman 2013). Finally, HBCUs should use social media as a platform to inform and educate the general public about their role in the American system of higher education.

## Challenges Specific to Teacher Education

Macrolevel challenges to the existence of HBCUs manifest themselves even more directly by specifically challenging the efficacy of teacher preparation programs at these institutions. Many of these challenges derive from contemporary changes in accreditation requirements and other pressures of program evaluation. Although all teacher education programs across the country are subject to these requirements and pressures, they present programs at HBCUs with a different set of challenges. In the current accountability-based climate, institutions that prepare PK–12 educators must provide specific statistical evidence of their effectiveness to maintain accredited status. Examples of accompanying evidence of an institution's effectiveness in meeting each standard include candidate GPAs, student work artifacts, retention rates, graduation rates, pass rates on licensure/certification exams, other quantitative/qualitative survey data of current and graduated students, and student loan default rates of currently matriculating and former students (American Council on Education 2014). This process focuses on the development of clearly quantifiable criteria that speak to the program's ability to meet the core standards. These new standards for the preparation of teachers may ultimately determine which programs survive and thrive in the years to come.

The Council for the Accreditation of Educator Preparation (CAEP; formerly the National Council for Accreditation of Teacher Education, or NCATE) fulfills the task of enforcing these standards. This group determines the efficacy of teacher preparation programs and requires that each institution provide a self-study report on its ability to produce competent, certified teachers (CAEP 2014). To maintain their status as accredited teacher preparation programs, institutions must present the results of their self-study during a CAEP site visit, which takes place every five years. The documentation contained in this report assures that each institution's licensure and certificate programs commit to a process of continuous improvement in a number of key areas. The organization charges teacher preparation programs with providing valid, empirical evidence of the strength of their course offerings, the viability of their partnerships with local area school districts, and the impact of their graduates in the field, among other areas.

Beginning in 2016, teacher preparation programs that successfully complete this process must provide evidence of each of the following (CAEP 2014):

- Standard 1: Content and Pedagogical Knowledge
    - Interns must be able to apply discipline-specific, empirically sound pedagogical practices.
- Standard 2: Clinical Partnerships and Practice
    - Interns must take part in "high-quality" clinical practice experiences.

- Standard 3: Candidate Quality, Recruitment, and Selectivity
  - Recruitment, admission, and retention of interns must be done according to a deliberately selective set of criteria.
- Standard 4: Program Impact
  - Interns who complete the certificate or licensure program will demonstrate an empirically discernable impact on PK–12 learning and development.
- Standard 5: Provider Quality, Continuous Improvement, and Capacity
  - Licensure and certificate programs are dedicated to the continuous pursuit of excellence.

CAEP standards represent an important move from the opportunities candidates have to develop professional skills toward actual demonstrations of these skills. The CAEP operationalization of quality, however, cannot necessarily capture the true positive impact of teacher training at HBCUs. The totality of the student experience, not simply a set of concrete, traditionally used metrics—for instance, GPA and graduation rates—presents the strengths of these institutions. While the quantitative measures that CAEP advocates may reflect a limited measure of programmatic quality, students who pursue teacher training at HBCUs undergo a transformative experience that contributes directly to their success in the field.

Though administrators and faculty at HBCUs support the commitment to quality espoused by CAEP, they nonetheless have several concerns about the proposed implementation of the five CAEP standards. According to B. Denise Hawkins (2013), the first of these concerns deals with the composition of the CAEP commission itself. Because the majority of individuals who comprise the group are not practitioners, there is a potential disconnect between the day-to-day needs of the field and the initiatives advanced by the commission. Additionally, the new standards will call for teacher candidates in a particular program to maintain a collective 3.0 GPA and achieve scores in the top third of all test takers on national standardized examinations like the GRE, SAT, or ACT, despite the fact that there is little to no empirical evidence of a relationship between these standards and teacher effectiveness. For teacher preparation programs at open-enrollment HBCUs (more than one-quarter of the total number of HBCUs), using metrics like retention, graduation rate, and GPA to assess program quality may be more than problematic.

This set of demographics will favor selective universities, but many HBCUs are open-enrollment institutions. As a result, HBCUs are more likely to enroll students who may have been rejected by other institutions—that is, students who may have graduated from less affluent K-12 school districts with limited resources and thus struggle academically or financially. While HBCUs have proven to be quite adept at working with students to close achievement gaps, they are often at a disadvantage when their students are compared to those at more selective colleges and universities.

Standard 5 (Provider Quality, Continuous Improvement, and Capacity) will establish harsh penalties for programs that enroll students who later default on student loans and for those who are not hired after graduating from a teacher preparation program. Although the proposed targets of this legislation, according to CAEP leadership, are for-profit teacher training programs that seek to gain financially without committing to the well-being of their students, this standard may have unintentional impacts on teacher preparation programs at HBCUs. According to Elizabeth Blume (2015) of the Postsecondary National Policy Institute, one-half of all HBCU graduates between 2000 and 2014 completed their program with more than $25,000 in debt, while only one-third of graduates from PWIs reported a similar level of debt; in fact, more than three-quarters of graduates from HBCUs left college with debt. Another factor that simultaneously influences compliance with standard 5 is job placement among HBCU graduates: in many major cities across the country (e.g., Cleveland, New York, Los Angeles, and Philadelphia) large districts have instituted hiring freezes to offset budgetary concerns. Therefore, disproportionate poverty, coupled with the difficulties of securing a teaching position in a difficult market, affects HBCU students at a higher rate. When applied indiscriminately, the Department of Education standards risk categorizing HBCUs and their graduates as inferior, especially if compared to institutions that prepare a more affluent student body.

Beyond these comparisons, the efforts by CAEP officials to create specific, measurable, outcome-based standards for teacher preparation programs may also work against the specific mission of HBCUs. Created as institutions to serve the communities of the poor and disenfranchised, HBCUs continue to serve today as vehicles of economic, social, and personal growth. It is difficult, if not impossible, to capture this impact through objective means like graduation rates and GPAs. Despite this difficulty, the proposed CAEP standards fail to consider the programmatic impact of teacher education on the community when evaluating the quality of each individual program.

This failure to consider a program's broader impact is particularly troubling for HBCUs because it deemphasizes what is perhaps the greatest strength of these institutions. Long before CAEP introduced standards for quality, HBCUs produced highly sought-after educators who proudly served urban, suburban, and rural school districts (Dilworth 2012). HBCUs provide not only remedial education to underprepared and underrepresented student populations but also opportunities to scores of students who may otherwise have lacked access to higher education (Palmer, Davis, and Gasman 2011). Perhaps even more important, HBCUs, emphasizing the personal and social development of men and women of color, contribute to the development of both high-quality teachers and high-quality, well-rounded individuals (Robinson and Albert 2008). This philosophy may not be reflected on CAEP's metrics, but it is nonetheless a core ideal of the HBCU institutional mission.

Although CAEP guides accreditation processes for programs, the teacher preparation rankings produced by National Council for Teacher Quality (NCTQ) are often more visible to the public through press releases and attention in media outlets. The NCTQ rankings illustrate another way that program evaluation frameworks can disadvantage HBCU teacher education programs by overlooking some of their key strengths. The NCTQ framework has received widespread criticism for its focus on surface inputs and simple documents associated with teacher education programs (Collins, Jenkins, and Strzelecka 2014; Darling-Hammond 2013). These criticisms are relevant to teacher education programs writ large, not only ones at MSIs. Alice Ginsberg and her colleagues (2015), however, pinpoint some ways that current evaluation frameworks, such as those of NCTQ, disproportionately and specifically affect HBCU teacher education programs; for instance, the researchers noted that out of 836 reviewed institutions, only one HBCU program ranked in the top one hundred, and only three ranked in the top two hundred.

The paper-review nature of NCTQ's approach, looking mostly at documents available online, presents a skewed perspective. NCTQ reviews course catalogue offerings, selected syllabi, readings and texts used in courses, and other documents related to programs. But this approach ignores the quality of instruction, evidence of student learning in programs, markers of teacher candidates' effectiveness as teachers, and other direct indicators related to the actual work of teaching. Ginsberg and her colleagues (2015) note that this approach adversely affects the evaluation of HBCU teacher education programs for a number of reasons. First, because many HBCUs are smaller, underresourced institutions, they frequently offer fewer courses than larger, better-resourced institutions offer. Programs with fewer course offerings still easily meet accreditation standards and produce effective teachers, yet a paper review privileges larger programs with a broader range of course offerings. Second, Ginsberg and her colleagues (2015) argue that documents like syllabi of courses in HBCU programs seldom account for the culturally relevant and justice-oriented components, many of which derive from the particular commitments of faculty members who choose to work at HBCUs.

Moreover, Ginsberg and her colleagues (2015) also give attention to how NCTQ's focus on program inputs at the cost of outputs misrepresents some strengths of HBCU teacher education programs. Output measures include a series of figures: employment placement after graduation, duration in the profession, and effectiveness in the classroom. Without a doubt, overlooking output measures like these ignores a key function of all teacher education programs, not just those of HBCUs or MSIs. Yet the researchers (Ginsberg et al. 2015)

note that output measures are particularly important for HBCU teacher education programs because of the ways these measures connect to key program
components; moreover, they find that values of freedom, activism, and community service through many HBCU programs often manifest in graduates'
decision to teach in racially diverse, high-poverty, and high-need schools. These
decisions tie into the larger trend in teacher employment research wherein
Black teachers and teachers of color are more likely than white teachers to
work and remain in hard-to-staff schools and among racially and economically
diverse student bodies (Achinstein et al. 2010). Teacher education program
evaluation frameworks, such as NCTQ, that do not consider output measures
overlook a distinct strength of HBCU programs.

A paper review and focus on program inputs also overlook how many
HBCUs anchor clinical field placements to larger values of service and equity.
Ginsberg and her colleagues (2015) note, "As HBCUs are deeply rooted in the
welfare and cultures of communities they serve, they recognize the importance
of having prospective teachers spend time in, and become intimately familiar
with these communities" (6). From this perspective, the research illuminates
the immense difference between preservice teachers sitting passively in field
placements to accumulate their required hours and preservice teachers using
field placements as a mechanism to invest in the welfare of the community
and students' lives. Program evaluation frameworks that do not account for
this quality of field placements overlook the strength of many HBCU teacher
education programs.

Despite the challenges that accreditation and evaluation frameworks pose
to teacher education programs at HBCUs, there are specific ways that programs
can remain true to their institutional missions.

## Keeping the Foundation: Service, Activism, and Social Justice

To best understand the future role of HBCUs, it is helpful to examine the principles upon which they were established and the concrete ways these principles
can manifest in their teacher education programs in the midst of contemporary
accreditation and evaluation pressures. Although they differed in their ideology
with respect to curricular decisions, W.E.B. Du Bois and Booker T. Washington
agreed that HBCUs were destined to be centers for the education of Black students who would ultimately use such training to benefit their communities.
Both intellectuals spoke quite directly to this foundational belief. Washington
(1900) spoke of "the broader education which comes from contact with the
public sentiment of the community in which one lives" (221); and Du Bois
(1903) affirmed that "[education] brought the masses of the Blacks in contact
with modern civilization, made Black men the leaders of their communities
and trainers of the new generation" (33). Contained in each man's profession

is an important ideal that guides the work of HBCUs in general and teacher preparation programs specifically: a commitment to the betterment of the community through service. This commitment derives from the larger, historical movement for Black education and liberation across churches, communities, and other social institutions (Anderson 1988; King 2005). These commitments manifest through a number of efforts across HBCUs, including preschool and tutoring programs, noncredit continuing education courses, community development initiatives, assistance for community-based organizations, health programs, and cultural activities (Jackson and Nunn 2003).

Commitment to the surrounding community at HBCUs is connected to values of social justice and activism that also ground many of these institutions. These values are often evident in the mission statements of institutions. For example, the mission statement of Cheyney University describes the role of the college as a "social equalizer, providing educational access to a population that has been marginalized by mainstream society" (Brown and Davis 2001, 33). Studying HBCU mission statements and campus leaders' perspectives, Terrell Strayhorn and Joan Hirt (2008) found an embrace of pluralism and service to the surrounding region, attention to students overcoming challenges related to systemic oppression, and confrontation of these systems in the larger world. Campus leaders and mission statements also made explicit references to race, ethnicity, age, and other identity markers and how these should not determine access to and opportunities for success in life. Many HBCU campus leaders experience justice and activism through the prism of spirituality and religion (Jean-Marie 2008). Cynthia L. Jackson and Eleanor F. Nunn (2003) concisely summarize the relationship among these values at many HBCUs for both faculty and students: "For HBCUs, activism and community service are mutually reciprocal: Black activism and service to Black communities, specifically, and to the entire community in which the HBCUs are located are part of the mission, role, and curriculum." (31).

In the midst of accreditation and evaluation pressures, there are tangible ways that HBCU teacher education programs can continue manifesting the principles of service, activism, and social justice. In fact, given their background upon these principles, HBCU teacher education programs are uniquely situated to lead the charge for the creation of a truly equitable society.

### Xavier University

Founded in 1915, Xavier University in New Orleans exists as the only higher education institution in the United States that is both Roman Catholic and an HBCU. By focusing on the conceptual framework that guides the university's Department of Education, Glenda Hembree and her colleagues (2013) discuss how commitment to service, activism, and social justice operates at Xavier University. In general, this framework extends students' university experience beyond the walls of campus and into the surrounding community in New Orleans.

The Department of Education at Xavier University considers spirituality first among the foundational principles of the conceptual framework that guides programs. Spirituality is defined as "each individual's ability to form meaningful relationships, explore personal values, and find meaning in the world" (Hembree et al. 2013, 25). In support of the emphasis on spirituality, faculty members challenge preservice teachers to develop and maintain key relationships to support the local community. The students complete a number of activities including tutoring, service learning, and other civic responsibilities in an effort to connect with others, strengthen the partnership schools, and invest in the surrounding neighborhoods. The introductory teacher education class requires all preservice teachers to create tangible teaching materials and leave these with their cooperating teachers after they complete the field experiences. These materials have included learning games for students, multicultural book lists, laminated products for classroom walls, and books. Framed as service learning, this requirement means that preservice teachers are not simply completing field internship requirements from the partner schools. Fulfilling these hours also means contributing to the school in some tangible way.

Hembree and her colleagues (2013) also describe how graduate education leadership students design and execute service-learning projects based upon the specific needs of schools. These projects have included "after-school tutoring for students, adult tutoring, landscaping to refurbish a school's exterior, and fundraising for an international humanitarian effort" (27). Because divisions between departments do not always correspond with community needs on the ground, counseling and education leadership students also collaborate on service-learning projects to understand community needs and then build school-based programs to address those needs. As a whole, the conceptual framework within the education programs at Xavier University direct students into service for the surrounding New Orleans community.

### *Savannah State University*

Savannah State University lost its teacher education program in 1979, owing not to underenrollment or underperformance but to the state of Georgia's desegregation plan for higher education. Desegregation plans such as these addressed possible program duplications among historically Black and white institutions in the same regions such as Nashville, Tennessee, Norfolk, Virginia, and Savannah (see Godard 1980). Possible solutions often included merging institutions, making one institution into a community college and the other a four-year college, or housing programs at separate institutions. As part of this plan in 1979, the state decided that it would house teacher education at nearby Armstrong State University (Armstrong State College at the time) and business administration at Savannah State University (Savannah State College at the time). Students at each institution could enroll in these programs through a joint agreement.

This background makes the reemergence of teacher education at Savannah State University notable and instructive to other HBCUs. Around 2010, Savannah State began planning to reestablish its teacher education program through a new School of Teacher Education working jointly with its College of Sciences and Technology. In order not to duplicate program offerings at nearby Armstrong State, an important part of this planning process included meeting with local and regional school systems to understand their needs. If needs existed in regional schools, then the university could make a case to the state of Georgia that a new program at Savannah State would not duplicate programs at other surrounding institutions but instead fill an important local and regional need. This planning process identified the need for teachers in STEM areas, particularly the need for teachers of color in these subject areas. Approved by the Georgia Professional Standards Commission in 2013, the program offers students majoring in biology, mathematics, civil engineering technology, and electronic engineering technology the option of taking courses to fulfill secondary education licensure requirements in a STEM field coordinated with their major (Savannah State University 2014).

Reestablishing a teacher education program at Savannah State cuts directly against the trend of teacher education programs at HBCUs, where they are often becoming endangered by pressures of accreditation and questions of relevance. The planning process notably centered on identifying needs in the surrounding community and using that as the leverage for program justification to larger bodies of approval at both the institution and the state levels. In addition, the range of certification options is narrow compared to those in many other teacher education programs at HBCUs and other institutions. This narrow range of options allows the program to build outward from its core strengths. This approach to program reestablishment can be instructive for HBCUs that do not in 2016 have teacher education programs but are exploring the possibility, and this approach can also be instructive for HBCUs with longstanding teacher education programs that are no longer robust across many different content areas, given their low enrollment. In these instances, scaling down the program to focus on a more narrow body of strengths can help sustain the program over a longer period of time.

### Coppin State University

HBCUs in Baltimore, such as Morgan State and Coppin State, have a lineage of protest and activism tied to civil rights (Walker 2015). This foundation is relevant not only to political actions but also to PK–16 initiatives. At Coppin State University, faculty and administrators in the School of Education launched the

Coppin Urban Education Corridor in 2003, an initiative that seeks to extend both the impact of the university to the Baltimore inner-city schools and the university's responsibility to the larger community it serves. A partnership between Coppin State and Baltimore City Schools started in 1998 when Coppin State took over management of the Rosemont Elementary/Middle School, ranked "the second-poorest-performing school in the state of Maryland" (Arrington 2006, 28). By 2016, following a dramatic turnaround, Rosemont is ranked among the top 10 percent of elementary schools in Baltimore (Urban Education Corridor 2015).

This transition was no small feat; in fact, only a careful partnership with the school and community accomplished this change. The School of Education worked with the staff of Rosemont to understand their needs, and the two instituted a professional development plan (Arrington 2006). The teachers had access to tuition-free courses at Coppin State in areas where they felt they needed development—for either personal development or content assistance with any licensure exams. The students at Rosemont benefited because the partnership created additional academic support programs as well as Saturday and summer enrichment programs. To make campus welcoming and its resources accessible, Rosemont students were able to attend any sporting or cultural events on campus for free; likewise, parents were able to take any GED or parenting classes tuition-free. Coppin State faculty and students staffed the programs as mentors and tutors.

The Rosemont and Coppin State partnership demonstrates the tenets of service, activism, and social justice wherein the communities support each other in various ways, while also deepening the experiences of the preservice teachers in the teacher education program. Although Rosemont was only one component, this partnership started the larger development of the Corridor into twelve programs. In 2005, the city established Coppin Academy, a Baltimore City public high school that is housed on Coppin's campus (Arrington 2006). The school is open to any resident of Baltimore City through a lottery draw. Rosemont and Coppin Academy provided the catalyst for instituting the other parts of the twelve programs: mentoring initiative, SAT Camp Project, urban education teacher training, parental involvement, Saturday academy for thinking, partnerships, enrichment program, rigorous academic instruction, health services, and evaluation (Urban Education Corridor 2015).

### Delaware State University

Delaware State University is one of the few HBCUs to be listed on NCTQs top one hundred schools for teacher education. The university is situated in Dover, Delaware, the second-largest city in the state. Delaware State provides service to the community, while also supporting its preservice teachers through its early childhood laboratory school. Laboratory schools are often connected to schools of education at large research-based institutions. It is quite common for well-resourced universities to have a laboratory school, but this arrangement is uncommon at HBCUs because they typically have fewer resources.

Moreover, laboratory schools tend to exclusively service families of faculty members at the institution, often limiting the availability to community members. But Delaware State's approach to their laboratory school is built around serving the community, an idea articulated in its mission and purpose: the early childhood laboratory school must "provide resources to parents and community members in child development and strategies for meeting the needs of special populations, including dual language learners" (Early Childhood Laboratory School 2015, 2). School tuition, adjusted based on family income between the months of September and June, makes it a much more affordable option for childcare for people in the community.

The education department based the curriculum of the laboratory school on nine essential areas in child development: art and writing, music and movement, building blocks, computer literacy, science and sensory, math and manipulatives, literacy and language, outdoor play, and dramatic play (Early Childhood Laboratory School 2015). Learning centers for each of the nine areas ground most of the instruction and student exploration. In addition, themed lesson plans purposefully incorporate the academic, physical, and social/emotional aspects to assist in the students' development on a daily basis.

The laboratory school, also an intricate part of preservice teacher development, provides a space for preservice teachers to learn while supporting the development of local children. The laboratory school specifically "aim[s] to lead through excellence and innovation as we train undergraduate and graduate students in child development theory, research and its applications, while implementing national and state standards for quality toddler, preschool, and kindergarten programs" (Early Childhood Laboratory School 2015, 2).

## Conclusion

The programs outlined in chapter 9 are especially important, given the current political climate. In the face of the growing economic disparity between the affluent and the impoverished in this country, hostile relations between law enforcement and communities of color, and a general distrust of political elites, HBCU students now more than ever are concerned with fulfilling their role as leaders in their communities. To this end, both internal and external adjustments to the teacher preparation programs at HBCUs can and should ensure their continuing relevance—particularly with respect to preparing educators who will address the key pedagogical, economic, and social issues that we face in the early twenty-first century.

First, there must be a deliberate effort to tie theoretical models of social justice to practice throughout the coursework sequence. Specifically, schools must initiate and evaluate internship experiences based upon the opportunities they present for students to exercise service, activism, and social justice. While HBCUs (like all teacher training programs at present) are limited by the measurable outcomes that must be in place to assure accountability to standards of accreditation, there is ample room for diversity in the types of experiences we create for students, especially by establishing partnerships with community-based organizations in addition to existing relationships with PK–12 schools. These partnerships provide ample opportunities to put theoretical models of social justice into action as students fulfill their pedagogical obligations and develop mutually beneficial relationships within the communities they serve. Ultimately, this will establish HBCUs as institutions at the forefront of serving traditionally undersupported populations.

Second, HBCUs must do a better job of publicizing their work to the larger academic community. For many years, successful social justice-influenced initiatives like those at Xavier University, Morgan State, Coppin State, and other HBCUs were well-kept secrets; while students and faculty at each college speak in superlative terms, few people outside each campus were aware of the work being done. Marybeth Gasman and Heather Collins (2014) speak to the need among HBCUs for a collaborative effort, extending to create a dissemination network, with respect to introducing their particular concerns to the federal government. Such a system of communication will assure that both policymakers and the general public are aware of the important work at these colleges and universities and their place at the forefront of teacher education.

While the realities of the teacher education reform movement may be inescapable for our nation's teacher preparation programs, there is reason for optimism among those who champion HBCUs. Time and again, exemplary institutions have demonstrated that a commitment to a mission based on principles of social justice, collaborative engagement, and community involvement need not preclude a strong program of teacher preparation. It is comforting to know that the HBCUs need not abandon this perspective to meet the demands of CAEP or any other accrediting body. Although this chapter highlights but a fraction of the work being done by HBCUs across the country, these examples evidence the continuing relevance of these institutions as well as their effectiveness in producing highly qualified teachers and well-rounded citizens.

### REFERENCES

Achinstein, Betty, Rodney T. Ogawa, Dena Sexton, and Casia Freitas. 2010. "Retaining Teachers of Color: A Pressing Problem and a Potential Strategy for 'Hard-to-Staff' Schools." *Review of Educational Research* 80: 71–107.

Allen, Walter R., and Joseph O. Jewel. 2002. "A Backward Glance Forward: Past, Present, and Future Perspectives on Historically Black Colleges and Universities." *Review of Higher Education* 25: 241–261.

American Council on Education. 2014. *Postsecondary Institution Rating System RFI.* http://www.acenet.edu/news-room/Documents/Higher-Ed-Assoc-PIRS-Comments.pdf.

Anderson, James. 1988. *The Education of Blacks in the South, 1860–1930.* Chapel Hill: University of North Carolina Press.

Arrington, Pamala. 2006. "Advancing an Urban Mission: The West Baltimore Pre-K to 16 Urban Education Corridor." *Journal of Higher Education Outreach and Management* 11: 23–39.

Blume, Elizabeth. 2015. "Focused on What Matters: Assessment of Student Learning Outcomes at Minority-Serving Institutions." *Postsecondary National Policy Institute.* https://www.newamerica.org/postsecondary-national-policy-institute/focused-on-what-matters-assessment-of-student-learning-outcomes-at-minority-serving-institutions/.

Brown, M. Christopher, and James E. Davis. 2001. "The Historically Black College as Social Contract, Social Capital, and Social Equalizer." *Peabody Journal of Education* 76: 31–49.

Collins, Heather, Shawn M. Jenkins, and Nika Strzelecka. 2014. "Ranking and Rewarding Access: An Alternative College Scorecard." *Penn Center for Minority-Serving Institutions.* http://www.gse.upenn.edu/pdf/cmsi/alternative_college_scorecard.pdf.

Council for the Accreditation of Educator Preparation. 2014. *CAEP Accreditation Standards and Evidence: Aspirations for Educator Preparation.* Washington, DC: CAEP Board of Directors.

Darling-Hammond, Linda. 2013. "Why the NCTQ Teacher Prep Ratings Are Nonsense." Palo Alto, CA: Stanford Center for Opportunity Policy in Education.

Dilworth, Mary. 2012. "Historically Black Colleges and Universities in Teacher Education Reform." *Journal of Negro Education* 81: 121–135.

Du Bois, W.E.B. 1903. "The Talented Tenth." In *The Negro Problem: A Series of Articles by Representative American Negroes of Today*, edited by Booker T. Washington, 31–76. New York: J. Pott.

Early Childhood Laboratory School. 2015. *Handbook.* Delaware State University. http://www.desu.edu/sites/default/files/u102/DSU_Labschool_Handbook13_0.pdf.

Fleming, Jacqueline. 2001. "The Impact of a Historically Black College on African American Students: The Case of LeMoyne-Owen College." *Urban Education* 36: 597–610.

Gasman, Marybeth. 2013. "The Changing Face of Historically Black Colleges and Universities." *Penn Center for Minority-Serving Institutions.* http://www.gse.upenn.edu/pdf/cmsi/Changing_Face_HBCUs.pdf.

Gasman, Marybeth, and Heather Collins. 2014. "The Historically Black College and University Community and the Obama Administration: A Lesson in Communications." *Change: The Magazine of Higher Learning* 5: 39–43.

Gasman, Marybeth, Andrés Castro Samayoa, and Felicia Commodore. 2015. "Black Colleges Matter: And We Have the Data to Prove it." *Newsweek,* August 27. http://www.newsweek.com/black-colleges-matter-and-we-have-data-prove-it-366306.

Ginsberg, Alice, Marybeth Gasman, Andrés Castro Samoya, and Francisco Ramos. 2015. "Re-assessing Teacher Education Quality: What NCTQ Isn't Telling Us about the Impact and Value of HBCUs." *Teachers College Record.* http://www.tcrecord.org ID Number: 18097.

Godard, James M. 1980. "Black and White Campuses in Urban Areas: Merger or Joint Planning?" Atlanta, GA: Southern Regional Education Board. http://files.eric.ed.gov/fulltext/ED197686.pdf.

Harper, Brian. 2007. "African American Access to Higher Education: The Evolving Role of Historically Black Colleges and Universities." *American Academic* 3: 109–128.

Harper, Shaun R. 2009. "Niggers No More: A Critical Race Counternarrative on Black Male Student Achievement at Predominantly White Colleges and Universities." *International Journal of Qualitative Studies in Education* 22: 697–712.

Hawkins, B. Denise. 2013. "Teaching Failure?" *Diverse Issues in Higher Education* 30: 14.

Hembree, Glenda, Alicia Costa, Timothy Glaude, Renee Akbar, and Rosalind P. Hale. 2013. "A Model That Works: An HBCU Preparing Teachers to Educate Diverse Students." *Journal of Intercultural Disciplines* 13: 23–48.

Irvine, Jacqueline Joyner, and Leslie T. Fenwick. 2011. "Teachers and Teaching for the New Millennium: The Role of HBCUs." *Journal of Negro Education* 80: 197–213.

Jackson, Cynthia L., and Eleanor F. Nunn. 2003. *Historically Black Colleges and Universities: A Reference Handbook.* Santa Barbara, CA: ABC-CLEO.

Jean-Marie, Gaetane. 2008. "Social Justice, Visionary, and Career Project: The Discourses of Black Women Leaders at Black Colleges." In *Historically Black Colleges and Universities: Triumphs, Troubles, and Taboos*, edited by Marybeth Gasman and Christopher L. Tudico, 53–74. New York: Palgrave Macmillan.

King, Joyce E., ed. 2005. *Black Education: A Transformative Research and Action Agenda for the New Century.* New York: Routledge.

McGee, Ebony, and Danny Martin. 2011. "'You Would Not Believe What I Have to Go Through to Prove My Intellectual Value!': Stereotype Management among Academically Successful Black Mathematics and Engineering Students." *American Educational Research Journal* 48: 1347–1389.

Nazaryan, Alexander. 2015. "Black Colleges Matter." *Newsweek*, August 18. http://www. newsweek.com/black-colleges-matter-363667.http://www.newsweek.com/black-colleges-matter-363667http://www.newsweek.com/black-colleges-matter-363667.

Palmer, Robert, Ryan Davis, and Marybeth Gasman. 2011. "A Matter of Diversity, Equity, and Necessity: The Tension between Maryland's Higher Education System and Its Historically Black Colleges and Universities over the Office of Civil Rights Agreement." *Journal of Negro Education* 80: 121–133.

Perry, Andre M. and Ivory Toldson. 2014. "Black Colleges are the Biggest Victims of States' Invasive New Funding Rules." *The Washington Post*, December 16. https://www .washingtonpost.com/posteverything/wp/2014/12/16/black-colleges-are-the-biggest-victims-of-states-invasive-new-funding-rules/.

Riley, Jason. 2010. "Black Colleges Need a New Mission." *Wall Street Journal*, September 28. http://www.wsj.com/articles/SB10001424052748704654004575517822124077834.

Robinson, Brooks, and Angela Albert. 2008. "HBCUs Institutional Advantage: Returns to Teacher Education." In *Understanding Minority-Serving Institutions*, edited by Marybeth Gasman, Benjamin Baez, and Caroline Sotello Viernes Turner, 183–202. Albany: State University of New York Press.

Roebuck, Julia, and Komanduri Murty. 1993. *Historically Black Colleges and Universities: Their Place in American Higher Education.* Westport, CT: Praeger.

Savannah State University. 2014. *Annual Report 2013–2014.* http://www.savannahstate.edu/ presidents-office/docs/Savannah-State-University-Annual-Report-2013_2014.pdf.

Strayhorn, Terrell, and Joan Hirt. 2008. "Social Justice at Historically Black and Hispanic-Serving Institutions: Mission Statements and Administrative Voices." In *Understanding Minority-Serving Institutions*, edited by Marybeth Gasman, Benjamin Baez, and Caroline Sotello Viernes Turner, 203–216. Albany: State University of New York Press.

Urban Education Corridor. 2015. Coppin State University. http://legacy.coppin.edu/leader/ Urban_Education_Corridor_Brochure.PDF.

Walker, Larry. 2015. "Social Justice and HBCUs: The Fight for Equality in Baltimore." *Diverse Issues in Higher Education*, May 3. http://diverseeducation.com/article/72318/.

Washington, Booker T. 1900. "Education Will Solve the Race Problem: A Reply." *North American Review* 171: 221–232.

# Conclusion

## Teacher Education beyond Minority-Serving Institutions

### EMERY PETCHAUER
### LYNNETTE MAWHINNEY

This volume presents chapters that speak to and reveal the important and varied teacher education work happening at Minority-Serving Institutions (MSIs). Some authors wrote of work happening *at* particular institutions. In doing so, they gave attention to the holistic perspective on preservice teacher development that MSIs often take. In some instances, this looks like anticipating the barriers—both professional and personal—their preservice teachers may experience so that the institutions may either establish supports before a crisis or develop them quickly when needs arise. Other authors attended to the ways that MSI teacher education programs grow deep roots in surrounding regions to develop teachers and serve the needs of the community through justice-oriented frameworks. As teacher education changes into the 2020s, it will be important for programs at all institution types to make convincing cases for their relevance and importance to surrounding communities. There is much more to learn from MSIs about how teacher education programs do this well.

Other authors in this volume presented work relevant *across* a particular strand of institutions, such as Historically Black Colleges and Universities or Tribal Colleges and Universities, with particular attention to the contemporary challenges teacher education faces at these institutions. As we noted in the introduction to this volume, Hispanic-Serving Institutions (HSIs) and Asian American and Native American Pacific Islander–Serving Institutions (AANAPISIs) are more recent classifications for institutions (particularly in the West and the Southwest) that are becoming more diverse along the lines of ethnicity, language, and documentation status. In the near future, there is much room to understand what teacher education can look like at these changing institutions and, for example, how they can become rich resources to develop the bilingual teachers the United States desperately needs.

Accomplishing this goal entails faculty members undergoing a conceptual shift in how they understand their institutions and their work at them. For example, because of the newness of these classifications, some faculty members at HSI and AANAPISIs are (understandably) not even aware that their institutions hold such a classification. We encountered this when talking to some colleagues at HSIs and AANAPISIs while assembling this volume. The significant contributions that HSIs and AANAPISIs can make to help shift teacher education over the next decades depend, in large part, on faculty members changing the ways they conceptualize their work. As service, activism, and justice have been threads woven through HBCU teacher education since their inception, cultural plurality, language rights, and pathways to the profession for undocumented students might become threads woven through teacher education programs at HSI and AANAPISIs in the future.

Also in this volume, some authors pushed toward understanding teacher education *among* MSIs as an entire institutional unit. Chapter 6 provided a clear example of this through the University of Illinois, Chicago (UIC), Monarch Center's initiative to improve special education programs among MSIs. What makes this work among MSIs particularly important is its provision of an alternative framework outside the Carnegie Classification system to build links among institutions and create access to resources. Working from a Research I Carnegie classification institution, scholars at UIC created a training center to support other MSIs who do not have access to such resources or grant opportunities. This perspective leads faculty members and administrators at MSIs to look not horizontally at other institutions of similar enrollment, endowment, and other empirical measures for meaningful partnerships. Instead, faculty members and administrators should look vertically—"up" and "down" the Carnegie classifications—toward other MSIs that might not neatly fit into the same preexisting classifications but nonetheless can jointly enrich teacher development. This perspective fits within the "lift as we climb" ethos present on campus at many HBCUs.

These three scales—*at, across*, and *among*—provide a useful framework to consider MSI teacher education research and practice. We also believe, however, that good reasons exist to consider teacher education *beyond* MSIs. Here we do not mean MSIs should lose their institutional identities as HBCUs, HSI, and the like in order to assimilate into the larger universe of higher education; instead, we mean that thinking beyond MSIs is considering the vital connections that can be built between teacher education programs at MSIs and Predominately White Institutions (PWIs), while still preserving the unique identity, history, and mission of MSIs.

We noted in the introduction to this volume that we began our careers as teacher educators in the same department at Lincoln University, an HBCU. Our career trajectories took us to the PWIs where we currently work, but for one year Lynnette worked at a PWI (The College of New Jersey) and Emery remained at Lincoln. This provided us with a short opportunity to explore the kind of teacher education partnership across MSIs and PWIs that we are recommending in this conclusion.

We took advantage of one opportunity through the Philadelphia Urban Seminar, a two-week immersion field internship for preservice teachers in the Pennsylvania and New Jersey region. Around fifteen institutions typically participate in the Urban Seminar, and preservice teachers experience the program with classmates from their institution. Our approach, however, was to run the classes from our separate institution as one. This meant that we co-taught our class sessions and fieldwork-debrief sessions. In doing so, we broke down any existing divisions between the institutions and the group of Black preservice teachers from Lincoln and the white preservice teachers from TCNJ. We also joined the nonacademic parts of the program, such as trips to the grocery store with students or sightseeing in Philadelphia and other functions over the weekend of the program. As an immersion program, preservice teachers from both institutions also stayed in the same housing unit. Most important, we organized preservice teachers into pairs for a series of crossinstitution and, consequently, crossrace dialogues and reflections. We created a conversational framework to help them reflect upon their ideas about urban education, motivations to become teachers, and the personal-professional implications of what was happening in their field experiences during the program. The conversations took place during mealtimes and lasted about thirty minutes. We approached this partnership guided by a belief that interpersonal interactions across differences often initiate conceptual shifts in the ways people understand equity and injustice related to race.

Over the course of the program, we saw evidence of shifts in our students' thinking that are often more difficult to orchestrate in traditional, racially segregated or predominantly white teacher education programs. During one weekend of the program, we held a cookout for our students at Lynnette's house in Philadelphia and invited some of the previous Urban Seminar students from Lincoln. Inviting past and current Urban Seminar participants was in line with the holistic, family approach to student development of HBCUs. In the midst of eating potato salad and barbecue chicken, we took some time for the group to discuss their experiences in the Urban Seminar so far with the alumni. One of the African American Lincoln alumni discussed a moment in the Urban Seminar the previous year when a Philadelphia school district teacher—perhaps not realizing that some people in the room (including Lynnette and the student) indeed lived in north Philadelphia—called that area of the city a "dirty place" and advised not living there. Upon hearing this story, two of the TCNJ students started asking honest questions of the Lincoln alumni about how to teach across racial differences in the city and what kinds of issues they, as white teachers, should be mindful of. Rather than assuming that the desire to teach in an urban area equated with knowing how, they acknowledged their position and sought direction.

Also notable to us in this conversation was the diversity of perspectives offered by the fifteen or so African American teachers and preservice teachers in the room. In other words, the conversation was not one of white preservice teachers tokenizing a single Black classmate or overgeneralizing the perspective and experience of a single Black classmate to be representative of Black experiences. The complexity and richness of experience was made evident by the balance between Black and white preservice teachers in the room. These interactions also gave the African American preservice teachers opportunities to speak authoritatively about their own experiences, rather than have those experiences approximated to white preservice teachers through multicultural teacher education reading and curricula.

These interactions between our students also started giving white preservice teachers an experiential framework to challenge other white preservice teachers about racism. This became evident during a diversity and antibias professional workshop toward the end of the Urban Seminar. Four of the TCNJ preservice teachers were sitting at a table with a group of other white preservice teachers from another institution. During a small group discussion, the TCNJ preservice teachers mentioned the Lincoln-TCNJ partnership and some of the lessons it was teaching them about diversity in public school classrooms. The white preservice teachers from another institution explained that this was not a valid connection because Lincoln preservice teachers were "not *really* Black but white on the inside" because "they talk like us." The TCNJ preservice teachers challenged these racist and white supremacist claims of their white peers by citing that some of the Lincoln students grew up in the very same neighborhoods as the students in the schools. In fact, some Lincoln students had given the TCNJ students tours of their home neighborhoods and the larger city that very week. Prior to the MSI-PWI partnerships that week, we are not sure the TCNJ group would have had this kind of experiential framework to challenge the assumptions of other white peers in these ways.

In sharing these instances, we are careful not to oversimplify or romanticize the kind of work that can happen through teacher education partnerships beyond MSIs. Without a doubt, our longstanding professional relationship from having been colleagues in the same HBCU department enabled us to plan and facilitate these learning experiences for our preservice teachers. Haphazardly combining courses across two institutions would not enrich these programs; raising racial consciousness is a messy, recursive process. Effective components of teacher education programs, however, happen through intentional, long-term planning. Effective partnerships between MSIs and PWIs can also happen through such planning. Institutions in the same regions have a natural opportunity for partnerships, particularly because they often place preservice teachers in the same school districts for field experiences and internships. These kinds of partnerships also fit within the growing study away experience (opposed to study abroad) in higher education where students study for a semester or a year at a different institution in the country. Teacher education programs can work within these initiatives that are growing in popularity to give their preservice teachers experiences at MSIs.

Although our collaboration worked across Black and white racial lines due to our student populations, teacher education partnerships between MSIs and PWIs can also work across a much broader set of variables. The chapters in this volume speak to many of these: language and language variation, socioeconomic class, heritage and culture, and place and relationship to land. Partnerships with HBCUs, TCUs, AANAPISIs, and HSIs, or studying at these institutions through study away programs, all have the capacity to enrich the education of preservice teachers by making these dimension of the human experience more salient aspects of their professional preparation.

# NOTES ON CONTRIBUTORS

**MARY BAY** is associate professor emeritus at the University of Illinois at Chicago. As the associate director of the Monarch Center, she was responsible for the program improvement strand. During her years as a faculty member, Dr. Bay was both an associate dean for student affairs and clinical experiences and the director of the Council on Teacher Education, where she oversaw the university's twenty-two certification programs. She is widely published in teacher education journals.

**JONATHAN BRINKERHOFF** spent eighteen years in public education teaching grades two through six, serving as a science education specialist within his own district—the San Luis Obispo County Schools Office and State Department of Education—and conducting teacher effectiveness trainings based on Madeline Hunter's models. He worked with student teachers for ten years and flirted with administration before receiving a PhD from Arizona State University and working fourteen years at the University of New Mexico.

**SANDRA BROWNING** taught mathematics in elementary school through high school for forty-four years. She also supervised mathematics and science teachers of grades prekindergarten through 12. Dr. Browning has a PhD in mathematics education and currently teaches mathematics methods, curriculum design, and classroom environment at the University of Houston–Clear Lake. Dr. Browning also supervises undergraduate interns and coordinates graduate interns.

**MAE S. CHAPLIN** is assistant professor for the College of Education at Sacramento State University. Dr. Chaplin teaches courses in the areas of literacy, language acquisition, social studies methods, and multicultural education, including a multicultural children's and young adult literature course at the undergraduate level as well as methods courses for the Multiple Subjects Teaching Credential Program. Dr. Chaplin, a former middle school teacher and literacy coach, is interested in the research and implementation of teaching methods designed to make the educational experience more equitable for English learners. Dr. Chaplin has presented her work related to educational equity and teacher preparation at national conferences, including the National

Association for Multicultural Education and the National Association for Bilingual Education. Her current work focuses on the use of transformative teaching methods to recruit, prepare, and retain educators from diverse backgrounds for careers in California's public schools.

**ANNETTE M. DAOUD** is professor in the School of Education at California State University, San Marcos, where she teaches courses in the areas of multicultural/multilingual education. Her class in the Single Subject (secondary) Credential Program, Secondary Multilingual Education, focuses on teaching credential candidates how to teach content and English-language development to their middle and high school English learners. She also teaches multicultural education courses at the undergraduate and master's degree levels. Dr. Daoud is the author of *Middle and High School English Learners and the Common Core: Equitable Instruction in Content Area Classrooms* (2015). Her research agenda includes improving the educational experiences of secondary English learners as well as issues of social justice and educational equity in teacher education. She is the principal investigator on a grant, Leading and Learning: Supporting English Learners with Effective Teacher Preparation and Professional Development, funded by the US Department of Education's Office of English Language Acquisition.

**LAURA M. GELLERT** is assistant professor of Mathematics Education/ Childhood Education at City College (CUNY). She has twenty years' experience teaching mathematics at all levels. She holds a master's degree in mathematics from the Courant Institute at New York University and a PhD in urban education from the CUNY Graduate Center. Dr. Gellert works extensively in mathematics teacher education. Her research has included in-service teacher mentorship, inclusive education with mathematics education, and STEM education.

**BRIAN HARPER** is associate professor in the department of Curriculum and Foundations at Cleveland State University. A former classroom teacher in the Philadelphia public school district and graduate of Cheyney University, Dr. Harper completed his doctoral work in educational psychology at The Ohio State University. His research interests include African American racial identity development and motivational psychology, particularly as it applies to students in urban settings. His current work focuses on African American students, counterfactual reasoning, and the factors that promote or inhibit academic self-regulation.

**JONI S. KOLMAN** is assistant professor of teacher education at California State University, San Marcos. Her research is situated at the intersection of urban teacher education, K–12 inclusive classroom practice, and education policy. Her work surfaces the ways in which school-level factors, in conversation with current education policies, contribute to the teaching, learning, and entry opportunities available to teachers and teacher candidates. Dr. Kolman's teaching focuses on inclusive education, learning in clinical experiences, and elementary teaching.

**CARMELITA LAMB**, a native Texan, was born in Austin and raised in San Antonio. She is of mixed blood—Hispanic and an enrolled member of the Lipan Band of Apache tribe of south Texas. She received her PhD in institutional analysis/occupational adult education in 2009. The title of her dissertation was "Cohort Model Learning Communities: The Tribal College Perspective of Best Practices in Teacher Education." Dr. Lamb is the department chair for Graduate Studies and Distance Education at the University of Mary, Bismarck, ND. She also serves in multiple educational capacities: Regional Advisory Committee under the direction of US Secretary of Education Arne Duncan, content expert for NCATE, proposal reviewer for SACNAS, testing developer/supervisor for Praxis examinations, and curriculum designer for Honoring Tribal Legacies (National Park Service, Lewis and Clark Trail) under the direction of Dr. Stephanie Wood, Oregon State University. Dr. Lamb is widowed and has three children: Dr. Lauren Dean Lamb, DVM; Felicia Marie Lamb, BS, MS, secondary science instructor; and Bianca Irene Lamb, first-year pediatrics resident at the Mayo Clinic in Rochester, MN.

**DANIELLE LANSING** (Navajo) is a faculty member in early childhood education at Southwestern Indian Polytechnic Institute (SIPI), a national tribal community college located in Albuquerque, NM. Dr. Lansing has served as an early childhood educator for fifteen years. She has spent the majority of her career teaching in Bureau of Indian Education and tribal contract schools in New Mexico and Arizona with various tribes such as the Navajo Nation, Salt River Pima Maricopa Indian Community, and the Pueblo of T'siya. She is currently the project director and principal investigator for the Wakanyeja "Sacred Little Ones" grant for SIPI. In this capacity, she has developed research initiatives that seek to create innovative practices in SIPI's ECE program and within the local community. Her research interests include qualitative research methodologies, such as phenomenological studies and Indigenous research methodologies. She is also greatly committed to contributing the Tribal College and University perspective within teacher education discourse.

**NORMA A. LOPEZ-REYNA** is associate professor of special education and director of the University of Illinois at Chicago's Educational Assessment Clinic. Her expertise is in bilingual special education, parental roles in understanding and teaching their children with disabilities, and teachers' decision making through the use of formative assessment. Dr. Lopez-Reyna has extensive experience directing not only research and personnel preparation grants but also the Monarch Center, the national technical assistance center for minority-serving institutions.

**LYNNETTE MAWHINNEY** is associate professor and coordinator of urban education at The College of New Jersey where her work focuses on the professional lives of aspiring and current urban teachers and urban schooling. She began her English teaching career at an American Indian boarding school in South Dakota that serviced fifteen reservations in three states and spent most of her career teaching in a Philadelphia high school. Dr. Mawhinney spent the first three years of her academic career in the teacher education department at Lincoln University (PA), the first degree-granting historically Black university in the United States. Her work has appeared in the *International Journal of Qualitative Studies in Education, Teaching and Teacher Education, The Negro Educational Review*, and other venues. She is the author of *We Got Next: Urban Education and the Next Generation of Black Teachers* (Peter Lang, 2014).

**DENISE L. MCLURKIN** is assistant professor and the undergraduate coordinator for the childhood education program at the City College of New York. Dr. McLurkin earned a master's degree in literacy education and a doctorate in the literacy, languages and cultures program at the University of Michigan, Ann Arbor. Her research focuses on improving literacy methods courses for preservice teachers and examining the lives of adult literacy learners. She currently teaches literacy methods courses and student teaching seminars, supervises student teachers, advises undergraduate candidates, and conducts workshops focused on New York State teaching certification exams for undergraduate and graduate candidates.

**EMERY PETCHAUER** is associate professor in the departments of English and Teacher Education at Michigan State University, where he also serves as coordinator of the English education program. He began his career teaching English at a majority Mexican high school near the US-Mexico border and spent the first six years of his academic career in the teacher education department at Lincoln University (PA), the first degree-granting historically Black university in the United States. Dr. Petchauer's scholarship has appeared in *Teachers College Record*; *Review of Educational Research*; the *Journal of Negro Education*; and other venues. His previous book projects include *Hip-Hop Culture in College Students' Lives* (2012) and *Schooling Hip-Hop: Expanding Hip-Hop-Based Education across the Curriculum* (2013).

**DEWITT SCOTT** is a doctoral candidate in educational leadership at Chicago State University and student success specialist at Moraine Valley Community College in Palos Hills, IL. His research focuses on critically examining the experiences of Black males in higher education administration and exploring alternative leadership strategies for Historically Black Colleges and Universities. In addition to being a community college administrator and doctoral candidate, Scott is a writer for *InsideHigherEd* and a communications instructor at Saint Leonard's Adult High School for formerly incarcerated adults on Chicago's west side. Scott is a member of a number of service organizations such as Chicago Books to Women in Prison, Liberation Library, and Black and Pink Chicago, an organization advocating for the elimination of violence and oppression of LGBTQ prisoners. He lives in Chicago with his wife, Cecelia.

**BYUNG-IN SEO** is associate professor in the doctoral studies department at Chicago State University. Before becoming a professor, she spent fifteen years teaching English and math to adolescents (grades 6 through 12) at Lasallian schools. Her research focuses on adolescent content area literacy, with a goal of bridging the learning divide between English and math. As a professor, she has taught a wide variety of courses from freshman-level educational foundations to doctoral-level statistics and curricular theory. In addition to being a professor, Dr. Seo facilitates reading/writing and math clubs and provides complementary ACT/SAT preparation classes to economically deprived students.

**CHERYL A. FRANKLIN TORREZ** is associate professor in the department of Teacher Education, Educational Leadership, and Policy at the University of New Mexico. Dr. Torrez has worked with and within PK–12/university settings for more than two decades. Her research interests and scholarship include clinical preparation, social studies education, and teacher education across the professional life span. She has received grants that focus on PK–12/university collaborations from the US Department of Education, the W. K. Kellogg Foundation, and other funders.

**ROSANNE WARD** is a research associate at the University of Illinois at Chicago. She is also an adjunct assistant professor for the special education department and regularly teaches courses in the characteristics of and methods for teaching students with exceptionalities. Dr. Ward, an award-winning teacher, taught students with special needs for thirty-five years in the public schools of Indiana, Colorado, and Illinois and collaborates extensively with general educators.

**IRENE WELCH** is a faculty member in the department of Teacher Education, Educational Leadership, and Policy at the University of New Mexico. She teaches literacy courses and has served as embedded faculty as part of the CTCS model. Dr. Welch received her PhD in language and literacy education from Georgia State University. Her teaching and research focus on issues related to teacher preparation, co-teaching, language and literacy development, bilingual education, and ESL.

# INDEX

Urban Seminar. *See* Philadelphia Urban
  Seminar
US Congress, III
US Department of Agriculture, 145
US Department of Education, III, 151–152,
  163, 166
US Department of Indian Education, 152
US-México border, 6
Ute Nations, 37

Wakanyeja. *See* Sacred Little Ones
whites, 51, 92, 137; American, 67;
  candidates, 136; female participant, 136;
  fragility, 134; male, 136; male participant,
  136; male preservice teacher, 136; male
teachers, 137; normative English, 134, 140;
  peers, 180; perspective, 27; preservice
  teachers, 135–139, 179–180; racial lines,
  181; schools, 6; students, 16, 17, 67, 130,
  162; supremacy, 134, 140; supremacists,
  180; teachers, 1, 5, 16, 168, 180; test
  takers, 88; whiteness, 133
W. K. Kellogg Foundation. *See under*
  charitable organizations
work-arounds, 123, 124
working-class students, 129, 132. *See also*
  low-income: students

Xavier University, 169–170, 174